WOMAN *and* HOME

SPECIAL
OCCASIONS

WOMAN and HOME

SPECIAL OCCASIONS

LUCY KNOX

HAMLYN

First published in Great Britain 1994 by
Hamlyn, an imprint of Reed Consumer Books Limited
Michelin House, 81 Fulham Road, London SW3 6RB
and Auckland, Melbourne, Singapore and Toronto.
Text and photographs copyright © 1994
Woman and Home
Design copyright © 1994
Reed International Books Limited

ISBN 0 600 58363 5

A CIP catalogue record for this book is
available at the British Library.

Printed in Spain

ACKNOWLEDGEMENTS

Art Director Jacqui Small
Design Manager Bryan Dunn
Designer Bobby Birchall, Town Group Consultancy
Executive Editor Susan Haynes
Editor Elsa Petersen-Schepelern
Jacket Photography Tim Imrie
Jacket Stylist Sue Russell

WOMAN AND HOME
Orlando Murrin Editor
Sue Dobson

RECIPE DEVELOPMENT
Lucy Knox Cookery Editor
Sarah Lowman Deputy Cookery Editor
Wendy Salmon Cookery Assistant

Linda Tubby, Linda Collister, Mary Gwynn,
Penny Baker, Elizabeth Winslade, Christine Baker

PHOTOGRAPHERS
Melvin Grey, Theo Bergström, Steve Baxter,
Simon Smith, Jerry Tubby, Jon Kevern,
Tim Imrie, Bill Richmond, Ian O'Leary,
Anthony Gould-Davies, Dave Jordan

STYLISTS
Carolyn Russell, Sue Russell, Kate Hardy,
Kay McGlone, Sandra Buckland

AUTHOR'S ACKNOWLEDGEMENT
I must say a huge thank you to my mother Gina,
for teaching me to cook, to my father Peter, for his
encouragement, and to Keith Richmond for all the
hours spent trying the recipes with me. And, finally, to
my Test Kitchen Team without whom this would not
have been possible.

CONTENTS

Introduction

This book is for everyone who enjoys entertaining and who wants to create a memorable occasion and leave a lasting impression.

We begin with an informal New Year's Brunch; celebrate Easter with a mouth-watering four course menu, and mark Christmas with a traditional Victorian meal.

One chapter is devoted to catering for a family wedding, another dedicated to a delicious Christening tea.

We have prepared two splendid menus for an elegant, sophisticated dinner party, and three simple meals for impromptu entertaining when time is at a premium.

Eat outdoors in style with our perfect picnic, and serve up our sensational bite-sized nibbles at your next cocktail party.

And we have a gourmet vegetarian dinner which is so delicious it will be enjoyed by both meat-eaters and vegetarians alike.

All these recipes have been double-tested by the expert team in the Woman and Home Test Kitchen and, where we can, we give detailed 'prepare ahead' instructions so as little as possible is left to the last minute.

Remember, entertaining is supposed to be as much for the host and hostess as it is for the guests you have invited around to wine and dine with you.

If you enjoy your party, your guests will too, and the purpose of this book is to help you do just that., whatever the special occasion. Look on it as a trusted friend when you cook to entertain and impress

New Year's Brunch Party

B runch is a glorious feast – an informal meal that starts about 11 o'clock, in which people can eat as much, or as little, as they like. It's a delightful way to celebrate the New Year.

Choose from buttery croissants and thick, home-made marmalade, traditional kedgeree or smoked salmon tartlets. Cook your favourite sausages to accompany our devilled kidneys or serve the best fish cakes you will ever have tasted.

We give prepare-ahead instructions to avoid last minute panic, leaving the morning free for cooking at leisure. Decorate the table with bowls of fruit to dip into between dishes, and serve plenty of tea and coffee, and freshly squeezed fruit juice. Also don't forget the classic breakfast cocktail, Buck's Fizz – 280 ml (½ pt) of orange juice and a bottle of Champagne fills eight glasses. Have a Happy New Year!

SERVES 15 TO 20

Haddock Kedgeree

Devilled Kidneys

– * –

Fresh Salmon Fish Cakes

or

Fish Cakes with Herby Tomatoes

Smoked Salmon Tartlets

– * –

Fruits of the Forest Jam

Wholemeal Muffins

Butter Croissants

Pain au Chocolat

Spicy Scones

Fruit Compôte

Oat Crunch Cereal

– * –

Bread and Cheese Pudding

Scrambled Egg Croustades

Muesli with Fresh Fruit and Yogurt

Mushroom and Bacon Tartlets

– * –

Brioche

Spicy Ginger and

Kumquat Marmalade

Cinnamon Coffee Bread

– * –

Fruit Refresher

Hot Orange Punch

HADDOCK KEDGEREE

This dish is perfect for breakfast – it can be prepared and chilled the night before. Place in the oven to reheat one hour before serving.

340 g (12 oz) long grain white rice
4 tablespoons freshly chopped parsley
455 g (1 lb) undyed, smoked haddock
280 ml (½ pt) milk
4 eggs, size 3, hard-boiled,
shelled and chopped
170 g (6 oz) unsalted butter, diced
Salt and freshly ground black pepper
4 tablespoons double cream
Flat-leaf parsley, to garnish

Bring a large saucepan of water to the boil, and add the rice. Cook for 15 minutes, or according to the packet instructions. Rinse the rice well under cold water for about 3 to 4 minutes

then drain it thoroughly. Add the chopped fresh parsley and stir it through the rice.

Place the fish and milk in a wide pan. Bring slowly to the boil, cover and cook slowly until the fish flakes – about 15 to 20 minutes. Drain the fish, reserving the liquid. Flake the fish, discarding the skin and bones. Layer the rice, fish, hard-boiled eggs and butter in an ovenproof dish, seasoning each layer with salt and freshly ground black pepper. Cover and chill in the refrigerator for up to 4 hours, or overnight.

Set the oven at Gas Mark 4, 350°F, 180°C. Spoon the cream and 3 tablespoons of the fish cooking liquid over the chilled kedgeree. Cover with buttered foil. Reheat in the oven for about 1 hour or until piping hot. Stir well. Garnish with flat-leaf parsley before serving.

Alternatively, you can substitute 110 g (4 oz) of wild rice for 110 g (4 oz) white rice, cook the two kinds of rice in two separate pans of boiling water. Cook the wild rice for about 25 minutes or according to the packet instructions.

DEVILLED KIDNEYS

SERVES 12

This quickly prepared dish is one of the truly great British breakfast classics.

24 lambs' kidneys
30 g (1 oz) butter
For the devil sauce:
2 tablespoons tomato ketchup
2 tablespoons Worcestershire sauce
2 tablespoons mustard powder
110 g (4 oz) butter, melted
Salt and freshly ground
white pepper
A pinch of cayenne pepper

Clean and halve the kidneys. Heat the butter in a pan and fry the kidneys for about 3 to 5 minutes on each side. Drain on absorbent kitchen paper. Arrange the kidneys in a flameproof serving dish and keep warm in a low oven. Carefully drain off any excess fat from the pan, leaving the meat juices.

To make the sauce, add the tomato ketchup, Worcestershire sauce, mustard and butter to the meat juices and heat until bubbling. Season to taste with salt, white pepper and cayenne pepper.

Spread the sauce evenly over the kidneys. Cook under a preheated grill for a minute or until piping hot.

FRESH SALMON FISH CAKES WITH LEMON AND DILL, OR WITH HERBY TOMATOES AND WATERCRESS

MAKES 24

570 ml (1 pt) milk
½ teaspoon mace (optional)
A bouquet garni
1 medium onion
680 g (1½ lb) potatoes, scrubbed
110 g (4 oz) butter
85 g (3 oz) flour
4 tablespoons double cream
2 tablespoons chopped fresh parsley
0.9 kg (2 lb) cooked salmon (weighed without skin and bones), flaked
2 tablespoons lemon juice
Salt, black pepper and cayenne pepper, to taste
6 tablespoons seasoned flour

2 eggs, size 3, beaten
340 g (12 oz) fresh white breadcrumbs
Oil for deep-frying
To garnish:
Lemon wedges
Sprigs fresh dill
VARIATION
To serve:
4 tablespoons olive oil
680 g (1½ lb) cherry tomatoes
3 tablespoons freshly chopped mixed herbs, such as parsley, marjoram and basil
Fresh watercress, to garnish

Heat the milk with the mace, bouquet garni and onion. Remove the saucepan from the heat just before the mixture begins to boil, then cover and leave to infuse for 30 minutes. Strain, and discard the flavourings.

Boil the potatoes in their skins until tender, then drain, skin and mash them thoroughly. Melt the butter in a heavy-based pan. Gradually stir in the flour, then the strained milk. Bring the mixture to the boil, stirring constantly. Continue cooking for 2 to 3 minutes, still stirring, to make a thick, smooth sauce. Remove the pan from the heat and stir in the cream and chopped parsley. Fold the sauce into the mashed potatoes, followed by the salmon and lemon juice, taking care not to break up the salmon flakes. Season to taste. Leave the mixture to cool, then chill for a few hours, or preferably overnight.

Using floured hands, shape the mixture into 24 fish cakes, each about 7.5 cm (3 in) in diameter. Dust with seasoned flour, brush with beaten egg and then coat with breadcrumbs. Chill until ready to cook. Cover the fish cakes with oiled cling film and chill overnight.

Fry a few cakes at a time in the hot oil in a deep fat fryer for 3 to 5 minutes each side, or until crisp and golden. Keep warm in a low oven while frying the remaining fish cakes. Serve garnished with lemon wedges and sprigs of fresh dill.

VARIATION

With Herby Tomatoes and Watercress
Heat oil in a heavy-based frying pan, add the tomatoes and cook for 3 to 4 minutes. Remove from the pan and toss with the herbs. Garnish the fish cakes with watercress and serve with the tomatoes.
TO FREEZE: open-freeze the fish cakes until firm, and then stack between sheets of greaseproof paper in a rigid plastic container.
TO USE FROM FROZEN: cook from frozen.

LEFT *Haddock Kedgeree, and Devilled Kidneys, served with sausages.*
PREVIOUS PAGE LEFT *A basket of brioches, large and small.*
PREVIOUS PAGE RIGHT *Ripe fresh fruit.*

SMOKED SALMON TARTLETS

Bake the pastry cases the night before and store in an airtight container. Warm through in a moderate oven before filling with the egg and smoked salmon mixture.

For the pastry:	110 ml (4 fl oz) double cream
170 g (6 oz) plain flour	Salt
A pinch of salt	Freshly ground black pepper
85 g (3 oz) butter	30 g (1 oz) butter
For the parsley butter:	*For the topping:*
40 g (1½ oz) butter, softened	60 to 110 g (2 to 4 oz) smoked salmon,
2 teaspoons chopped, fresh parsley	cut into strips
For the filling:	Fresh herbs, to garnish (optional)
6 eggs, size 3	Patty tins

To make the pastry, sift the flour and salt into a bowl, then rub in the fat to form the texture of breadcrumbs. Stir in some ice-cold water to make a soft but not sticky dough. Roll the pastry out on to a lightly floured surface and use to line the tins. Prick each pastry base lightly, then chill for 10 to 15 minutes.

Set the oven at Gas Mark 6, 400°F, 200°C and warm a baking tray in the oven. Line the pastry cases with greaseproof paper and fill with baking beans. Bake 'blind' for 10 minutes, remove the paper and beans. Bake for 5 to 10 minutes further, until the pastry is golden.

To make the parsley butter, beat the butter with the chopped parsley. When mixed thoroughly, place on a piece of greaseproof paper and shape into a short log. Chill for up to 12 hours, until ready to use.

When ready to serve, make the filling. Beat the eggs thoroughly with the cream and seasoning. Melt the butter in a heavy pan until foaming. Add the egg mixture and cook over a very gentle heat, stirring constantly with a wooden spoon until the mixture starts to curdle. When the mixture becomes soft and creamy, remove the pan from the heat and beat the mixture well. Immediately spoon into the warm pastry cases. Arrange the smoked salmon on top. Dot each one with a knob of parsley butter. Flash the tartlets under a hot grill for about 30 seconds to a minute, to melt the butter. Serve at once, garnished with fresh herbs, if wished.

NOTE: it is not recommended to serve soft-cooked eggs to people who are elderly, very young, infirm, or to pregnant women.

OPPOSITE *Clockwise from top right: fresh fruit, Spicy Ginger and Kumquat Marmalade, a basket of Brioche, Butter Croissants, Pain au Chocolat, Wholemeal Muffins and Spicy Scones, Fruits of the Forest Jam, Smoked Salmon Tartlets, Fish Cakes with Herby Tomatoes, and Fruit Compote.*

WHOLEMEAL MUFFINS

These can be served with a wide variety of both sweet and savoury toppings, so are ideal to freeze in batches and use at any time of day.

455 g (1 lb) strong, plain
white flour
230 g (8 oz) wholemeal flour
1 teaspoon salt
1 sachet easy-blend yeast
570 ml (1 pt) milk, warmed
A little melted fat
A griddle or heavy-based frying pan

Sift the flours and salt into a large, warmed bowl, returning any bran left in the sieve to the bowl. Stir in the yeast. Add the milk and mix to a soft sticky dough. Cover the bowl with oiled cling film and leave to prove in a warm place until doubled in size – about 1 hour.

Turn the dough out on to a well-floured work surface and divide it into 16 equal-sized pieces. Shape each piece of dough into a round measuring about 6.5 cm (2½ in) in diameter. Place on a well-floured board or baking tray and leave in a warm place for 10 to 15 minutes, until slightly risen.

Lightly grease the griddle with melted fat, then heat. Cook the muffins in batches on a low heat until golden brown on each side, turning them halfway through the cooking time. (Each muffin takes about 20 to 25 minutes.) Split the muffins in half and toast. Serve hot with butter.

TO FREEZE: place the cold muffins in plastic bags. Seal and freeze for up to 1 month.

TO USE FROM FROZEN: thaw at room temperature for 2 hours, then split and serve toasted with butter.

BUTTER CROISSANTS

MAKES 14

455 g (1 lb) strong, plain,
unbleached white flour
1 teaspoon salt
1 teaspoon caster sugar
230 g (8 oz) unsalted butter

1 sachet easy-blend yeast
1 egg, size 3, beaten
260 ml (9 fl oz) milk,
warmed
Beaten egg to glaze

Sieve the flour and salt into a warmed mixing bowl, then stir in the sugar. Rub in 60 g (2 oz) of the butter, then stir in the yeast. Whisk the egg into the milk. Make a well in the centre of the flour and beat well to form a soft and sticky dough. Turn the dough on to a lightly floured work surface and knead thoroughly for 10 minutes, or until the dough is firm and elastic.

Roll out the dough to a rectangle 51 by 20.5 cm (20 by 8 in) and 15 cm (¼ in) thick. Beat the remaining butter to soften it, and divide into 3 equal portions. Leaving a small border around the edge of the dough, carefully spread 1 portion of butter on one-third of the dough and fold down the remainder, as if making puff pastry. Seal the edges by pressing gently with a rolling pin. Turn the dough so the fold is on the left-hand side. Twice more roll out the dough to the same size as before, and repeat the procedure with the other 2 portions of butter followed by the folding and rolling (to give a total of 3 rolls and folds). Cover the dough with oiled cling film and chill for about 30 minutes.

Turn out on to a floured work surface, roll out, and repeat the rolling and folding a further 3 turns, Chill again for at least 1 hour (at this stage the dough can be kept tightly covered in the fridge for 1 to 2 days).

Roll out on a lightly floured surface to a rectangle about 53 by 30.5 cm (21 by 12 in), and trim the edges. Cut the dough in half lengthways. With a sharp knife, mark points 12.5 cm (5 in) apart along one side of each strip. On the opposite side of each strip mark points 12.5 cm (5 in) apart, but start 6.5 cm (2½ in) in from the end. Make diagonal cuts between the marks to produce even triangles.

Starting at the base of each triangle, roll up very tightly, and tuck the tip of the triangle underneath. Curve the ends into crescents. Place well apart on several greased baking trays. Cover with oiled cling film and leave to prove for about 1 hour or until doubled in size – or chill overnight.Set the oven to Gas Mark 7, 425°F, 220°C. Brush the croissants with the egg to glaze, and bake for 15 minutes until crisp and brown. Serve warm. Eat within 24 hours.
TO FREEZE: cool completely, open-freeze until firm, then freeze for up to 3 months.
TO USE FROM FROZEN: warm through in a moderate oven from frozen.

PAIN AU CHOCOLAT

MAKES 20

1 quantity croissant dough
(see above)

230 g (8 oz) plain chocolate
1 egg, size 3, beaten, for glazing

Make the croissant dough as described in the previous recipe. After chilling, roll out to a rectangle 102 by 25.5 cm (40 by 10 in). Cut the dough in half lengthways and cut each section into 10 rectangles 10 by 12.5 cm (4 by 5 in).

Cut the plain chocolate into strips. Place a strip of chocolate in the centre of each rectangle and wrap the dough around. Place the pain au chocolate on baking trays and leave to prove for 1 hour, or until doubled in size.

Set the oven at Gas Mark 7, 425°F, 220°C. Brush the pastries with the beaten egg and cook for 15 to 20 minutes until golden. Serve warm.
TO FREEZE: follow the directions for Butter Croissants, above.

SPICY SCONES

MAKES ABOUT 9 SCONES
Although usually a teatime favourite, these large, spicy scones make a delightful breakfast treat.

230 g (8 oz) white flour
230 g (8 oz) wholemeal flour
2 teaspoons baking powder
A pinch of salt
½ teaspoon mixed spice
85 g (3 oz) caster sugar
85 g (3 oz) butter
2 eggs, size 3, made up to
280 ml (½ pt) with milk

Set the oven at Gas Mark 7, 425°F, 220°C. Sift the flours, baking powder, salt and spice into a mixing bowl, then stir in the caster sugar. Rub in the butter until the mixture resembles fine breadcrumbs. Add the egg and milk mixture and mix to a smooth, soft but not sticky dough.

Knead lightly on a floured work surface, and then roll out to 2 cm (¾ in) thick. Using a 7.5 cm (3 in) fluted cutter, stamp out the scones, rerolling the trimmings as necessary. Arrange on several greased baking trays. Bake for about 15 minutes or until well risen and golden brown. Serve warm.
TO FREEZE: pack the scones into a plastic container and freeze for up to 1 month.
TO USE FROM FROZEN: place on a wire rack and thaw at room temperature for 2 to 2½ hours. Warm the scones gently before serving.

RIGHT *Fruit Compote and Oat Crunch Cereal, served with milk or yogurt.*
OVERLEAF *From left: fresh fruit, Scrambled Egg Croustades, Hot Orange Punch, Fresh Salmon Fish Cakes, Haddock Kedgeree, Smoked Salmon Tartlets.*

FRUIT COMPOTE

This is a delicious and unusual brunch or breakfast dish.
The citrus tea brings out the flavours of the fruits.

110 g (4 oz) no-need-to-soak
dried figs
110 g (4 oz) dried apple
110 g (4 oz) no-need-to-soak
dried pears
110 g (4 oz) no-need-to-soak
dried apricots
The juice of 1 lemon
6 whole cloves

1 cinnamon stick
1 small pineapple
1 citrus-flavoured tea bag
2 tablespoons honey, or to taste
60 g (2 oz) white seedless grapes
60 g (2 oz) black seedless grapes
2 oranges, peeled and sliced
110 g (4 oz) fresh dates, stoned
and quartered

Place the dried fruit in a large, heavy-based pan with 850 ml (1½ pt) of cold water, the lemon juice, cloves and cinnamon stick. Bring the mixture to the boil, stirring occasionally. Reduce the heat and simmer for 10 minutes or until the fruit is plump.

Meanwhile, peel, slice and core the pineapple and cut into chunks. Remove the Fruit Compote from the heat and add the tea bag, honey and remaining fruit.

Cover and leave to stand for 15 minutes to allow the flavours to infuse. Remove the cinnamon stick and tea bag. Pour into an attractive glass bowl, and serve warm.

OAT CRUNCH CEREAL

A crunchy cereal, delicious served either with milk or thick Greek yogurt.

230 g (8 oz) jumbo oat flakes, toasted
30 g (1 oz) oat bran, toasted
1 teaspoon cinnamon
60 g (2 oz) demerara sugar
85 g (3 oz) clear honey
85 g (3 oz) raisins
60 g (2 oz) flaked almonds, toasted
30 g (1 oz) pumpkin seeds, toasted
60 g (2 oz) banana chips

Set the oven at Gas Mark 4, 350°F, 180°C. Mix together the oat flakes, oat bran, cinnamon and sugar. Stir in the honey. When well mixed, spread evenly over a lightly oiled baking tray. Bake in the oven for 10 to 15 minutes until golden brown and crunchy. Stir occasionally. Leave to cool.

Break the mixture into small pieces and add the remaining ingredients. Oat Crunch Cereal can be stored for up to 3 days in an airtight container.

Serve with milk or thick Greek yogurt and honey, if wished.

BREAD AND CHEESE PUDDING

SERVES 12

Prepare this simple and most spectacular savoury pudding the night before and bake just before serving – it will puff up just like a soufflé.

30 g (1 oz) butter
16 slices medium-sliced
white bread
455 g (1 lb) mature Cheddar
cheese, grated
455 g (1 lb) Cheshire
cheese, grated
1.15 litres (2 pt) milk
6 eggs, size 3, beaten
3 tablespoons snipped chives
3 tablespoons chopped parsley
Salt and freshly ground
white pepper
A 3.15 litre (5½ pt) ovenproof dish

Grease the ovenproof dish thoroughly with the butter. Remove the crusts from the bread. Line the base of the dish with half the bread. Mix the cheeses together and sprinkle half over the top of the bread. Place the remaining bread over the top, then add the rest of the cheese. Beat together the milk, eggs, chives, parsley, salt and freshly ground white pepper. Pour over the cheese and bread layers, cover and chill overnight.

The next day, set the oven at Gas Mark 4, 350°F, 180°C. Bake for about 1 to 1¼ hours or until the pudding is crisp, puffed and golden. Serve at once.

SCRAMBLED EGG CROUSTADES

MAKES 32

For a real treat, add small strips of smoked salmon to the scrambled eggs before spooning into the croustades.

For the croustades:
30 g (1 oz) unsalted butter, melted
8 slices wholemeal bread
For the filling:
4 eggs, size 3, beaten
85 ml (3 fl oz) double cream

Salt and freshly ground
black pepper
15 g (½ oz) unsalted butter
Fresh chervil, to garnish
Patty tins
A 5 cm (2 in) round cutter

Set the oven at Gas Mark 8, 450°F, 230°C. Lightly brush the tins with a little of the melted butter. Use the cutter to cut out four circles from each slice of bread. Roll and flatten each bread circle with a rolling pin, then carefully press into the tins to line completely. Brush the inside of the bread with the remaining melted butter and bake for 10 minutes until crisp and golden. Repeat until there are 32 croustade bases.

Meanwhile, to make the filling, beat the eggs thoroughly with the cream and season with salt and freshly ground black pepper. Melt the butter in a heavy-based pan until foaming. Add the egg mixture and cook over a very gentle heat, stirring constantly with a wooden spoon until the mixture starts to curdle. When the mixture becomes soft and creamy, remove the pan from the heat and beat the mixture well. Immediately spoon into the warmed croustades. Serve the croustades at once, garnished with a little fresh chervil.

NOTE: the croustade bases can be made in advance. Store in an airtight container – then heat through at Gas Mark 6, 400°F, 200°C for about 5 minutes before filling with the scrambled eggs.

MUESLI WITH FRESH FRUIT AND YOGURT

Try this wonderfully light and healthy alternative to porridge.

170 g (6 oz) rolled oats
170 ml (6 fl oz) fresh milk
30 g (1 oz) oat bran
170 ml (6 fl oz) natural yogurt
30 g (1 oz) flower blossom honey
60 g (2 oz) unblanched hazelnuts, toasted

15 g (½ oz) unblanched almonds, toasted
1 red apple, cored
1 Cox's Orange Pippin, or other
crisp eating apple, cored
230 g (8 oz) fresh berries,
such as raspberries or blueberries

Soak the rolled oats in the fresh milk overnight in the fridge. The next morning, stir and add the oat bran, yogurt and honey. Roughly chop the nuts and add to the muesli mixture. Grate the apples and add to the mixture. Spoon into a large, glass serving dish and arrange the fresh berries on top. Serve with a jug of double cream.

MUSHROOM AND BACON TARTLETS

MAKES 16

These buttery crisp pastries are filled with creamy mushrooms
and topped with bacon. They are delicious for a special breakfast or brunch, and also
make good canapés for parties or cocktail parties.

For the pastry:
170 g (6 oz) plain flour
A pinch of paprika
85 g (3 oz) unsalted butter
For the filling:
8 rashers of smoked streaky bacon
30 g (1 oz) unsalted butter

170 g (6 oz) button mushrooms, sliced
1 teaspoon plain flour
140 ml (¼ pt) double cream
Salt and freshly ground
black pepper
A pinch of ground nutmeg
16 small patty tins

To make the pastry, sift the flour and paprika into a large bowl. Rub in the butter until the mixture resembles fine breadcrumbs. Add enough cold water to make a stiff dough. Knead lightly then wrap in cling film and chill for 15 minutes.

Set the oven at Gas Mark 6, 400°F, 200°C. Place a baking tray in the oven to heat.

Roll the pastry out on to a lightly floured work surface and use to line the patty tins. Prick the pastry bases with a fork and chill for 10 to 15 minutes. Line the pastry with greaseproof paper, fill with baking beans and bake 'blind' for 10 minutes. Remove the beans and greaseproof paper, and return to the oven for 10 minutes more.

Meanwhile, to make the filling, using the back of a knife, carefully stretch the bacon. Cut each rasher in half and roll up. Place in a roasting tin and bake for 10 to 15 minutes or until crisp, turning occasionally. Melt the butter, add the mushrooms and cook until softened. Stir in the flour and cook for 1 minute. Gradually add the cream, stirring continuously. Heat the sauce very gently until thickened. Season to taste with salt, pepper and nutmeg. Spoon a little of the mushroom sauce in each warmed pastry case and top with a bacon roll.

NOTE: the pastry cases can be made in advance. Store in an airtight container, and when ready to use, place on a baking tray to warm through while making the filling.

FRUITS OF THE FOREST JAM

MAKES 3.28 KG (7 LB 4 OZ) OR
2.85 LITRES (5 PT)

The joy of this jam is that
it can be made at any time of the year.
Packets of frozen fruits of the forest are
available from large supermarkets;
alternatively, make your own
mixture of raspberries,
redcurrants, blackcurrants
and blackberries.

1.8 kg (4 lb) frozen fruits of the forest
1.8 kg (4 lb) sugar with pectin
Sterilised jam jars, waxed discs,
Cellophane covers, elastic bands
and labels

Put the frozen fruit into a saucepan and cook gently until the fruit is pulpy. Add 570 ml (1 pt) water and mix well. Stir in the sugar, dissolve over a very low heat, stirring frequently. Bring to the boil, and boil rapidly for 15 minutes or until setting point is reached. Allow the jam to stand and cool for a few minutes. Pot, seal and label.

BRIOCHE

455 g (1 lb) strong, plain, unbleached
white flour
1 sachet easy-blend yeast
1 teaspoon salt
60 g (2 oz) caster sugar

4 eggs, size 3, at room temperature
170 ml (6 fl oz) milk
110 g (4 oz) butter, softened
Beaten egg to glaze
Brioche moulds, greased

Sieve the flour into a mound on a clean work surface and carefully mix in the yeast. Make a large well in the centre and spoon in the salt and caster sugar. Using the fingers of one hand, pinch together the salt, sugar and the eggs, broken in one by one. Gradually draw in the flour, adding the milk in small quantities. Continue working in the flour to give a smooth batter.

When all the flour has been incorporated, continue to work the mixture, beating it with your fingers for 10 minutes. Note that the batter will be very sticky at this stage. Turn the dough into an oiled bowl, cover with oiled cling film and leave to prove in a warm place until doubled in size – about 1 to 1½ hours.

Knock back the risen dough and knead in the softened butter by dotting pieces of butter on to the dough and kneading thoroughly.

When well combined, return the mixture to the oiled bowl, cover and refrigerate for at least 4 hours (the dough can be left in the fridge overnight at this stage).

When ready to cook, set the oven at Gas Mark 8, 450°F, 230°C. Knock back the chilled, risen dough and divide into 12 equal pieces, or 1 large and 6 small brioches, or 2 large brioches. To make each brioche, cut off one-quarter of the dough. Shape the larger piece into a ball and place in a prepared mould, then shape the small piece into a pear shape.

With a floured finger, make a hole in the centre of the dough in the tin. Set the pointed end of the pear-shaped piece of dough into the hole. Cover with oiled cling film and leave to prove until doubled in size.

Glaze with the beaten egg. Bake for about 10 minutes for the small brioches and 20 minutes for the larger brioche or brioches. Transfer to a wire rack and leave to cool. The brioches should be eaten within 24 hours and are delicious served warm. TO FREEZE: cool completely, open-freeze until firm, then freeze for up to 3 months. TO USE FROM FROZEN: warm through from frozen in a preheated oven for about 5 to 10 minutes if small, and 10 to 12 minutes if large.

SPICY GINGER AND KUMQUAT MARMALADE

MAKES 3.4 KG (7 LB 8 OZ) OR 2.85 LITRES (5 PT)

There is nothing better to serve with delicious, freshly baked breads and pastries than a lightly spiced, fresh fruit marmalade.

The grated rind and juice of
1 orange
1.1 kg (2 ½ lb) kumquats
2.05 kg (4 ½ lb) granulated
sugar, warmed
5 tablespoons stem ginger syrup
85 g (3 oz) stem ginger,
finely chopped
2 teaspoons ground cloves
A small piece of muslin or cloth
Sterilised jam jars, waxed discs, Cellophane
covers, elastic bands and labels

Put the grated orange rind and juice into a preserving pan. Wipe the kumquats with a damp cloth, then halve the fruit and remove the pips. Tie the pips in a square of muslin.

Transfer the kumquats to a food processor and blend on 'pulse' setting until coarsely chopped (or put through a mincer). Tip into the preserving pan, add the muslin bag and 2.6 litres (4½ pt) water, stir well. Bring the mixture slowly to the boil – this will take about 1 hour. Cover the pan with a baking tray and simmer the fruit until softened and transparent – about 25 to 35 minutes.

Using the back of a wooden spoon (or two plates), squeeze any excess juice from the muslin bag back into the marmalade, then discard the bag. Add the sugar, syrup, ginger and cloves. Stir over a gentle heat until the sugar has dissolved, then bring to the boil. Continue boiling rapidly until setting point is reached. Stirring occasionally. Skim and leave to stand for about 10 to 15 minutes. Pot, seal and label.
NOTE: make 3 weeks ahead of serving or as far in advance as possible to allow the flavour to mature.

OPPOSITE *Cinnamon Coffee Bread.*

FRUIT REFRESHER

*Mangoes and peaches
complement the orange juice to make
this the perfect refresher for
your brunch.*

2 large mangoes, peeled and stoned
2 peaches, peeled and stoned
1.15 litres (2 pt) freshly squeezed
orange juice
1.15 litres (2 pt) carbonated
mineral water

Place the mangoes and the peaches in a
liquidiser or food processor and
process until smooth. Add to the
orange juice and mineral water. Serve
well chilled with masses of ice.

HOT ORANGE
PUNCH

Warming and delicious.

2 orange-flavoured tea bags
570 ml (1 pt) freshly squeezed
orange juice
115 ml (4 fl oz) Grand Marnier
2 oranges, sliced

Add the tea bags to 1.15 litres (2 pt) of
boiling water and leave to infuse for
about 10 minutes. Remove the tea
bags. Bring the orange juice to the boil,
add the tea and the Grand Marnier.
Pour immediately into heated mugs or
glasses over slices of orange.

CINNAMON COFFEE BREAD

MAKES ONE 0.9 KG (2 LB) LOAF

2 tablespoons instant coffee
280 ml (½ pt) milk, warmed
455 g (1 lb) strong, plain flour
A pinch of salt
60 g (2 oz) unsalted butter
30 g (1 oz) soft, light
brown sugar

1 teaspoon ground cinnamon
1 sachet easy-blend yeast
To complete:
60 g (2 oz) soft, light brown sugar
2 teaspoons ground cinnamon
30 g (1 oz) walnuts, chopped
30 g (1 oz) Brazil nuts, chopped

Dissolve the coffee in the warmed milk. Sift the flour and salt into a warmed mixing bowl
and rub in the butter. Stir in the sugar, cinnamon and yeast. Add the milk mixture and mix
to form a soft dough. Turn out on to a lightly floured work surface and knead thoroughly
for 10 minutes. Place in a lightly oiled bowl, cover with oiled cling film, and leave to
prove in a warm place until doubled in size – about 1 hour. Divide the dough into 8 even-
sized pieces and shape into fingers.

To complete, mix together the sugar, cinnamon and nuts. Brush each finger of
dough with a little melted butter and then roll in the nut mixture to coat. Place 4 of the
dough fingers in the base of the prepared tin, leaving a small space between each
finger. Place the remaining fingers on top. Cover with oiled cling film and leave to
prove in a warm place until doubled in size – about 45 minutes.

Set the oven at Gas Mark 6, 400°F, 200°C. Bake in the oven for 30 to 40 minutes.
Cover the loaf with a sheet of foil after 10 minutes if it starts to brown too quickly.
Turn out on to a wire rack and leave to cool. Best eaten within 24 hours served warm.
TO FREEZE: wrap in greaseproof paper and foil, and freeze for up to 1 month.
TO SERVE FROM FROZEN: thaw at room temperature for 2 to 3 hours and warm
through in a preheated oven set at Gas Mark 5, 375°F, 190°C for 10 to 15 minutes.

An Elegant Dinner Party

Chilled Fennel and

Coloured Pepper Soup

Cheese Crispies

— ∗ —

Herb Crêpes with Fresh Asparagus

and Yellow Oyster Mushrooms

and Orange Dressing

— ∗ —

Poached Salmon in Aspic

Twice-dressed Baby Red

and White Potatoes

Salad of Shredded Beetroot

and Mouli

Steamed Marsh Samphire

— ∗ —

Celebration Raspberry Savarin

Hazelnut Meringue Gâteau

Dine in the grand style with our elegant, sophisticated dinner party menus to delight and impress your friends.

We have prepared two splendid menus. A fabulous light summer meal for relaxed, alfresco entertaining; and a truly magnificent, more substantial winter dinner to serve when the weather may be cold but the company and conversation sparkle with warmth.

CHILLED FENNEL AND COLOURED PEPPER SOUP

SERVES 8

Served with cheesy melt-in-the-mouth biscuits and garnished with fresh fennel leaves and fine strips of brightly coloured pepper, this delicate soup makes a gourmet start to any celebration.

3 tablespoons sunflower oil
1.10 kg (2½ lb) Florence fennel, chopped
(reserve green tops)
1 large onion, chopped
1 large orange pepper
1 large yellow pepper
Salt and freshly ground
white pepper
570 ml (1 pt) good-quality chicken stock

Heat the oil in a heavy-based pan. Add the fennel and onion cook over a gentle heat for 5 minutes or until softened but not coloured. Deseed and chop all except one 40 g (1½ oz) strip of each colour pepper. Reserve these strips and add the rest of the peppers to the pan and stir.

Turn the heat up to medium and soften the vegetables for 10 minutes, stirring occasionally. Season with salt and freshly ground white pepper and add stock and 570 ml (1 pt) cold water. Bring to the boil, reduce the heat and simmer for about 20 minutes until the vegetables are softened.

Purée in a blender or food processor until smooth. Cover and then chill. Cut the reserved strips of pepper into fine slivers and use a little of each colour to garnish the individual soup bowls along with the reserved green frond of fennel.

PREVIOUS PAGE RIGHT *Freshly picked flowers are a must for an elegant lunch or dinner table.*
PREVIOUS PAGE LEFT *Poached Salmon in Aspic – sumptuous for a summer lunch.*

CHEESE CRISPIES

MAKES 30

Featherlight biscuits that will keep for up to 2 days in an airtight container in the fridge.

85 g (3 oz) plain flour	1 egg, size 3, beaten
¼ teaspoon celery salt	30 g (1 oz) Parmesan cheese, finely grated
60 g (2 oz) unsalted butter	2 baking trays, greased
60 g (2 oz) mature Cheddar cheese, grated	5 cm (2 in) plain cutter

Set oven at Gas Mark 8, 230°C, 450°F. Sift the flour and celery salt into a bowl, rub in the butter and add grated Cheddar cheese. Work the mixture together to form a dough. Chill for 2 hours. Cut the dough in half and roll out, a small piece at a time, very thinly, on a lightly floured surface. Stamp out the biscuits using the cutter and place on the prepared baking sheet. Brush with egg and sprinkle a little Parmesan on the top. Bake for 5 minutes until golden. Leave to cool on a baking tray for about 10 seconds before transferring to a wire rack to finish cooling.

HERB CRÊPES WITH FRESH ASPARAGUS AND YELLOW OYSTER MUSHROOMS AND ORANGE DRESSING

SERVES 8

Allow one crêpe per person with 3 asparagus spears and a helping of mushrooms.

For the crêpes:	3 tablespoons sunflower oil
110 g (4 oz) plain flour sifted	Freshly ground black pepper
A pinch of salt	A pinch of salt
1 egg, size 3	*For the filling:*
1 egg yolk, size 3	24 fresh asparagus spears
8 tablespoons milk	1 tablespoon sunflower oil
60 g (2 oz) unsalted butter, melted	A knob of unsalted butter
Butter, for greasing the pan	A pinch of crushed garlic
For the orange dressing:	455 g (1 lb) yellow oyster mushrooms
The juice of ½ an orange	A pinch of salt
1 tablespoon virgin olive oil	8 fronds of chervil, to garnish

To make the crêpe batter, place flour and salt in a bowl, make a well in the centre, add the egg, egg yolk and milk. Using an electric beater whisk the mixture in the well, gradually incorporating the flour to make a smooth batter. Stir in 2 tablespoons of melted butter and 170 ml (6 fl oz) water, cover and leave to stand for 2 hours.

To cook the crêpes, heat a small 12.5 cm (5 in) crêpe pan, and add a little butter to coat. Pour in a small amount of batter and swirl round to the edges of the pan. Cook the crêpe until pale and golden on each side, then layer between pieces of greaseproof paper on a plate set over a pan of gently simmering water to keep warm.

To make the orange dressing, put all the ingredients in a screw-topped jar and shake until well emulsified.

To cook the asparagus, scrape off the v-shaped scales and any hard outer skin, tie in even bundles and stand upright, tips uppermost, in a narrow deep pan or asparagus steamer with about 7.5 cm (3 in) of boiling salted water. Cook for 5 to 10 minutes (depending on the thickness) – then remove and drain thoroughly.

To cook the mushrooms, heat a frying pan, add the oil, the knob of butter and the garlic. When it sizzles, add the mushrooms, and tear any large ones in half. Add salt and stir-fry until wilted and cooked lightly.

To assemble, place a crêpe on each plate, add 3 asparagus spears, and some mushrooms. Fold the crêpe over, sprinkle with dressing, and garnish with chervil.

POACHED SALMON IN ASPIC

SERVES 8

A glorious centrepiece for a lavish buffet – garnished with lime and lemon slices, flat-leaf parsley and edible flowers (available from most large supermarkets), then topped with aspic, flavoured with homemade fish stock made from a crisp, white, German wine.

A fresh salmon weighing 2.3 g (5 lb), cleaned
For the fish stock:
455 g (1 lb) fish head and bones from non-oily fish
1 onion, sliced
2 sticks celery, sliced
1 bayleaf
A pinch of salt
280 ml (½ pt) Gewurztraminer wine
To assemble the salmon:
85 ml (3 fl oz) Lime Mayonnaise (see recipe for
Twice-dressed Baby New Potatoes)
For the aspic:
2 sachets gelatine
1 egg white and shell, crushed
60 ml (2 fl oz) Gewurztraminer wine
To garnish:
2 lemons, washed
2 limes, washed
30 g (1 oz) edible flowers
Flat-leaf parsley, to garnish

To poach the fish, cut the salmon in half across the middle, just above the fins, so that the heavier, head end is slightly smaller. Arrange 2 pieces of double thickness foil in the bottom of a deep roasting tin so the two pieces of fish can be placed on top.

Place the onion, celery, bayleaf, lime, peppercorns and parsley stalks in the tin and place the two pieces of fish on top of the foil. Pour over the wine and top up with water just to cover. Wrap the tin tightly with foil then carefully transfer to the hob and bring to the boil. Reduce the heat and simmer very gently for 10 minutes. Remove from the heat and leave to cool. Place in the fridge overnight with all the cooking liquid to allow all the flavours to infuse with the salmon.

To skin and bone the fish, lift out the two pieces, holding the foil carefully at each end. Start work on the tail end. Slit the skin along the back of the fish. Remove the fins with all the bones attached. Peel off the skin using a sharp knife and scrape away any of the brown curd from the centre backbone or sides of the fish. Carefully turn the tail over and repeat the same method for removing the skin. Trim the tail.

Carefully remove the fillets from the bone and set aside. Don't worry if the fillets fall apart, as you will easily be able to position the flakes back together in the fish shape, using the aspic. Lift up the backbone, peeling it towards the tail and cut it free. Make sure there are no bones left in the flesh.

Spread a little of the lime mayonnaise over the tail fillets and replace the upper fillets. Carefully place the tail end on to the serving plate.

Now work on the head end. Pull off the small fin from behind the head. Slit the skin along the back of the headpiece on the side of the fish. Peel off the skin in the same way as you did with the tail. Repeat on the other side of the head. Carefully remove the fillets from the bone and set aside. Lift up the backbone carefully and snip at the end near the head. Make sure there are no bones left in the flesh. Spread a little of the lime mayonnaise over the fillets and replace the upper fillets. Put the two pieces of fish back together again on the serving plate. Smooth the lime mayonnaise into all the joints with a palette knife until all the surfaces are flat again. Chill whilst making the aspic.

Meanwhile, to make the fish fumet, put all the ingredients except the wine in a large pan. Bring gradually to the boil and, without stirring, skim off any scum that rises to the surface. Reduce the heat and simmer gently for 15 minutes. Add the wine and continue to simmer for a further 15 minutes. Strain the fumet through a sieve into a clean bowl. Do not press any solids through, otherwise the liquid will be cloudy.

To make the aspic, strain the fumet again into a bowl through a sieve lined with muslin, and chill until the sediment sinks to the bottom of the bowl. Carefully ladle off the clear liquid into a large pan leaving the sediment behind. Place the pan of stock over a low heat. Meanwhile, to clarify the stock to make aspic, whisk the egg white until frothing. Add to the pan with crushed shell.

Increase the heat to medium to allow the mixture to boil slowly up the sides of the pan. Remove it from the heat and let the foam subside.

Do not stir or move the foam. Stand for 10 minutes. Gently move the pan back on to the heat and repeat the process. Leave for 10 minutes. Line a sieve with a double thickness of damp muslin or kitchen paper. Place over a bowl. Carefully tip the contents of the pan into the sieve. Remove the sieve and you will have a clear liquid in the pan. Place 4 tablespoons of cold water in a small heatproof bowl, sprinkle over the gelatine and leave to absorb for about 5 minutes. Warm the fumet gently.

Dissolve the gelatine by standing the bowl in a pan of very hot water. Add the dissolved gelatine and wine. Remove from the heat and chill almost to setting point.

Paint all over the top of the prepared salmon with almost-gelling aspic. Slice the lemons and limes carefully and thinly, and place down the centre of the salmon. Dip the parsley briefly into boiling water then ice-cold water (to set the colour and make it floppy). Dip into aspic and arrange on the salmon. Take the petals from the flowers, dip in the aspic and apply to the salmon, reforming the flower shape. Paint over with aspic to finish glazing. Chill for 20 minutes. Soften the remaining aspic slightly by setting the bowl in a pan of hot water if necessary. Apply about 3 coats of thin aspic to ensure the jelly has set well over all the garnishes.

Chill for 10 minutes before serving. Arrange more flowers and herb leaves around the sides of the fish.

TWICE-DRESSED BABY RED AND WHITE POTATOES

SERVES 8

*Small red potatoes, such as Roseval,
are wonderful for cold potato dishes.
Team them up with Jersey Royals or other
small waxy white potatoes, to make this
a pretty and subtle potato salad.*

**455 g (1 lb) small red skinned potatoes,
washed
455 g (1 lb) small Jersey
Royals, washed
3 tablespoons sunflower oil
1 teaspoon white wine vinegar
Salt and freshly ground
white pepper**
For the lime mayonnaise:
**280 ml (½ pt) good-quality mayonnaise
1 to 2 tablespoons lime juice
Edible flowers or fresh herbs,
to garnish**

Cook the potatoes in boiling, salted
water for 15 to 20 minutes then drain.
Place the oil, vinegar, salt and pepper
in a screw-topped jar and shake until
well-emulsified. Pour over the hot
potatoes and toss.

Spoon the mayonnaise into a small
bowl and stir in the lime juice to
flavour it and make the mayonnaise
slightly thinner. Season to taste with
salt and freshly ground white pepper.

When the potatoes are completely
cold, fold 5 tablespoons of mayonnaise
into the potatoes. Serve the remaining
mayonnaise separately in a small bowl
to accompany the salmon if wished.
Garnish the hot potatoes with edible
flowers or fresh herbs.

LEFT *An elegant alfresco lunch with
(clockwise from left) Twice-dressed Baby
Red and White Potatoes, Salad of
Shredded Beetroot and Mouli, Steamed
Marsh Samphire, Hazelnut Meringue
Gâteau, Celebration Raspberry Savarin,
Herb Crêpes with Fresh Asparagus, Yellow
Oyster Mushrooms and Orange Dressing,
Poached Salmon in Aspic, and Chilled
Fennel and Coloured Pepper Soup.*

SALAD OF SHREDDED BEETROOT AND MOULI

SERVES 8

Colourful and fresh, this salad offsets the richness of salmon.

1 raw beetroot, about
280 g (10 oz) in weight, peeled
1 mouli (long white radish) about
280 g (10 oz) in weight, peeled
2 tablespoons sunflower oil
Juice of ½ lemon
10 g (¼ oz) fresh chives, chopped

Finely slice the beetroot in a processor or by hand and then finely shred and rinse in a colander under cold running water. Drain well. Repeat this process with the mouli. Cover both and chill separately until just before serving.

Combine the beetroot and the mouli in a bowl and add all the remaining ingredients. Toss well and then serve.

STEAMED MARSH SAMPHIRE

SERVES 8

Samphire grows on salt marshes by the sea and is high in minerals and vitamins. It is available, or can be ordered, from good fishmongers.

340 g (12 oz) fresh samphire
2 teaspoons sunflower oil

Sort through the samphire, throw away any brown bits, and cut off any tough looking stalks (although, when fresh at this time of year, there is usually little to discard). Rinse thoroughly to remove sand and excess salt, and place in a steamer or colander set over a pan of gently simmering water. Steam until just tender, about 2 to 5 minutes. Refresh briefly under cold water to set the colour and stop the cooking process. Toss in oil and serve warm or cold with the salmon.

Do not add any salt to this recipe, as the samphire contains natural salt from the sea marshes.

CELEBRATION RASPBERRY SAVARIN

SERVES 10 TO 12

This lively dessert may seem quite a lot of trouble to make, but the result is truly delectable. The savarin should be light, soft and moist with syrup.

For the savarin batter:
2 teaspoons dried yeast
5 tablespoons milk, heated to blood heat.
170 g (6 oz) strong white flour, sifted
4 teaspoons caster sugar
A pinch of salt
85 g (3 oz) unsalted butter
3 eggs, size 3, beaten
For the syrup:
230 g (8 oz) caster sugar

6 tablespoons raspberry liqueur
For the coulis:
340 g (12 oz) fresh raspberries
3 tablespoons icing
sugar, sifted
To decorate:
455 g (1 lb) fresh raspberries
Raspberry leaves
A savarin mould 24 cm (9½ in) diameter,
lightly oiled even if non-stick

Set the oven to Gas Mark 6, 400°F, 200°C. To make the savarin batter, place the dried yeast in a medium-size mixing bowl and spoon over the milk. Do not mix, but cover and leave in a warm place for 10 minutes. Mix 30 g (1 oz) of the flour and 1 teaspoon of the sugar into the yeast and milk. Use fingertips to smooth out any lumps. Place in a warm place for 20 minutes. The mixture will have a swollen, smooth appearance and bubbles may begin to break the surface.

In another bowl place the remaining 140 g (5 oz) flour and 3 teaspoons of sugar. Add the butter cut up into pieces and smooth it into the flour and sugar. When the yeast mixture is ready, add the butter mixture and eggs and beat with an electric beater until the batter becomes completely smooth, about 2 minutes. Pour evenly into the prepared savarin mould. Cover with cling film and leave the mixture to rise to within 5 mm (¼ in) of the top. This takes about 30 to 40 minutes.

Place in the oven and bake for 20 minutes or until golden and just beginning to leave the sides of the mould. While the savarin is rising and cooking, make the syrup by placing the sugar in a heavy based pan and adding 200 ml (7 fl oz) of water. Gently heat to dissolve the sugar and when the liquid is clear bring to the boil for about 5 minutes.

After 2 minutes unmould the savarin carefully on to a wire rack. Place on a plate. After a few minutes spoon over the cooled syrup. Cool completely and pile the fresh raspberries in the centre. Remove from the heat and add the raspberry liqueur.

Prepare the coulis by rubbing the raspberries and icing sugar through a sieve until only seeds are left behind. When cool, spoon over the savarin. Decorate with raspberry leaves just before serving.

OPPOSITE *Hazelnut Meringue Gâteau and the delicious Celebration Raspberry Savarin.*

HAZELNUT MERINGUE GÂTEAU

SERVES 8

*A fabulous version of an all-time favourite,
sandwiched with caramel coffee cream. You can prepare
and store the meringue in an airtight container up to two days in
advance. Assemble an hour before serving and place in the
fridge to chill which also allows the centre to go
a little gooey!*

4 egg whites, size 3
230 g (8 oz) golden caster sugar
110 g (4 oz) blanched hazelnuts, finely ground
For the filling:
85 g (3 oz) caster sugar
4 tablespoons hot black coffee
570 ml (1 pt) double cream, whipped
To decorate:
8 to 10 whole blanched hazelnuts, toasted
2 sheets silicone paper with a 20 cm (8 in)
diameter circle drawn on each
2 baking trays

Set the oven to Gas Mark ½, 250°F, 130°C. Place the egg whites and sugar in a bowl. Bring a large pan of water to a fast boil (using a pan just large enough to support the base of the bowl without the bowl touching in the water).

Remove the pan from the heat, place the bowl over the water and, using an electric beater, whisk the egg whites and gradually add the sugar until very stiff. Remove the bowl from the heat and carry on whisking for a further 3 minutes until it cools slightly. Fold in the ground hazelnuts. Put the meringue mixture into a piping bag fitted with a 1.5 cm (¾ in) plain nozzle and pipe on to the prepared silicone sheets in a spiral starting from the centre.

Bake for 2½ to 3 hours until firm and crisp. Remove from the oven, transfer to wire racks until cool enough to peel off the silicone paper and then cool completely.

To prepare the filling, place the sugar with 5 tablespoons cold water in a heavy-based pan. Heat the mixture gently to dissolve the sugar, then turn up the heat and cook to a pale caramel colour. Remove the pan from the heat and add all the coffee at once, taking great care as it will splutter up the pan. Stir to dissolve the caramel, returning it to the heat to do this if necessary. Set aside to cool.

Fold the coffee-caramel mixture carefully into the cream and spread three-quarters of it carefully over the meringue base. Place the second meringue on top and dust with icing sugar. Put the remaining cream into a piping bag fitted with a 1 cm (½ in) star nozzle and pipe 8 to 10 rosettes around the top edge. Place a toasted hazelnut on top of the rosettes.

WINTER MENU

SERVES 12

Cocktails:
Victoria, Sidecar and Lace

— * —

Trio of Melon
Warm Scallops with Radicchio

— * —

Pink Champagne Sorbet

— * —

Celebration Spiced Beef
Pommes de Terre Dauphinoise
Pastry Cases Filled with Beetroot
Confits and Horseradish
Mayonnaise

— * —

Petit Jardin
Leafy Salad with Tiny Cheeses

— * —

Chocolate and Coffee Galettes
Hazelnut Fudge
Cream and Cherry Fudge
Mango and Lime Meringue Pie
with Fresh Fruit Coulis

COCKTAILS

An excellent way to start a formal party,
these three drinks are sure to be a success.
Don't forget the low-alcohol recipe for
non-drinkers.

VICTORIA

SERVES 6

185 ml (6½ fl oz) gin
185 ml (6½ fl oz) dry vermouth
60 ml (2 fl oz) apricot brandy
Ice
1 tablespoon grenadine

Pour the gin, vermouth, brandy and ice into a large jug and mix well. Strain into serving glasses with lots of crushed ice. Drop the grenadine down through the centre of the drink to give a red glow. Serve with a cocktail stirrer.

SIDECAR

SERVES 6

1 egg white, size 3
60 g (2 oz) caster sugar
Crushed ice
170 ml (6 fl oz) brandy
115 ml (4 fl oz) Cointreau
115 ml (4 fl oz) lemon juice

Dip the rim of the glass in the egg white, then in the sugar. Combine the rest of the ingredients in a cocktail shaker and give a brisk shake. Strain into glasses and then serve.

LACE

SERVES 6

1 egg white, size 3
30 g (1 oz) caster sugar
310 ml (11 fl oz) low-alcohol white wine
185 ml (6½ fl oz) natural cream of coconut
355 ml (12½ fl oz) pineapple juice
Crushed ice

Dip the rim of the glass in the egg white and then in the sugar. Combine the rest of the ingredients in a cocktail shaker and give a brisk shake. Alternatively, quickly whizz in a blender. Strain into glasses and serve.

TRIO OF MELON

SERVES 12

It's certainly worth looking out
for the three differently coloured melons
to make this colourful, light and
refreshing supper.

1 Charentais melon
(orange flesh)
1 honeydew melon
(pale green flesh)
1 watermelon
(red flesh)

Halve and carefully scoop out the seeds from the Charentais and honeydew melons. Halve the watermelon.

Use a melon baller to scoop balls from each melon, avoiding the seeds from the watermelon.

Arrange in a large glass bowl. Chill for up to 4 hours.

Bring to room temperature about 45 minutes before serving – no earlier, or the flavour will be lost. Serve the Trio of Melon in individual chilled wine glasses.

WARM SCALLOPS WITH RADICCHIO

SERVES 12

*The slightly bitter radicchio complements the
richness of the scallops wonderfully, to make a light and flavoursome
first course.*

12 large fresh scallops,
removed from shells
140 ml (¼ pt) extra virgin olive oil
2 cloves garlic, bruised
2 branches of rosemary

3 heads of radicchio, shredded
30 g (1 oz) unsalted butter
1 teaspoon caster sugar
1 tablespoon balsamic vinegar
1 tablespoon olive oil

Remove the piece of tough white muscle from the side of each scallop along with any dark membrane clinging to it. Rinse the scallops well under cold water, then drain and pat them dry with absorbent kitchen paper. Remove the pink corals to cook separately; cover and chill.

To make the pattern on top of the scallops, line up the white parts of the scallops on a flat board and brush with a little oil. Place a thin, metal skewer over a gas flame or hob until very hot. Wrap an old, clean, rolled-up cloth around the end of the skewer to protect your hand from burning. Place the skewer on the scallops in diagonal lines, reheating the skewer as necessary.

Heat 3 tablespoons of the oil in a large, flat pan or wok. Fry the garlic and the rosemary branches to flavour the oil, removing them before they burn.

Reduce the heat to medium. Put the shredded radicchio into the pan or wok and stir-fry until it just begins to wilt. Remove from the wok with a slotted spoon, set aside and keep warm.

In a frying pan, heat 2 tablespoons of the oil, and fry the corals on both sides without colouring them. Remove them from the pan and put aside in a warm place. Reserve the juices.

Wipe out the pan, add 5 tablespoons of oil and fry the scallops quickly, sealing the patterned side first. This should take 2 to 3 minutes – do not allow the scallops to over-brown or over-cook. Remove from the pan and keep warm.

Add the coral juices to the pan to heat, and add the butter to thicken the juices slightly. Add the sugar, balsamic vinegar and 1 tablespoon of olive oil, and mix well, seasoning to taste. At this stage, none of the ingredients should be kept warm for more than 3 to 5 minutes.

To serve, toss the radicchio in the pan juices and spoon a little on to each warm plate. Place a scallop and a coral in the centre and then garnish with tiny sprigs of fresh rosemary.

PINK CHAMPAGNE SORBET

SERVES 12

*Perhaps a little extravagant, but an
exciting way to cleanse the palate – and
very refreshing too.*

8 tablespoons icing sugar
2 bottles good-quality
pink champagne

Sift the icing sugar into the champagne and stir together. Pour the mixture into a rigid container and place in the freezer until slushy. Remove the sorbet from the freezer, and then churn in a food processor until 'creamy'.

Return to the freezer, then repeat this process once more.

Remove the sorbet from the freezer 15 minutes before you wish to serve it, and allow it to soften slightly. Fill tulip-shaped glasses and keep in the freezer.

This sorbet is best eaten as soon as possible after making.

OVERLEAF LEFT *A traditional
English dish from Elizabethan times –
Celebration Spiced Beef.*
OVERLEAF RIGHT *Pastry Cases filled
with Beetroot Confits and Horseradish
Mayonnaise.*

CELEBRATION SPICED BEEF

SERVES 12

*Dating back to Elizabethan times, this dish has
a wonderfully mellow, spicy flavour. Choose traditionally
reared beef, well marbled and rich in colour. The meat
will take 10 days to cure – but the final result is
well worth the time.*

3.2 kg (7 lb) topside or silverside of beef,
cut and tied ready for curing
170 g (6 oz) soft dark brown sugar
110 g (4 oz) coarse sea salt
2 teaspoons ground mace
30 g (1 oz) black peppercorns
20 g (¾ oz) allspice berries
40 g (1½ oz) juniper berries
2 cloves
4 bayleaves
Sprigs of thyme and flat-leaf parsley, to garnish

Rub the meat all over with 110 g (4 oz) of the sugar, pressing it in well. Place in a crock, enamel dish or non-aluminium tray, cover with cling film and leave in a cool place or a fridge for 2 days, rubbing with the sugar daily.

On day 3, mix the remaining sugar, salt and mace. Coarsely grind the remaining ingredients in a coffee grinder and combine with the sugar mixture. Rub well into the meat and leave for 8 days, covered as before. Rub the mixture into the meat daily, and turn. The mixture will turn liquid over the days, but still work well into the meat; don't drain any off.

On Day 11, pat the meat dry, removing any spices. Set the oven at Gas Mark 1, 275°F, 140°C. Place the meat in a deep, oval, cast-iron pot just large enough for the meat. Pour in 230 ml (8 fl oz) cold water, cover with 2 layers of aluminium foil, and seal well. Put the lid on the pot. Place in the oven and cook for about 4 hours. Do not open the pot during cooking otherwise the moisture will escape and the meat will dry out. When cooked, take the pot out of the oven, but do not remove the lid. Leave to stand in a cool place for 2 hours.

Pour off the liquid and wrap the meat in aluminium foil. Place on a board, place another board on top and put weights on top of this. Store in a cool place or chill until the next day. If storing in the fridge, take the beef out 2 hours before serving.

The meat will keep well for several days. When ready to use, place on a carving board and slice very thinly. Serve garnished with sprigs of fresh thyme and flat-leaf parsley.

POMMES DE TERRE DAUPHINOISE

Try our version of this classic French potato dish. It is quick and simple to prepare, sumptuous to eat, and excellent served with beef, pork, lamb or poultry.

1 clove garlic
85 g (3 oz) unsalted butter
1.35 g (3 lb) medium-sized potatoes, peeled
Salt and freshly ground white pepper
570 ml (1 pt) double cream
2 small bunches mixed fresh herbs, to garnish
Two 23 cm (9 in) round oven-to-table dishes

Set the oven at Gas Mark 2, 300°F, 150°C. Rub the dishes with the garlic and a third of the butter.

Slice the potatoes thinly into rounds. Carefully arrange the slices in concentric circles in the dishes.

Mix the salt and freshly ground white pepper into the cream and pour evenly over the potatoes. Dot with the remaining butter.

Cook for about 1½ hours or until the potatoes are tender. Increase the oven temperature to Gas Mark 6, 400°F, 200°C and cook for 10 minutes more, to crisp and brown the top.

Remove the potatoes from the oven and garnish with bunches of mixed fresh herbs just before serving.

PASTRY CASES FILLED WITH BEETROOT CONFITS AND HORSERADISH MAYONNAISE

SERVES 12, MAKES 24

These tartlets make the perfect accompaniment to the Celebration Spiced Beef opposite.

For the pastry cases:
340 g (12 oz) plain flour
A pinch of salt
170 g (6 oz) unsalted butter, cubed
Twenty-eight 5.5 cm (2¼ in) patty tins
For the beetroot confits:
30 g (1 oz) unsalted butter
2 tablespoons sunflower oil
Six 170 g (6 oz) cooked beetroot, peeled and cut into julienne strips
60 ml (2 fl oz) fresh orange juice
1 teaspoon fresh thyme,

finely chopped
A pinch of salt
Freshly ground black pepper
Fresh thyme, to garnish
For the horseradish mayonnaise:
2 egg yolks, size 3
½ teaspoon English mustard
A pinch of salt
½ teaspoon caster sugar
200 ml (7 fl oz) sunflower oil
1 teaspoon cider vinegar
2 tablespoons creamed horseradish

To make the cases, sift the flour and salt into a mixing bowl. Rub in the butter until the mixture resembles fine breadcrumbs. Add enough cold water to make a soft but not sticky dough. Wrap the pastry in cling film and chill for 15 minutes. Meanwhile, set the oven at Gas Mark 5, 375°F, 190°C.

Roll out the pastry on a lightly floured work surface and cut out 28 circles to fit the patty tins. Chill the pastry for 5 to 10 minutes. Line with greaseproof paper, fill with baking beans and bake 'blind' for 10 to 15 minutes. Remove the beans and put the patty tins back in the oven for a further 5 minutes to cook through. Transfer to a wire rack and leave to cool.

To make the beetroot confits, melt the butter and oil in a heavy-based pan. Add the beetroot and sweat gently with the lid on for 10 minutes, stirring occasionally. Turn up the heat slightly and add the other ingredients for the confits. Continue cooking for a further 5 minutes. Cool, cover and chill until ready to use.

To make the horseradish mayonnaise, whisk the egg yolks together with the mustard, salt and sugar, using a hand whisk. Gradually whisk in the oil drop by drop. As the mayonnaise begins to thicken, add the vinegar and remaining oil as before. Stir in the horseradish. Cover and store in the fridge. Use within 24 hours.

To serve the cases, spoon a little of the beetroot confits into 14 of the cases and garnish with leaves of fresh thyme. Spoon the horseradish mayonnaise into another 14 cases and arrange one of each on individual serving plates.

PETIT JARDIN

SERVES 12

A wide variety of fresh vegetables
that can be partly prepared in advance and stored,
covered, in the fridge, until just before serving.

2 bunches or packs (about 36) baby
carrots, peeled or scrubbed
12 baby turnips,
peeled or scrubbed
24 Brussels sprouts, trimmed
12 baby corn, neatened
1 red pepper, deseeded and cut into
julienne strips
1 yellow pepper, deseeded and cut into
julienne strips

36 baby mange tout, topped
and tailed
24 round radishes
(a little green top left on, if possible),
washed
85 g (3 oz) unsalted butter
Salt
Freshly ground black pepper
Flat-leaf parsley leaves to garnish
(optional)

Have 2 large pans and 1 medium-sized pan of boiling, salted water ready on the stove. In one of the large pans, cook the carrots and turnips for about 3 to 5 minutes until almost cooked but still slightly crisp. Drain and refresh by plunging into cold water for 1 minute, drain and put into more cold water until cool, then drain.

In the other large pan, cook the Brussels sprouts and baby corn for 2 minutes, add the peppers and mange tout for 1 minute, then drain and refresh as before.

Then, in the medium-sized pan, cook the radishes for 2 minutes, then drain and refresh in the same way as before.

When almost ready to serve, have a large pan of boiling salted water on the heat, together with a wok containing the butter melting slowly. Put all the vegetables except the mange tout into the water and heat for 45 seconds, add the mange tout for 5 seconds and then drain well.

Add all the vegetables to the wok and stir for 1 minute or until well glazed. Season to taste with salt and freshly ground black pepper. Tip out on to a serving platter, garnish with flat-leaf parsley and serve immediately.

LEAFY SALAD WITH TINY CHEESES

SERVES 12

Follow the French tradition and serve this dressed salad and cheese course
before the pudding.

2 Little Gem lettuces
2 lollo rosso
1 bunch watercress
1 packet fresh chervil
For the dressing:
1 tablespoon raspberry vinegar

5 tablespoons sunflower oil
Salt and freshly ground
black pepper
To complete the salad:
A 320 g (11¼ oz) jar Bio Greek or other
small yogurt cheeses in oil

Wash and spin all the leaves until dry and arrange on a serving plate. Place all the ingredients for the dressing in a screw-top jar and shake vigorously until emulsified.

Just before serving, toss the leafy salad with the dressing and arrange the mini cheeses on top.

CHOCOLATE AND COFFEE GALETTES

SERVES 12

Copy the stencils below to complete this simple but spectacular dessert.

230 g (8 oz) good quality
plain chocolate
For the filling:
60 g (2 oz) caster sugar
60 g (2 oz) blanched mixed nuts,
roughly chopped
4 teaspoons coffee powder

430 ml (¾ pt) double cream
A baking tray lined with foil
and oiled
A piping bag fitted with
a 1 cm (½ in) star nozzle
For the decoration:
4 tablespoons icing sugar

Break the chocolate into a bowl and melt over a pan of hot water. Using a pencil and ruler, draw a rectangle 25.5 by 32 cm (10 by 12½ in) on a large piece of greaseproof paper. Mark off into twenty 6.5 cm (2½ in) squares, extending the lines from the outer edge by about 5 cm (2 in) to give cutting guidelines.

Place the sheet of greaseproof paper on to a cool, flat work surface, pour the melted chocolate into the centre and spread evenly with a palette knife. Leave to harden. Have a long, sharp knife, a jug of hot water and a clean damp cloth ready.

Cut the chocolate into neat squares, following the guidelines marked on the greaseproof paper, by first dipping the knife into hot water, wiping it, then cutting cleanly through the chocolate. Wipe the knife and repeat the process until all the squares are cut. Place in layers between sheets of silicone paper in an airtight container, and store in the fridge.

To make the filling, make some praline by placing 2 tablespoons of water and the sugar in a heavy-based pan. Dissolve the sugar over a low heat, turn the heat up and boil the syrup until it turns golden. Remove the pan from the heat, add the nuts, mix well and pour on to the prepared baking tray. Leave to harden and cool, then place in a blender or food processor and whizz until quite fine.

Dissolve the coffee powder in 1 teaspoon of cold water. Whip the cream until soft peaks form, then fold in the coffee and praline. Place the mixture in the piping bag.

To assemble, lay 6 chocolate squares on a tray that will fit inside an airtight box. Pipe a swirl of cream mixture on to each, then place another chocolate square on top set at a slight angle. Repeat with cream and a final square.

Place a stencil on top and carefully sieve some icing sugar over it, using a tea strainer. Remove the stencil carefully and place each gallette in the airtight box. Store in the fridge for up to 12 hours. Remove the tray from the box and, using a cake slice, gently lift each gallette on to a serving plate.

HAZELNUT FUDGE

MAKES 36 SQUARES

170 ml (6 fl oz) milk
455 g (1 lb) caster sugar
60 g (2 oz) unsalted butter
A 397 g (14 oz) can sweetened
condensed milk
110 g (4 oz) toasted hazelnuts, chopped
A 16.5 cm (6½ in) square tin, oiled and
base-lined

Place the milk, sugar and butter in a large, heavy-based pan and place over a very gentle heat. Allow the sugar to dissolve and the butter to melt very slowly. Stir the mixture if necessary to prevent it sticking, but be careful not to let it splash up the sides of the pan.

Once the sugar has completely dissolved, add the condensed milk and increase the heat. Continue stirring until the mixture is smooth. Stir in the hazelnuts and bring the mixture to the boil. Boil for 35 minutes. The mixture should darken slightly, but be careful not to let it burn. When the mixture begins to thicken and darken, remove from the heat and start to beat with an electric whisk until it is thick and fudge-like.

Pour the fudge mixture into the prepared tin and leave for 15 minutes. When almost set, gently mark into squares, and allow the fudge to cool completely before cutting into squares and removing from the tin. Store the fudge in an airtight container in the fridge for up to 2 weeks.

ABOVE *Stencils for Chocolate and Coffee Galettes*

CREAM AND CHERRY FUDGE

MAKES 36 SQUARES

Rich, buttery, home-made fudge
is a real treat. Take time choosing pretty
boxes and petits fours cases to fill with
these delicious sweets. You could
make several batches of both
fudge recipes to give a
good assortment.

110 g (4 oz) unsalted butter
455 g (1 lb) icing sugar, sifted
A 170 g (6 oz) can evaporated milk
140 ml (¼ pt) double cream
60 g (2 oz) glacé cherries, washed
and halved
A 14 cm (5½ in) square tin, oiled
and based-lined

Melt the butter in a heavy-based pan. Remove the pan from the heat and stir in the icing sugar, followed by the evaporated milk and cream. Return the pan to the heat and bring slowly to the boil, stirring constantly.

Reduce the heat and cook until the fudge reaches 240°F, 116°C (the soft ball stage) – about 20 to 30 minutes. Add the glacé cherries and mix well. Pour the mixture into the prepared tin and leave to cool. When almost set, mark into squares. Store in an airtight container for up to 1 week.

MANGO AND LIME MERINGUE PIE WITH FRESH FRUIT COULIS

SERVES 12

Serve this superb pie at room temperature with a little of the
coulis for a truly tempting treat.

For the pâte sucrée:
230 g (8 oz) plain flour
A pinch of salt
110 g (4 oz) unsalted butter, at room
temperature, cubed
60 g (2 oz) caster sugar
4 egg yolks, size 3
A 20.5 cm (8 in) loose-based,
fluted flan tin
For the filling:
7 small limes
60 g (2 oz) caster sugar

2 ripe mangoes
60 g (2 oz) cornflour
4 egg yolks, size 3
For the meringue:
4 egg whites, size 3
A pinch of salt
230 g (8 oz) caster sugar
A piping bag fitted with a 1 cm (½ in)
star nozzle
For the coulis:
2 ripe mangoes, peeled
and diced

To make the pâte sucrée, sift the flour and salt on to a clean, cool work surface, make a well in the centre and add the butter, sugar and egg yolks. Using the fingertips of one hand, 'peck' the butter, sugar and the egg yolks together to form a paste, then gradually bring the flour from the edges and work into the paste until all the flour has been incorporated. Knead briefly until smooth, but do not overwork. Cover with cling film and chill for about 30 minutes. Set the oven at Gas Mark 5, 375°F, 190°C.

Roll out the pastry on a lightly floured work surface and use to line the flan tin. Prick the pastry base with a fork and chill for 20 minutes. Line the pastry case with greaseproof paper, fill with baking beans and bake 'blind' for 15 minutes. Remove the beans and return the pastry case to the oven for 5 minutes. Remove from the oven and leave to cool completely.

To make the filling, grate the rinds from 2 of the limes and place in a small, heavy-based pan with 570 ml (1 pt) water and the sugar. Slowly dissolve the sugar, increase the heat and boil for 1 minute. Remove the pan from the heat and leave to infuse for 15 minutes. Remove the flesh from the mangoes.

Squeeze the juice from the limes. Blend the cornflour with a little of the lime juice and put into a blender or food processor with the rest of the lime juice and the flesh from the mangoes. Strain the lime and sugar syrup into the purée, discarding the rind, and blend well.

Pour into a heavy-based pan and heat gently until the mixture thickens, stirring constantly. Remove the pan from the heat and leave to cool for 2 minutes. Gradually whisk in the egg yolks, then leave to cool.

To make the meringue, whisk the egg whites and salt until stiff but not dry. Gradually whisk in the sugar until stiff and glossy. Set the oven at Gas Mark 7, 425°F, 220°C.

To assemble, spoon the lime and mango filling into the pastry case. Put two-thirds of the meringue into the piping bag. Spoon the rest on top of the filling and smooth out as much as possible. Pipe swirls around the top.

Bake for 10 to 15 minutes or until the meringue is lightly browned. Remove from the oven and cool. Serve within 2 hours of cooking.

To make the fruit coulis, purée the diced mango flesh and lime juice together until smooth. Pour into a jug and serve with the Mango and Lime Meringue Pie.

PREVIOUS PAGES *Petit Jardin, and Leafy Salad with Tiny Cheeses.*

CHAPTER THREE

Impromptu Entertainment

W hen time is short, ideas for good, fast food are more than welcome. We've come up with some smart time plans. Busy cooks can create these three easy and delicious meals for two, four or six people from start to finish in around half an hour.

CRISPY POUSSINS WITH SALAD AND RICE

SERVES 2

Mediterranean Salad

— * —

Crispy Poussins
Stir-fry Vegetables with Mango
Herby Rice

— * —

Easy Trifle

COUNTDOWN

Set the oven at
Gas Mark 7, 425°F, 220°C.

Thaw the mixed fruits for Easy Trifle
in the microwave or as far in
advance as possible.

30 minutes before
Roast poussins.

25 minutes before
Make Easy Trifle, chill.

20 minutes before
Prepare vegetables for stir-fry.

15 minutes before
Pour glaze over poussins.

10 minutes before
Cook rice and egg for salad.

5 minutes before
Arrange and serve salad.

MEDITERRANEAN SALAD

SERVES 2

A refreshing, easy starter.

I egg, size 3
2 slices Parma ham
6 slices salami
Mixed salad leaves
8 black olives
For the dressing:
I teaspoon white wine vinegar
I tablespoon olive oil
A pinch English mustard
½ clove garlic, crushed
I teaspoon snipped chives
Salt and freshly ground
black pepper

Cook the egg in boiling water for 9 to 10 minutes, drain and rinse under cold water, then peel them, halve and slice. Arrange the sliced egg, the cold meats, mixed salad leaves and the olives on to chilled plates.

Place all the dressing ingredients into a screw top jar. Shake vigorously until well emulsified, then drizzle over the salad. Serve at once.

CRISPY POUSSINS

SERVES 2

These succulent tiny chickens are available from butchers and most supermarkets.

2 Poussins	I tablespoon golden syrup
2 teaspoons five spice powder	30 g (1 oz) unsalted butter
Salt	2 teaspoons dark soy sauce
I small lemon, quartered	4 tablespoon sweet sherry
Fresh coriander	Fresh coriander to garnish

Set the oven at Gas Mark 7, 425°F, 220°C. Liberally sprinkle the poussins inside and out with the five spice powder and salt. Stuff the centre of the bird with the lemon wedges and coriander. Transfer to a roasting tin and roast for 15 minutes.

Meanwhile melt together the golden syrup, the butter, soy sauce and the sherry. Brush liberally over the poussins and roast for a further 15 to 20 minutes, basting frequently. The poussins are cooked when the juices run clear when the thickest part of the thigh is pierced with a skewer.

Skim off any fat from the gravy and simmer until reduced and thickened if necessary. Pour over poussins. Garnish with fresh coriander and serve at once.

TOP RIGHT *Crispy Poussins, Stir-fry Vegetables with Mango and Herby Rice.*
OPPOSITE *Easy Trifle.*
PREVIOUS PAGE RIGHT *Fruity Crème Brûlée (recipe page 45).*
PREVIOUS PAGE LEFT *Mediterranean Salad.*

STIR-FRY VEGETABLES WITH MANGO

SERVES 2

Prepare all vegetables before you begin cooking.

I tablespoon sesame oil
2 small onions, cut into 8
I clove garlic, crushed
I carrot, cut into matchsticks
I stick celery, cut into matchsticks
I tablespoon white wine vinegar
I teaspoon soft brown sugar

½ mango, peeled and sliced
60 g (2 oz) mange tout
I courgette, cut into matchsticks
3 tablespoons ready made chicken stock
Salt and freshly ground black pepper
60 g (2 oz) cashew nuts, toasted

Heat the oil in a heavy based frying pan. Add the onions, garlic, carrots and celery, stir fry until lightly browned.

Stir in the white wine vinegar, sugar, mangoes, mange tout, courgette and chicken stock, stir-fry for 5 minutes or until vegetables are tender. Season to taste and stir in the cashew nuts.

HERBY RICE

SERVES 2

Use dried herbs to save preparation time.

140 g (5 oz) long grain white rice
1 tablespoon dried parsley

Salt and freshly ground black pepper

Wash the rice. Put into a pan of boiling, salted water, add the dried parsley and cook for 10 minutes or until tender. Drain thoroughly, and turn into a warmed serving dish. Stir through a little seasoning. Keep the rice warm until ready to serve.

EASY TRIFLE

SERVES 2

Use shop-bought Madeira cake for speed to make this delicious dessert.

85 g (3 oz) Madeira cake, broken in pieces
170 g (6 oz) fresh or frozen mixed fruit, thawed

2 to 3 tablespoons sweet sherry
140 ml (¼ pt) double cream, whipped

Break the Madeira cake into small chunks and divide evenly between 2 long glasses. Add the mixed summer fruit then pour over the sherry. Spoon over the whipped cream. Transfer to the fridge until ready to serve.

HALIBUT STEAKS AND SYLLABUB

SERVES 6

Warm Goats' Cheese Filo Parcels

— * —

Halibut Steaks with Tomato and
Rosemary Sauce
Buttered Pasta
Sugar Snap Peas

— * —

Ginger and Brandy Syllabub

COUNTDOWN

Assemble all the ingredients and set
the oven at Gas Mark 6, 400°F, 200°C.

30 minutes before
Boil pans of water for the pasta and
sugar snaps. Top and tail the sugar
snaps. Make the filo parcels.

20 minutes before
Make the syllabub, transfer to serving
dishes and leave in the fridge to chill.

15 minutes before
Prepare the salad. Chop the onion.
Cook the Halibut Steaks with Tomato
and Rosemary Sauce.

7 minutes before
Place the filo parcels in the oven.
Cook the pasta and sugar snaps.

5 minutes before
Decorate the syllabub. Drain the
pasta and sugar snaps.

WARM GOATS' CHEESE FILO PARCELS

SERVES 6

Pretty filo parcels contain a rich cheese filling.

12 sheets filo pastry
170 g (6 oz) goats' cheese
60 g (2 oz) unsalted butter,
melted
An 80 g (2¾ oz) bag of
mixed salad leaves

For the dressing:
2 tablespoons olive oil
1 tablespoon walnut oil
1 tablespoon white wine vinegar
A pinch of salt and sugar
A pinch of powdered mustard

Set the oven at Gas Mark 6, 400°F, 200° C. Cut the filo pastry into twenty-four
15 cm (6 in) squares. Allowing 4 squares per parcel, place on top of each other at a
45°angle.

Divide the goats' cheese into 6 and place a portion in the centre of each square.
Brush the pastry with a little melted butter. Draw up the edges of the pastry to make
the parcel around the goats' cheese. Press the edges of the pastry to seal, then brush
with a little melted butter and bake for 3 to 4 minutes.

To make the dressing, place all the ingredients in a screw-topped jar and shake
vigorously until emulsified. Place the filo parcels on individual serving plates with
salad leaves, pour over a little of the dressing and serve at once.

HALIBUT STEAKS WITH TOMATO AND ROSEMARY SAUCE

SERVES 6

Halibut is a firm textured fish and this simple sauce is the perfect accompaniment.

2 tablespoons olive oil
1 large onion, finely chopped
6 halibut steaks, each weighing about
170 g (6 oz)

680 g (1½ lb) tinned chopped tomatoes
2 tablespoons freshly chopped rosemary
Salt and freshly ground white pepper
Fresh rosemary, to garnish

Heat the oil in a large pan. Add the onion and cook until softened but not coloured. Add the halibut steaks, chopped tomatoes and chopped rosemary, and bring to the boil. Reduce the heat and cover the pan with a tightly-fitting lid. Simmer gently for 8 to 10 minutes, or until the fish has turned white.

Garnish with sprigs of rosemary and serve with Buttered Pasta and Sugar Snaps.

BUTTERED PASTA

SERVES 6

Buy fresh tagliatelle which cooks very quickly and can be frozen to be used at any time.

680 g (1½ lb) fresh tagliatelle with garlic
60 g (2 oz) unsalted butter

Salt and freshly ground
black pepper

Bring a large pan of salted water to the boil and add the pasta. Return to the boil and simmer for 3 to 4 minutes. Drain the pasta thoroughly, then toss in the butter. Season with salt and freshly ground black pepper, and serve at once.

SUGAR SNAP PEAS

SERVES 6

Sugar snap peas have very tender pods and are prepared in the same way as mange tout.

340 g (12 oz) sugar snap peas
or mange tout
Salt and freshly ground black pepper

Bring a large pan of slightly salted water to the boil. Top and tail the sugar snaps, and boil for 3 to 5 minutes until just tender. Drain well, season to taste and serve at once.

GINGER AND BRANDY SYLLABUB

SERVES 6

Rich, creamy and quite potent – a wonderful way to end the meal.

430 ml (¾ pt) double cream
3 tablespoons brandy
3 tablespoons syrup from
stem ginger
40 g (1½ oz) stem ginger, finely chopped
Gold or silver almonds,
to decorate

Place all the ingredients in a bowl and, using an electric beater, whisk until the mixture is thick and light. Divide the mixture between 6 glass serving dishes and chill until ready to serve. Decorate with gold or silver almonds and serve with dessert biscuits of your choice.

OPPOSITE *Warm Goat's Cheese Filo Parcels.*
LEFT *Halibut Steaks with Buttered Pasta and Sugar Snap Peas*

PESTO, PASTA AND MORE: A VEGETARIAN FEAST FOR FOUR

SERVES 4

Herby Spiced Mushrooms

– * –

Pesto Pasta

– * –

Fruity Crème Brûlée

COUNTDOWN

Preheat the grill, line the grill pan
with a sheet of foil.
Assemble all the ingredients.
Put a large pan of water on to boil for
the pasta.

30 minutes before
Cook the pasta for 10 minutes. Dice
the feta cheese and make up the pasta
sauce.

25 minutes before
Make up the crême brûlée and brown
under the grill.

20 minutes before
Drain the pasta, rinse well and place in
a bowl of cold water.

15 minutes before
Assemble the mushrooms and grill for
12 to 15 minutes.

7 minutes before
Assemble the pasta dish.

HERBY SPICED MUSHROOMS

SERVES 4

*Serve this quick, simple and
delicious dish with crusty bread as a
substantial starter. Made with smaller
button mushrooms, it also makes
an unusual canapé.*

**8 large flat cup mushrooms, wiped
and trimmed
2 cloves garlic, crushed
1 chilli, deseeded and
finely chopped
3 tablespoons freshly
chopped parsley
2 tablespoons olive oil
Salt and freshly ground
white pepper**

Preheat the grill. Place the mushrooms
stalk side up on a shallow baking tray.
Mix together the garlic, chilli and the
parsley and spread over the top.
Season and drizzle over a little oil.
Place under the hot grill for about 12 to
15 minutes.

Add salt and freshly ground black
pepper to taste, and serve hot with
crusty French bread.

RIGHT *Herby Spiced Mushrooms.*

PESTO PASTA

SERVES 4

*Everyone loves penne – here
they are served with sun dried tomatoes
soaked in olive oil (available in most large
supermarkets) and a mixture of herbs,
to make a tasty light pasta dish
with a wonderful flavour.*

170 g (6 oz) penne (pasta quills)
2 tablespoons ready-made pesto sauce
4 tablespoons olive oil
1 tablespoon white wine vinegar
A 285 g (10 oz) jar sun dried tomatoes
in oil, drained
110 g (4 oz) black olives, pitted (optional)
170 g (6 oz) feta cheese, cubed
A few whole basil leaves, to garnish

Cook the pasta in a large saucepan of
boiling, salted water for 10 minutes or
according to the packet instructions.

Drain and rinse well with cold
water, then drain and leave to cool.

Place in a large mixing bowl. Whisk
together the pesto, oil and vinegar and
mix into the pasta. Add the remaining
ingredients and place on a serving
plate. Garnish with basil leaves just
before serving.

FRUITY CRÈME BRÛLÉE

SERVES 4

*Laced with raspberries,
this is a rather special change from
the old favourite.*

230 g (8 oz) fresh raspberries,
or frozen ones, thawed
140 ml (¼ pt) double cream, whipped
60 g (2 oz) demerara sugar
30 g (1 oz) chopped
toasted hazelnuts

Preheat the grill. Divide the raspberries
between 4 ramekin dishes. Spoon the
whipped double cream over the top of the
raspberries and sprinkle the sugar
mixture over the top. Place under the
grill for 5 minutes or until the sugar has
caramelised. Sprinkle with hazelnuts
while the caramel is still hot. Leave to
cool before serving.

45

CHAPTER FOUR

Easter Lunch

A Selection of Canapés:
Spinach Roulade
Mixed Cheese Bites

– * –

Quails' Egg and Pine Nut Salad
or
Broccoli and Smoked Bacon Soup

– * –

Stir-fry of Mixed Cabbage
with Garlic
Broad Beans with Lemon
and Herbs
Root Vegetable Dauphinoise
Lamb in Pastry
Rowan Jelly

– * –

Chestnut Soufflé with
Rum Cream
Apple and Calvados Crumble
Mississippi Mud Pie

Easter Sunday is a time for special celebrations. We have devised a four course menu that's simply bursting with flavour. The delicious canapés can be served with pre-lunch drinks or at any time during the Easter weekend.

There is a choice of starters (a light salad or hearty soup); traditional Easter lamb encased in crisp puff pastry and served with seasonal vegetables and, to finish, a choice of three rich, robust puddings.

Plan ahead and you'll have lots of time to entertain your guests.

SPINACH ROULADE

MAKES 32 PIECES

Prepare the day before required and store, uncut and tightly wrapped in cling film, in the refrigerator overnight.

For the roulade:
230 g (8 oz) frozen chopped spinach, thawed
4 eggs, size 3, separated
½ teaspoon finely grated nutmeg
Salt and freshly ground black pepper
For the filling:
110 g (4 oz) cream cheese
A 20.5 by 30.5 cm (8 by 12 in) Swiss roll tin, lined with foil and well greased
4 rectangles of greaseproof paper about 10 by 15 cm (4 by 6 in)

Set the oven at Gas Mark 7, 425°F, 220°C. To make the roulade, drain the spinach, squeezing well to remove as much water as possible, then place in a large bowl. Add the egg yolks, the grated nutmeg and seasoning and mix well. In a spotlessly clean bowl, whisk the egg whites until stiff but not dry.

Carefully fold the egg whites into the spinach mixture. Pour into the prepared Swiss roll tin and level the surface. Bake the roulade for about 15 to 20 minutes until well risen and golden brown. Leave in the tin to cool.

Turn the roulade out on to a clean work surface and tear off the foil in strips. Cut the roulade into 4 pieces and lay each piece on top of a rectangle of greaseproof paper.

To make the filling, beat the cream cheese until softened, and divide it between the 4 pieces of roulade. Spread the cheese out to the edges and roll up each piece tightly like a Swiss roll. Wrap each roll carefully in cling film, twisting the ends tightly, and then refrigerate the roulade for at least 30 minutes before serving.

Just before serving, unwrap the roulades, trim the ends and cut each roll into 8 pieces. Arrange on a large platter with the other canapés.

TO FREEZE: freeze for up to 3 months.
TO USE FROM FROZEN: thaw on a wire rack for 3 to 4 hours.

MIXED CHEESE BITES

MAKES ABOUT 24

A selection of colourful canapés which are quick and easy to make – and taste absolutely delicious.

230 g (8 oz) cream cheese
Salt and freshly ground black pepper
60 g (2 oz) walnut pieces, finely chopped
2 tablespoons sesame seeds, toasted
2 tablespoons snipped chives

Beat the cream cheese until soft, and season with salt and freshly ground black pepper. Cover and chill the mixture until firm – about an hour. (The mixture can also be left in a sealed container and chilled overnight).

Divide the cheese mixture into 24 equal portions, each about the size of a walnut, and form into balls. Roll one-third of the balls in the walnuts, one-third in the sesame seeds and the final third in the snipped chives. Chill until ready to serve – up to 4 hours. Arrange on a large platter with the Spinach Roulade and Pumpernickel. A cocktail stick can be inserted into each ball for easy serving.

For another, quick, extra canapé, top some rounds of pumpernickel with a teaspoon of sour cream, and garnish with a little lumpfish roe.

QUAILS' EGG AND PINE NUT SALAD

SERVES 6

This crunchy spring salad with quails' eggs makes a stunning start to this celebratory lunch.

1 dozen quails' eggs
2 medium-sized carrots
140 g (5 oz) salad leaves such as lamb's lettuce, oak leaf, spinach, and watercress, washed
40 g (1½ oz) pine nuts, toasted
For the dressing:
1 teaspoon finely chopped root ginger
1 teaspoon sugar
3 tablespoons red wine vinegar
5 tablespoons sunflower oil
2 teaspoons freshly chopped parsley

Put the eggs in a saucepan, cover with water and bring to the boil. Boil for 3 minutes. Drain and rinse thoroughly in cold water. Leave to cool.

Peel the carrots and cut into fine strips using a vegetable peeler. Shell and halve the eggs. Spin the salad leaves in a salad spinner and gently pat dry with a clean tea towel. Arrange on 6 individual chilled serving plates. Arrange with the strips of carrot. Sprinkle over the toasted pine nuts.

Put all the ingredients for the dressing into a screw-topped jar and shake vigorously until well emulsified. Pour over the salad just before serving.

BROCCOLI AND SMOKED BACON SOUP

SERVES 4 TO 6

When buying broccoli, choose those with crisp, fresh-looking heads and stalks which snap easily.

6 rashers of smoked bacon, cut into cubes
30 g (1 oz) broccoli,
cut into florets
1 medium potato, peeled and grated
850 ml (1½ pts) good-quality
vegetable stock
Salt and freshly ground black pepper
60 g (2 oz) Emmental cheese,
coarsely grated

Put the cubed bacon in a large, heavy-based pan (preferably non-stick) and let it fry in its own fat until crisp and golden. Add the butter and when melted, add the broccoli, potato and stock. Season to taste and cook for about 15 minutes until the broccoli is soft, stirring occasionally. Remove about half of the broccoli florets from the pan with a slotted spoon. Purée the remaining broccoli and bacon in a liquidiser or a food processor until smooth. Tip the puréed soup back into a rinsed-out pan. Stir in the reserved broccoli florets and reheat.

Ladle into warmed bowls, sprinkle the cheese on top and serve at once.

STIR-FRY OF MIXED CABBAGE WITH GARLIC

SERVES 6

Cooking this cabbage quickly helps retain its crispy texture.

30 g (1 oz) unsalted butter
1 large onion, chopped
1 to 2 cloves garlic, crushed
0.9 kg (2 lb) mixture of red and
green cabbage
Salt and freshly ground
black pepper

Melt the butter in a large, heavy-based saucepan. Add the onion and garlic and cook until softened but not coloured, stirring occasionally.

Meanwhile, trim, core and finely shred the cabbage. Add to the pan and season with salt and freshly ground black pepper. Mix well and cover with a tightly-fitting lid for 5 to 10 minutes, stirring frequently. Serve piping hot with the Lamb in Pastry on page 50.

BROAD BEANS WITH LEMON AND HERBS

SERVES 6

Shelling broad beans is a time-consuming activity – but the rewards are well worth all that time and effort.

1.35 kg (3 lb) broad beans, shelled
The grated rind of 1 lemon
Salt and freshly ground
black pepper
2 tablespoons chopped mixed fresh herbs

Place the broad beans in a saucepan of boiling, salted water with the lemon rind. Simmer gently for 3 to 5 minutes. Drain well. Season with salt and freshly ground black pepper, and serve them garnished with chopped mixed herbs.

ROOT VEGETABLE DAUPHINOISE

SERVES 6

A new version of this classic potato dish, which takes only half the time to cook and has a much lighter and fresher taste

0. 9 kg (2 lb) potatoes or parsnips, peeled
Salt and freshly ground
black pepper
430 ml (¾ pt) milk
¼ teaspoon nutmeg
A large sprig of rosemary
60 g (2 oz) Cheddar cheese, grated
Fresh rosemary to garnish
A large, ovenproof dish, greased

Set the oven at Gas Mark 7 425°F, 220°C. Cut the potatoes or parsnips into 6 mm (¼ in) thick slices. Do not rinse or soak in water. Lightly season the slices and put them into a large, heavy-based pan with the milk and the nutmeg. Pluck the rosemary leaves from the stalk and add to the pan. Bring to the boil and simmer gently for about 7 to 10 minutes, stirring occasionally to prevent the mixture from sticking to the sides of the pan.

Carefully pour into the prepared dish. Sprinkle with grated cheese. The potatoes can be prepared to this stage and kept covered and chilled for up to 4 hours. Bake for 15 to 20 minutes or until bubbling and golden brown. Serve garnished with fresh rosemary sprigs.

PREVIOUS PAGE RIGHT *Chestnut Soufflé and Apple and Calvados Crumble.*
PREVIOUS PAGE LEFT *A Selection of Canapés; Mixed Cheese Bites and Spinach Roulades.*

LAMB IN PASTRY

SERVES 6

*Carefully arrange the pastry
leaves over the lamb to create an
impressive centrepiece for your Easter
lunch. To make the leg of lamb easy
to carve, ask your butcher to
remove the H-bone for you.*

A 1.35 kg (3 lb) leg of lamb,
H-bone removed
2 cloves garlic, finely sliced
2 to 3 tablespoons olive oil
1 onion, finely chopped
230 g (8 oz) field mushrooms,
wiped and sliced
1 to 2 tablespoons creamed horseradish
60 g (2 oz) fresh brown breadcrumbs
Salt and freshly ground
black pepper
570 g (1¼ lb) puff pastry, thawed if frozen
Beaten egg to glaze

Remove any gristle and fat from the meat. Make slits down the length of the lamb and insert the slivers of garlic.

Heat the oil in a large, heavy-based pan and fry the meat briskly on all sides until completely browned. Carefully remove from the saucepan and drain thoroughly on absorbent kitchen paper. Leave to cool, then chill for 1 hour.

Meanwhile, fry the onion and the mushrooms in the remaining oil and meat juices for 5 minutes until softened but not coloured. Tip into a liquidiser or food processor with the horseradish, breadcrumbs and seasoning, and blend until smooth. Leave to cool.

Set the oven at Gas Mark 7, 425°F, 220°C. Roll out the pastry on a lightly floured work surface to a rectangle large enough to cover the leg of lamb completely. Spread the mushroom mixture down the centre of the pastry and place the lamb in the centre. Brush the pastry rim with the beaten egg and draw up the pastry to enclose the lamb completely. Brush with the beaten egg and garnish with the pastry trimmings, glazing the pastry as necessary.

Bake the lamb for 1½ to 1¾ hours, covering with foil after 20 minutes to prevent the pastry from overbrowning. Serve at once garnished with glazed spring vegetables.

ROWAN JELLY

MAKES 680 G (1½ LB)

*If you have difficulty buying
rowan berries, substitute cranberries
for them. This soft-set jelly can be
made at least one week
in advance.*

**455 g (1 lb) cooking apples
455 g (1 lb) rowan berries
Granulated sugar (see recipe)
Sterilised jam jars, covers
and labels**

Cut any blemishes off the apples and roughly chop them, including peel and cores, and place in a non-aluminium preserving pan with the rowan berries. Add 850 ml (1½ pts) cold water to cover the fruit. Bring to the boil, cover and simmer, stirring occasionally, until very soft. Strain the fruit overnight in a jelly bag.

Measure the liquid and weigh out 455 g (1 lb) of sugar for each 570 ml (1 pt). Put the liquid and sugar into a clean preserving pan and stir well. Stir over a low heat until the sugar has completely dissolved. Bring to the boil and boil rapidly for 10 to 15 minutes or until the setting point is reached. Skim if necessary, and pot in warmed jam jars. Cover, label and store the jars in a cool, dry cupboard.

LEFT *Lamb in Pastry, with Rowan Jelly,
and Quails' Egg and Pine Nut Salad.*

FROM LEFT *Root Vegetable
Dauphinoise, Chestnut Soufflé, Apple and
Calvados Crumble, Stir-fry of Mixed
Cabbage with Garlic, and
Rowan Jelly (centre).*

CHESTNUT SOUFFLÉ WITH RUM CREAM

SERVES 6

*A strongly flavoured rum cream is the
perfect accompaniment to this wonderfully light, hot soufflé.*

280 ml (½ pt) milk
60 g (2 oz) caster sugar
A pinch of salt
30 g (1 oz) plain flour
4 eggs, size 3, separated

10 g (¼ oz) unsalted butter
85 g (3 oz) chestnut purée
A few drops vanilla essence
2 marrons glacés,
roughly chopped

Heat 6 tablespoons of milk with the sugar and salt until scalding. Blend the flour with the remaining milk and stir into the sweetened milk. Return to the rinsed-out pan and bring to the boil, stirring all the time, reduce the heat and simmer for 2 to 3 minutes. Remove the pan from the heat. Leave to cool for 2 minutes. Beat in the egg yolks, butter, chestnut purée, vanilla essence and marrons glacés.

Whisk the egg whites until stiff but not dry and carefully fold them into the chestnut mixture. Pour into the soufflé dish and bake in the oven for 35 minutes or until well risen and golden. Very lightly whip the cream until it just holds itself, add the rum and sugar and whip the mixture to a soft dropping consistency. Serve the soufflé immediately with the rum-flavoured cream.

MISSISSIPPI MUD PIE

SERVES 8
One of our favourite recipes!

For the base:
280 g (10 oz) chocolate digestive biscuits
85 g (3 oz) unsalted butter
For the filling:
4 tablespoons milk
255 g (9 oz) marshmallows
340 g (12 oz) good-quality plain chocolate
2 teaspoons instant coffee
430 ml (¾ pt) double cream
To decorate:
30 g (1 oz) good-quality white chocolate
A 21.5 cm (8½ in) spring-clip cake tin,
base-lined

To make the base, crush the biscuits into fine crumbs. Melt the butter and stir in the biscuit crumbs. Carefully line the base and sides of the tin with the biscuit crumbs. Chill while making the filling.

To make the filling, place the milk and the marshmallows in a heavy-based saucepan, and heat gently until the marshmallows have melted. Remove the saucepan from the heat and leave to cool completely.

Melt the plain chocolate in a bowl set over a pan of gently simmering water. Leave to cool. Dissolve the coffee in 2 tablespoons of boiling water and leave to cool. Whip the cream until soft peaks form.

Fold the cooled chocolate and coffee into the marshmallow mixture and add the whipped cream. Mix well and pour into the prepared tin. Smooth the surface with a palette knife or the back of a metal spoon.

To decorate the pie, melt the white chocolate as described above. Drop small amounts on top of the chocolate mixture and drag a cocktail stick across the surface to make swirls. Chill for about 2 or 3 hours or until set.

Carefully unmould from the tin and transfer to a chilled serving plate.

TO FREEZE: remove from the tin and open-freeze for up to 1 month.

TO USE FROM FROZEN: thaw overnight in the fridge, or at room temperature for about 8 hours.

APPLE AND CALVADOS CRUMBLE

SERVES 6

Calvados is an apple-based brandy that is matured slowly in old oak casks. Used in combination with apples it will make this everyday dish into something very special.

1.35 kg (3 lb) cooking apples,
peeled, cored and roughly chopped
110 g (4 oz) light muscovado sugar
3 to 4 tablespoons Calvados
30 g (1 oz) unsalted butter
For the crumble:
170 g (6 oz) unsalted butter

340 g (12 oz) plain flour, sifted
½ teaspoon cinnamon
170 g (6 oz) light muscovado sugar
The grated rind of 1 lemon
A 1.15 litre (2 pt) ovenproof dish,
well greased

Set the oven at Gas Mark 4, 350°F, 180°C. Put the apples, the sugar, Calvados and butter into a heavy-based pan, cook over a gentle heat for about 10 minutes or until the apples are softened, stirring frequently. Spoon into the ovenproof dish.

To make the crumble, rub the butter into the flour and cinnamon until the mixture resembles breadcrumbs. Stir in the sugar and the lemon rind. Sprinkle the crumble mixture on top of the apple. Bake in the oven for 30 to 40 minutes or until golden brown. Serve hot with whipped cream or custard.

TO FREEZE: assemble in a freezer/ovenproof dish, and freeze before cooking.

TO USE FROM FROZEN: thaw at room temperature for 3 to 4 hours before cooking as described above.

Catering for a Wedding

A fork buffet of eye-catching cold dishes is usually considered appropriate for a Wedding Breakfast starting at midday or in the early afternoon, while bite-size pop-in-the-mouth finger food is more suitable for a teatime reception. Here are two spectacular spreads – perfect for either an elaborate or a simple celebration.

A WEDDING BUFFET

Asparagus and Brie Quiche

Celebration Salmon

Olive-studded Duck Terrine

Roast Beef with
Horseradish Sauce

Jambon Persillé

Chicken Filo Tartlets

Cheesy Gougère with
Turkey Divan Filling

— ∗ —

Sesame Mushroom Salad

Oriental Salad

Sprouted Salad

Potato & Bacon Salad

Mixed Pepper Salad with
Herb Dressing

— ∗ —

Iced Amaretti Soufflé

Summer Strawberry Tart

Hazelnut Gâteau

Chocolate Mousse Cake

— ∗ —

Tiers of Joy:
Traditional Wedding Cake

ASPARAGUS AND BRIE QUICHE

MAKES ONE 10 INCH QUICHE, SERVES 12 TO 16

For the pastry:
230 g (8 oz) plain flour
A pinch of salt
110 g (4 oz) butter
For the filling:
230 g (8 oz) fresh asparagus
110 g (4 oz) ripe Brie, rind removed
140 ml (¼ pt) single cream
140 ml (¼ pt) Greek-style yogurt
4 eggs, size 3, beaten
Salt, cayenne pepper and nutmeg
A 25.5 cm (10 in) loose-based quiche tin

Set the oven at Gas Mark 6, 400°F, 200°C. To make the pastry, sift the flour and salt into a mixing bowl, and rub in the butter until the mixture resembles fine breadcrumbs. Stir in enough icy water to make a soft but not sticky dough. Wrap and chill for 10 minutes, until firm.

Roll the pastry out on a lightly floured surface to a circle about 30.5 cm (12 in) across and use to line the tin. Line the pastry case with greaseproof paper, fill with baking beans and bake 'blind' for 10 minutes. Remove the baking beans and greaseproof paper and bake the pastry for a further 10 to 15 minutes. Remove the pastry case from the oven and cool slightly (do not remove from the tin). Put a baking tray in the oven to heat up.

Meanwhile, remove the woody ends from the asparagus, then trim the tough outer layer with a vegetable peeler, and remove the v-shaped spurs. Cut into 4 cm (1½ in) lengths and blanch the asparagus in boiling salted water for 3 to 5 minutes. Drain and refresh with cold water. Drain thoroughly and dry with absorbent kitchen paper. Reduce the oven temperature to Gas Mark 4, 350°F, 180°C.

Beat the brie with the cream until softened, mix in the yogurt, eggs and plenty of seasoning (this can be quickly done in a food processor). Arrange the asparagus spears in the pastry case, pour over the Brie mixture. Place the quiche on the hot baking sheet and bake for about 35 to 40 minutes until golden and set. Serve warm.

The quiche can be made up to 2 days ahead, stored in the refrigerator, then gently reheated when required.

CELEBRATION SALMON

SERVES 10 TO 12

Poached salmon goes a long way and is very easy to serve. Here it is mixed with a herby mayonnaise and layered with marinated cucumbers and slices of egg.

4 large cucumbers, total weight about
1.35 kg (3 lb), washed
2 tablespoons sea salt
6 tablespoons white wine vinegar
60 g (2 oz) caster sugar
4 tablespoons roasted sesame oil
A salmon piece, about 680 g (1½ lb)
280 ml (½ pt) mixture of dry white wine
and water
6 peppercorns
A slice of onion
A few sprigs of parsley
For the mayonnaise:
85 g (3 oz) fresh parsley, finely chopped
2 tablespoons dill, chopped
280 ml (½ pt) soured cream
570 ml (1 pt) good quality mayonnaise
Salt and freshly ground black pepper
To complete:
8 hard-boiled eggs, sliced
A little diced cucumber
Salmon roe (optional)

Halve the cucumbers lengthways and, using a teaspoon, hollow out and discard the seeds and pulpy centres. Cut the cucumbers lengthways again, and then into 1 cm (½ in) cubes. Tip the cubes into a large bowl and sprinkle with the salt. Leave to stand at room temperature for 2 hours. Drain the cucumbers well, squeezing out any excess water with your hands. Transfer to a clean bowl, add the vinegar and sugar and mix well. Heat the oil and then pour over the cucumber. Mix , cover and leave to stand for a further 4 hours or overnight.

To cook the salmon, set the oven at Gas Mark 4, 350°F, 180°C. Put the salmon in a roasting tin or ovenproof dish. Pour over the wine and water mixture, add the peppercorns, slice of onion and the parsley sprigs. Cover with foil and bake for 20 to 25 minutes or until the salmon flakes when tested. Leave the fish to cool in the liquid, then remove, discard skin and bones and flake the fish into large chunks (the liquid can be saved for use in other fish recipes). Cover and chill the fish until ready to assemble. Mix together all the ingredients for the mayonnaise, season to taste and chill.

To assemble, fold the salmon into the mayonnaise. Spoon a layer of salmon mixture into the bottom of a glass serving bowl. Place a layer of sliced egg on top. Drain the cucumbers and arrange a layer of cucumber on top of the eggs. Continue layering, finishing with a layer of salmon. Cover and chill until required (up to 12 hours). Just before serving garnish with diced cucumber and salmon roe (if wished).

OLIVE-STUDDED DUCK TERRINE

MAKES ONE 0.9 KG (2 LB) TERRINE, CUTS INTO 10 SLICES

280 g (10 oz) duck flesh, free from skin
and bones
230 g (8 oz) fat pork
230 g (8 oz) minced veal
60 g (2 oz) duck liver, from the bird
30 g (1 oz) unsalted butter
2 cloves garlic, or to taste, crushed
2 tablespoons brandy

Salt and freshly ground black pepper
To complete:
18 to 20 rashers streaky bacon
2 bayleaves
4 to 6 juniper berries
1½ to 2 jars (185 g (6½ oz) size)
pimento-stuffed green olives
A 0.9 kg (2 lb) loaf tin or terrine, greased

Neatly dice the duck flesh and coarsely mince the fat pork. Mix these together with the veal. Lightly brown the duck liver in the heated butter, then leave to cool. Dice the liver, add to the meat mixture with crushed garlic and brandy and thoroughly combine. Season well. Cover and chill for 24 hours, stirring occasionally.

The next day, set the oven at Gas Mark 4, 350°F, 180°C. Remove the rind from the bacon, then stretch the rashers with the back of a round-bladed knife. Arrange the bay leaves and juniper berries in the base of the loaf tin. Neatly line the tin with the bacon rashers, leaving the ends hanging over the sides. Stir the duck mixture well, then put half into the tin and press down well to form an even layer. Arrange a layer of stuffed olives on top, then cover with the remaining duck mixture and spread evenly. Wrap the ends of the bacon over the mixture to encase.

Stand the loaf tin in a roasting tin. Pour boiling water into the roasting tin to a depth of 2.5 cm (1 in). Cook for about 2½ hours or until the juices run clear. Remove the loaf tin from its water bath. Cover with a double layer of foil, then top with weights. Leave to cool, then chill for 2 days to allow the flavours to develop.

TO FREEZE: when cold, remove from the tin, wrap and freeze for up to 2 months.
TO USE FROM FROZEN: thaw in fridge for 1 to 2 days.

ROAST BEEF WITH HORSERADISH SAUCE

SERVES 10 TO 12

A buffet meal is simply not complete without delicious, home-cooked roast beef.

2 cloves garlic
2.3 kg (5 lb) joint of lean sirloin or
entrecôte steak
Salt and freshly ground black pepper
140 ml (¼ pt) red wine
A large bunch of thyme
For the sauce:
140 ml (¼ pt) double cream
4 tablespoons horseradish sauce
Sprigs of fresh thyme,
to garnish

Set the oven at Gas Mark 7, 425°F, 220°C. Cut the garlic into fine slivers. Using a sharp knife, make a number of deep cuts in the joint and insert the slivers of garlic. Season the joint with salt and freshly ground black pepper, and place in a roasting tin. Pour over the red wine and arrange the thyme on top of the joint. Cover the meat completely with foil and roast for 1 hour for a rare joint, or if you prefer it medium or well done allow about 15 to 30 minutes extra. Remove from the oven and leave covered with foil until completely cold. Remove the thyme and leave in the fridge overnight.

To make the horseradish sauce, whip the cream until it just holds its shape and fold into the horseradish sauce. Taste and adjust the seasoning as necessary, then spoon into a small serving bowl.

Arrange slices of beef on a serving platter (up to 2 hours in advance), or leave the joint whole and allow guests to carve for themselves. Garnish with sprigs of fresh thyme and leave in the fridge until just before serving.

JAMBON PERSILLÉ

SERVES 10 TO 12

A festive ham and parsley terrine, which is very popular in France.
Use good quality uncooked ham and plenty of fresh parsley. The ham is fiddly
to shred, but this recipe is very simple and can be made
well in advance.

2.3 kg (5 lb) piece ham (we used shank)
455 g (1 lb) veal bones
2 large onions, halved
A large bouquet garni
2 black peppercorns
1 leek, trimmed and split
3 stalks celery, sliced
2 carrots, quartered
A 750 ml (1¼ pts) bottle dry white wine
6 shallots, finely chopped
6 tablespoons finely chopped fresh parsley
Salt and freshly ground white pepper
A 24 g (0.85 oz) packet aspic
Snipped mustard and cress, to garnish
A 2 litre (3½ pt) terrine, oiled and lined with
greaseproof paper

Soak the ham in cold water for 12 hours or overnight, changing the water once or twice. Blanch the veal bones in a large pan of boiling water for 5 minutes, then drain. Singe the onion halves over an electric plate or gas ring until very dark (this will add colour and flavour to the stock). Put the ham, bones, bouquet garni, peppercorns, browned onions, leek, celery, carrots, 570 ml (1 pt) of the white wine and enough water to cover into a large, heavy-based pan (not aluminium). Bring slowly to the boil, skim well and simmer partially covered for 2½ to 3 hours (skimming the pan frequently), until the ham is tender enough to be pulled apart with a fork. Top up with more boiling water, if necessary, to keep the meat covered. Remove the pan from the heat and leave to cool for 30 minutes. Carefully lift out the ham and discard the skin. Boil the ham stock until the cooking liquid is reduced to about 1.15 litres (2 pt).

Meanwhile, pull the meat into large shreds with 2 forks (see the photograph above for the texture of the meat) and mix with the remaining white wine, chopped shallots, parsley and a little white pepper.

Strain the reduced liquid through fine muslin or a coffee filter paper, and taste for seasoning – if the mixture has enough salt, add pepper only. Dissolve the aspic in the strained liquor according to packet instructions and leave to cool.

Arrange a layer of ham mixture in the base of the prepared terrine, and spoon over enough of the aspic liquid barely to cover, but allowing the aspic to seep between the pieces of meat. Chill until set. Continue layering until all the ingredients are used. Pour over enough liquid to cover. Cover and chill the ham aspic overnight. It can be chilled for up to a week.

To serve, loosen the sides of the mould with a palette knife, unmould on to a chilled serving platter and garnish with mustard and cress just before serving. Serve the ham thickly sliced.

CHICKEN FILO TARTLETS

SERVES 12

These light and delicate filo pastry cases can be made the day before use and filled with the chicken, celery and orange mayonnaise two hours before serving. It's worth making extra pastry cases to allow for breakages.

3 sheets filo pastry
60 g (2 oz) unsalted butter, melted
For the filling:
4 oranges
4 sticks celery, chopped
1 tablespoon tarragon, chopped
4 spring onions, trimmed and chopped
4 tablespoons good quality mayonnaise
455 g (1 lb) cooked chicken breasts, free
from skin and bone
Salt and freshly ground black pepper
12 Yorkshire pudding tins, buttered

Set the oven at Gas Mark 6, 400°F, 200°C. Cut each filo sheet into eight 12.5 cm (5 in) squares. Place 1 square of filo in the base of each tin, brush the base only with butter. Place the second sheet of filo on the top, set at a different angle to the first. Again, brush the base only with butter and prick the pastry bases with a fork. Bake for 3 to 4 minutes or until crisp and just golden. Carefully remove and leave to cool on a wire rack.

To make the filling, peel and segment the oranges over a bowl (to catch any juice). Mix the segments with the celery, tarragon and spring onions. Mix the mayonnaise with the orange juice. Slice the chicken breasts into thin strips and add to the celery mixture with the mayonnaise. Taste and adjust the seasonings, cover the mixture and chill until required. Stir well before use. Fill the pastry cases with the chicken mixture no more than 2 hours before serving and keep cool. Garnish with celery leaves.

ABOVE *Jambon Persillé.*
OPPOSITE *Olive-studded Duck Terrine.*
PREVIOUS PAGE *Celebration Salmon, made with mayonnaise.*

CHEESY GOUGÈRE WITH TURKEY DIVAN FILLING

SERVES 10 TO 12

A savoury cheese choux pastry ring with an unusual cold filling.

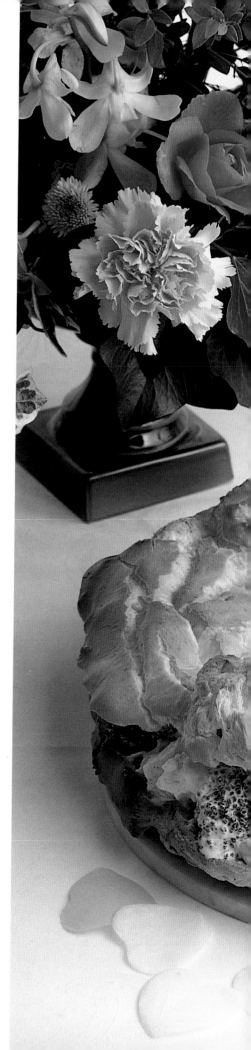

For the choux pastry:
70 g (2½ oz) unsalted butter, diced
100 g (3½ oz) plain flour, sifted
½ teaspoon salt
4 eggs, size 3, beaten
60 g (2 oz) Gruyère cheese, finely chopped
or diced
Freshly ground black pepper
and grated nutmeg,
to taste

For the filling:
455 g (1 lb) broccoli, trimmed into florets
680 g (1½ lb) cooked turkey meat, free
from skin and bone
280 ml (½ pt) Greek-style yogurt
280 ml (½ pt) good quality mayonnaise
1 tablespoon mild curry paste, or to taste
60 g (2 oz) toasted cashew nuts, or to taste
A large baking tray, greased and floured,
marked with a 25.5 cm (10 in) circle

Set the oven at Gas Mark 7, 425°F, 220°C. To make the choux pastry ring, put 170 ml (6 fl oz) water in a medium-sized, heavy-based pan and add the butter. Heat gently until the fat has melted, then quickly bring to the boil. Remove the pan from the heat and add the flour and salt to the hot liquid. Beat thoroughly with a wooden spoon. Return to a gentle heat and continue beating until the mixture is smooth and forms a ball in the centre of the pan (1 to 2 minutes). Remove from the heat, tip the mixture into a large bowl and cool for a few minutes. Gradually beat in the eggs, using a hand-held or electric mixer, followed by the cheese, pepper and nutmeg.

The choux paste should be thick and glossy, with a piping consistency. Using a dessertspoon, spoon the choux paste around the marked circle on the prepared baking tray to form a thick ring. Bake the gougère for 15 minutes, then reduce the oven temperature to Gas Mark 6, 400°F, 200°C. Continue cooking for a further 10 to 15 minutes, or until puffed and golden. Make small slits in the gougère to allow steam to escape, return to oven for 5 minutes, or until crisp. Cool on a wire rack. Store in an airtight tin and use within 24 hours

Meanwhile, to make the filling, blanch the broccoli in boiling, salted water for 5 minutes or until just tender. Drain and refresh under cold water. Drain thoroughly, then leave on a tray lined with absorbent kitchen paper. Cube the turkey meat. Mix the remaining ingredients for the filling together and season to taste. Fold in the broccoli and turkey. Carefully slit the gougère in half horizontally, and fill with the turkey mixture. Cover and chill until ready to use – up to 4 hours. If keeping for more than a couple of hours, it's best to add the broccoli just before serving.

TO FREEZE: freeze the gougère for up to 2 months.

TO USE FROM FROZEN: thaw on a wire rack, crisp up in the oven for a few minutes, then cool again before filling.

SESAME MUSHROOM SALAD

SERVES 10

680 g (1½ lb) button mushrooms, sliced
For the dressing:
2 tablespoons white wine vinegar
1 teaspoon Dijon mustard

1½ teaspoons light soy sauce
2 tablespoons toasted sesame seeds
Pinch of soft, light brown sugar
6 tablespoons olive oil

Put the mushrooms into a large bowl. Whisk together the vinegar, mustard, soy sauce, sesame seeds and brown sugar. Add the oil in a slow steady stream, whisking all the time until emulsified. Pour the dressing over the mushrooms and toss gently. Cover and chill until required – up to 6 hours. Toss gently before serving.

ORIENTAL SALAD

SERVES 10

Colourful, refreshing and full of flavour – this lovely salad can be made several hours in advance.

455 g (1 lb) white cabbage
230 g (8 oz) red cabbage
6 spring onions, thinly sliced on the diagonal
A 2.5 cm (1 in) piece fresh root ginger, peeled and finely chopped or grated
3 carrots, peeled and grated
110 g (4 oz) shelled roasted peanuts
For the dressing:
2 tablespoons light soy sauce
1 tablespoon roasted sesame oil
3 tablespoons sunflower oil
2 tablespoons white wine vinegar
½ teaspoon Dijon mustard
1 teaspoon soft, light brown sugar
Freshly ground black pepper

Finely shred the white and red cabbage (the shredding attachment on the food processor can do this quickly and easily). Mix the shredded cabbage with the chopped spring onions, ginger, grated carrots and roasted peanuts.

Put all the ingredients for the salad dressing in a screw-top jar and shake vigorously until well emulsified. Pour the dressing over the salad and toss gently. Taste and adjust the flavouring as necessary. Cover and chill until required – up to 6 hours. Toss the salad gently before serving.

LEFT *Cheesy Gougère with Turkey Divan Filling.*
OVERLEAF *The Wedding Buffet table, including (from left) a selection of salads, Iced Amaretti Soufflé, Tiers of Joy Wedding Cake, Summer Strawberry Tart, Roast Beef with Horseradish Sauce, Celebration Salmon, Olive-studded Duck Terrine, Cheesy Gougère and Jambon Persillé.*

SPROUTED SALAD

SERVES 8

A large pink grapefruit
A 110 g (4 oz) packet alfalfa sprouts
A 350 g (12½ oz) packet bean sprouts

1 teaspoon caster sugar (optional)
1 tablespoon sunflower oil
Salt and freshly ground black pepper

Peel and segment the grapefruit over a bowl to catch any juice. Rinse and thoroughly drain the alfalfa and bean sprouts. Taste the grapefruit juice and add sugar if needed, then stir in the oil and a little seasoning. Arrange the grapefruit segments, alfalfa and bean sprouts in a serving dish. Pour over the grapefruit juice dressing, and toss lightly. Chill until ready to serve – up to an hour. Toss gently before serving.

POTATO & BACON SALAD

SERVES 12 TO 15

1.35 kg (3 lb) new potatoes, scrubbed
230 g (8 oz) bacon, rind removed
4 sticks celery, washed and sliced
4 spring onions, washed and chopped
140 ml (¼ pt) good quality mayonnaise

Salt and freshly ground
black pepper
2 to 3 tablespoons freshly chopped
coriander (optional)
Celery leaves, to garnish

Cut any large potatoes in half. Cook in a large pan of boiling salted water for 10 to 15 minutes or until tender. Drain, refresh under cold water, drain again and leave to cool.

Meanwhile, grill the bacon on both sides until very crispy. Leave to cool slightly and. using your fingers, crumble the bacon into small pieces, then leave to cool completely. Mix the crumbled bacon, sliced celery and chopped spring onions together with the mayonnaise, plenty of seasoning and chopped coriander, if using. Stir in the potatoes and mix. Cover and chill overnight.

When ready to serve, mix again and spoon into a serving dish. Garnish with celery leaves. Serve the salad at room temperature

MIXED PEPPER SALAD WITH HERB DRESSING

SERVES 10 TO 15

Pasta salad with peppers and herby vinaigrette. The flavour improves when left to stand.

455 g (1 lb) pasta shapes, twists or bows
1 teaspoon olive oil
1 green pepper,
deseeded and chopped
1 yellow pepper,
deseeded and chopped
4 spring onions, trimmed and very
finely chopped

For the dressing:
85 ml (3 fl oz) olive oil
30 ml (1 fl oz) tarragon vinegar
¼ teaspoon Dijon mustard
2 tablespoons each chopped fresh basil,
parsley and chervil
Salt
Freshly ground black pepper

Cook the pasta in boiling salted water with the oil for 10 minutes (or according to the packet instructions), until just tender. Drain, then rinse with plenty of cold water. Drain thoroughly. Mix the pasta with the peppers and spring onions in a bowl.

Put all the dressing ingredients in a screw-top jar and shake well until emulsified. Pour over the salad and toss well. Taste for seasoning. Cover and chill for at least 4 hours or overnight. Taste again for seasoning and toss before serving.

ICED AMARETTI SOUFFLÉ

SERVES 10 TO 12

Dark chocolate with a fluffy soufflé glacé.

340 g (12 oz) good quality plain chocolate
30 g (1 oz) unsalted butter
110 g (4 oz) amaretti biscuits, broken
into pieces
3 tablespoons Amaretti liqueur
The grated rind and juice of 1 orange
1 tablespoon gelatine
8 eggs, size 3, separated
230 g (8 oz) golden caster sugar
420 g (¾ pt) double cream, lightly whipped
To decorate:
Cocoa powder, sieved
White chocolate curls
A 23 cm (9 in) deep-sided cake tin,
oiled and lined

Melt the chocolate with 2 tablespoons water and the butter in a bowl set over a pan of barely simmering water. Remove from the heat and beat until smooth and glossy. Using a large pastry brush, brush the chocolate over the inner sides and base of the prepared tin. Leave to set. Meanwhile, soak the crushed biscuits in Amaretto while preparing the filling.

Put the orange juice in a heatproof bowl. Sprinkle over the gelatine and leave to soak for about 5 minutes. Dissolve the gelatine by standing the bowl in a pan of hot water. Whisk the egg yolks, the orange rind and sugar together until pale and very thick, and the whisk leaves a distinct trail when lifted. Fold in the biscuit mixture, the gelatine and the cream. Whisk the egg whites until stiff but not dry and fold them into the amaretti mixture. Spoon the soufflé mixture into the chocolate case and freeze for at least 12 hours – or up to 2 weeks.

To serve, quickly dip the tin in a pan of hot water to loosen, then remove the soufflé. Carefully remove the greaseproof paper. Just before serving, dust the soufflé fairly thickly with cocoa powder, then decorate with white chocolate curls (easily made by shaving good quality white chocolate with a potato peeler). Serve slightly frozen, cut into slices.

SUMMER STRAWBERRY TART

CUTS INTO 12

A disc of shortbread-like pastry is topped with strawberries, glazed and then piped with cream.

For the pastry:
170 g (6 oz) plain flour
A pinch of salt
85 g (3 oz) caster sugar
85 g (3 oz) unsalted butter, diced
3 egg yolks, size 3
For the topping:
5 tablespoons redcurrant jelly
1 tablespoon strawberry or blackcurrant liqueur
455 g (1 lb) strawberries, washed, hulled and halved
280 ml (½ pt) double cream

Sift the flour with the salt on to a cold work surface. Make a well in the centre and add the sugar, butter and egg yolks. With the very tips of your fingers, work in the sugar, butter and egg yolks together until they resemble scrambled eggs. Gradually work in all the flour around the sides. Knead the pastry lightly until smooth (the pastry can also be made in a food processor). Wrap and chill for an hour. On a lightly floured surface, roll out the pastry to a small circle, transfer to the baking tray and continue rolling or shaping to a 25.5 cm (10 in) circle. Pinch the edge of the pastry using your finger to give a fluted edge. Prick the pastry with a fork and chill for about 30 minutes (the pastry can be frozen at this stage).

Meanwhile, set the oven at Gas Mark 5, 375°F, 190°C. Bake the pastry for about 10 to 15 minutes or until golden. Cool for a minute on the baking tray, then carefully transfer to a wire rack and leave to cool completely. Store in an airtight tin for up to 4 days. (The pastry can be frozen at this stage, but breakage may occur.)

To assemble, transfer the pastry sheet to a large, flat serving plate. Melt the redcurrant jelly with the liqueur over a gently heat, beating well until smooth. Brush a little over the pastry. Neatly arrange the strawberries on top. Reheat the remaining jelly mixture until boiling, then brush liberally over strawberries to form a thick, even glaze. Leave to set for about 10 minutes. Whip the cream until thick enough to pipe, then pipe a rope of cream around the edge of the strawberries. Chill until ready to serve – up to 2 hours.

BELOW *Summer Strawberry Tart and Hazelnut Gâteau.*

HAZELNUT GÂTEAU

MAKES A 23 CM (9 IN) GÂTEAU, CUTS INTO 16 SLICES

For the sponge:
8 eggs, size 3
170 g (6 oz) soft, light brown sugar
170 g (6 oz) plain flour, sifted
60 g (2 oz) butter, melted and cooled
For the filling:
280 ml (½ pt) double cream
A vanilla pod
4 egg yolks, size 3
455 g (1 lb) unsalted butter
230 g (8 oz) icing sugar, sifted
200 g (7 oz) hazelnuts, roasted and chopped
To complete:
85 g (3 oz) hazelnuts, roasted and halved
A 23 cm (9 in) deep, round cake tin, greased and base-lined

Set the oven at Gas Mark 4, 350°F, 180°C. Put the eggs and sugar in a large mixing bowl set over a pan of hot water. Using an electric hand whisk, whisk the mixture until pale, light and thick enough to leave a distinct trail when the whisk is lifted. Remove from the heat and continue whisking until cool.

Gently fold in the flour using a large metal spoon, then gently fold in the melted butter. Pour the batter into the prepared tin and bake for 50 to 60 minutes or until it is springy to the touch and shrinks slightly from the sides of the tin. Turn out on to a wire rack and leave to cool. Fill within 24 hours.

To make the filling, heat the cream and vanilla pod until scalding hot. Cover, leave to infuse for 5 minutes. Remove the vanilla pod and whisk in egg yolks. Beat the butter until softened, then gradually beat in the hot cream and icing sugar alternately in 2 or 3 batches. Continue beating until light and fluffy. Mix the hazelnuts into two-thirds of the buttercream. Leave the remaining cream plain. Cover and chill – up to 48 hours – until ready to use.

To assemble the cake, use a long serrated knife and cut the cake into 3, horizontally. Sandwich the cake layers together using half the hazelnut icing. Spread the remaining hazelnut icing on the top and sides of the cake to cover it completely. Pipe swirls of plain buttercream on the top of the cake using a piping bag fitted with large star tube. Fill centre with roasted halved hazelnuts. Dust with icing sugar before serving. The cake can be prepared up to 24 hours ahead. Chill until required.

CHOCOLATE MOUSSE CAKE

CUTS INTO 12 SLICES

For the sponge:
60 g (2 oz) unsalted butter
3 eggs, size 3
85 g (3 oz) golden caster sugar
85 g (3 oz) plain flour, sifted
For the chocolate mousse:
280 g (10 oz) good quality plain chocolate
60 g (2 oz) golden caster sugar
1 tablespoon gelatine
6 eggs, size 3
280 ml (½ pt) double cream, lightly whipped
For the chocolate ganache:
70 g (6 oz) good quality plain chocolate
60 g (2 oz) unsalted butter
140 ml (¼ pt) double cream
To decorate:
Raspberries or strawberries
A 20.5 by 30.5 cm (8 by 12 in) Swiss roll tin, greased and lined
A 1.45 litre (2½ pt) terrine, oiled and lined

Set the oven at Gas Mark 6, 400°F, 200°C. Melt the butter, remove from the heat and cool slightly. Meanwhile, put the eggs and sugar in a bowl set over a saucepan of hot water. Whisk until pale and thick enough to leave a ribbon-like trail. Remove the bowl from the heat and continue whisking until cool. Pour half the cooled butter around the edge of the cake mixture with half of the flour and gently but thoroughly fold

in. Repeat with the remaining butter and flour. Pour into the prepared Swiss roll tin and bake for 10 to 12 minutes, or until risen and firm to the touch. Turn out to cool on a wire rack.

To make the chocolate mousse, break the chocolate into small pieces and melt in a bowl set over a pan of hot water. Cool slightly. Dissolve the sugar in 60 ml (2 fl oz) water and boil for 2 minutes. Sprinkle the gelatine over 3 tablespoons water in a heatproof bowl and leave to soak for 5 minutes. Dissolve by standing the bowl in a pan of hot water.

Meanwhile, whisk the eggs slightly. Add the sugar syrup in a thin, stream, whisking all the time. Beat for a further 5 to 10 minutes or until the mixture has cooled and thickened. Gently but quickly fold in the melted chocolate and the dissolved gelatine. Cover and chill for 30 minutes. Fold the cream into the mousse mixture.

To assemble the cake, cut the sponge into 3 strips to fit the prepared terrine. Put 1 strip into the base of the tin, pour in half the mousse mixture, top with another strip of cake, followed by the remaining mousse mixture, and finally the remaining strip of cake. Cover and chill overnight.

To make the ganache, carefully melt all the ingredients over a gentle heat, remove from the heat and beat until glossy. Continue beating until cooled and thickened. Chill until thick enough to spread, then unmould the cake and spread the ganache over the top and sides of the cake. Chill until ready to serve – up to 24 hours. Decorate with fresh raspberries or strawberries. Serve thickly sliced.

TEMPLATE 1

TEMPLATE 2

TEMPLATE 3

TIERS OF JOY:
TRADITIONAL WEDDING CAKE

Our traditional, three-tier, moist, rich and golden fruit cake is covered in marzipan, then in ready-made white fondant icing. We recommend Renshaw's Regalice, available from larger supermarkets and specialist cake decorating shops. The cake is decorated with delicate lacy piping using a template as a guide, and finished with sprays of minute, wired, fresh rosebuds and leaves, to match the bride's bouquet and head-dress. This cake is simple, yet very striking in its charm and elegance. It can be attempted by everyone other than a complete beginner, as no specialist skills are needed. However, we do suggest that you practise piping the template design to perfect your technique before starting to decorate the cake.

Wedding Cake	Square – 15 cm	Square – 23 cm	Square – 30.5 cm
Ingredients for the cake:	(6 in) tin	(9 in) tin	(12 in) tin
Currants	200 g (7 oz)	455 g (1 lb)	0.9 kg (2 lb)
Sultanas	200 g (7 oz)	455 g (1 lb)	0.9 kg (2 lb)
Raisins	255 g (9 oz)	512 g (1 lb 2 oz)	795 g (1¾ lb)
Mixed peel	30 g (1 oz)	60 g (2 oz)	110 g (4 oz)
Glacé cherries	110 g (4 oz)	230 g (8 oz)	455 g (1 lb)
Almonds	85 g (3 oz)	140 g (5 oz)	280 g (10 oz)
Butter	170 g (6 oz)	395 g (14 oz)	765 g (1 lb 11 oz)
Soft light brown sugar	170 g (6 oz)	395 g (14 oz)	765 g (1 lb 11 oz)
Eggs, size 3, beaten	3	7	13
Plain flour, sifted	200 g (7 oz)	455 g (1 lb)	825 g (1 lb 13 oz)
Mixed spice	1 teaspoon	2 teaspoons	1 tablespoon
Sherry/brandy	1 tablespoon	3 tablespoons	5 tablespoons
Cooking time Gas Mark 3, 325°F, 170°C	3 to 3½ hours	3½ to 4 hours	5 to 5 ½ hours
Bought white marzipan	680 g (1½ lb)	1.10 kg (2½ lb)	1.80 kg (4 lb)
Boiled, sieved, apricot jam, to glaze			
Cake boards	20.5 cm (8 in)	28 cm (11 in)	35.5 cm (14)
Bought fondant (sugar paste)	680 g (1½ lb)	1.10 kg (2½ lb)	1.80 kg (4 lb)

1 each 15 cm (6 in), 23 cm (9 in), and 30.5 cm (12 in) square cake tin

For the Royal Icing:

1 egg white, size 3

230 g (8 oz) icing sugar, sifted

EQUIPMENT

Greaseproof paper or non-stick baking parchment
Brown paper and string
Soft pencil
Small greaseproof paper piping bags
No.2, No.0 and No.1 Bekenal piping tubes
Fine paintbrush

8 dowels
8 pillars
Small saw
Enough 1 cm (½ in) wide ribbons to decorate each cake board
Double-sided sticky tape
Wired fresh flowers

LEFT *Tiers of Joy: Traditional Wedding Cake, and templates for decoration.*

1. Fill any holes with marzipan.

TO LINE
THE CAKE TINS

For the base, place each tin on a double thickness of greaseproof paper and draw around each base with a pencil. Cut out the squares just inside the line. Then, to line the sides of each tin, put the tin on its side on to a long, wide strip of double thickness greaseproof paper. Mark the corners with a pencil, and roll the tin's 4 sides along the greaseproof paper. Add 5 cm (2 in) to allow for the join. Cut this strip to fit the tin, making sure it is 5 cm (2 in) wider than the depth of the tin. Fold up the bottom edge of the paper 2.5 cm (1 in) along its length. Fold the paper along the pencil-marked corners to get a good, firm crease. Snip up to the fold at each corner, to fit neatly.

Grease tins with a little melted fat and fit one of the base linings in each tin, followed by the double-thickness side lining. Grease base with a little more fat and fit other base on top.

TO MAKE
THE CAKES

It is usually easiest to make the 3 cakes one at a time. Prepare the dried fruits, peel, glacé cherries and almonds in advance. Thoroughly rinse the dried fruit, drain well and leave to dry

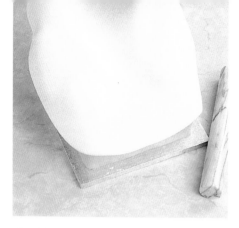

2. Lift the marzipan over the cake.

overnight on sheets of absorbent kitchen paper. Finely chop the mixed peel. Wash, drain and halve the cherries. Dry thoroughly. Roughly chop the almonds. Ensure the butter and eggs are at room temperature.

Set the oven at Gas Mark 3, 325°F, 170°C. Cream the butter until soft, then add the sugar and beat until light and fluffy. Gradually add the beaten eggs, beating well after each addition. Gently fold in the sifted flour and mixed spice using a large metal spoon. Stir in all the remaining ingredients.

Spoon the cake mixture into the prepared cake tin. Make a slight hollow in the centre of the mixture so that the cake will rise evenly during baking. Wrap the tin in a double layer of brown paper and tie securely with string. Check the chart on page 67 for the cooking times of each cake. These times are approximate, as each oven will vary. Check the cakes 1 hour before the end of cooking and, if necessary, cover the cakes with a layer of brown paper to prevent the top of the cakes becoming overbrown. The cakes are cooked when a warm skewer inserted in the centre comes out clean.

Leave the cakes to cool completely in the tins, then remove the lining paper. Cover with fresh greaseproof

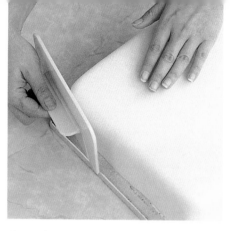

3. Polish with an icing smoother.

paper and foil, and store in a cool, dry place. The cakes will stay fresh for up to 3 months.

TO MARZIPAN
THE CAKES

Remove all your rings and bangles to prevent any marks and dents. Lightly dust a work surface with icing sugar and knead the marzipan until smooth. Brush the border of the top of the cake with a little boiled and sieved apricot jam. Roll a long, thin sausage of marzipan and attach it to the glazed edge of the cake. Press the marzipan sausage on to the cake with a palette knife to secure it and to ensure the surface is completely level.

Turn the cake upside down on the board, using a little royal icing to secure it, so that the flat base is now the top. Trim the marzipan sausage (now at the bottom of the cake) flush with the sides of the cake using a sharp knife.

Fill any holes in the cake with marzipan (**Step 1**). Brush the sides and top of the cake with more boiling hot apricot glaze.

Roll out the remaining marzipan to a square large enough to cover the entire cake (the top and sides) allowing for a little surplus. Carefully slide your left hand, palm upwards under the left side

7. Pipe over the traced lines.

8. Mark the centre of each cake.

9. Place the pillars over the dowels.

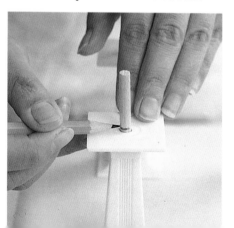

4. Pin the template to the cake.

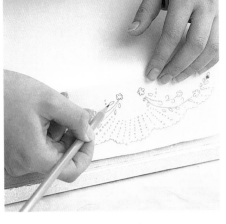

5. Carefully draw over the pattern.

6. Pipe a 'snail's trail' around the base.

of the marzipan. Lift the marzipan sufficiently to slide the right hand under beside the left, palm upwards. Keeping your fingers straight, lift the sheet of marzipan centrally over the cake (Step 2); allow the edge furthest away just to touch the board. Slowly withdraw your right hand, and then use this hand to smooth the top surface as you withdraw your left hand.

Gently flare out the corners, making sure the marzipan is not stretched too much. Smooth, and fit the marzipan to the corners by 'cuddling', cupping your hands and using an upward movement to prevent tearing the marzipan. Then smooth the sides. Trim the marzipan flush to the board using a large smoother or a sharp knife. Polish the marzipan with your hands or with an icing smoother (Step 3). Allow the marzipan to dry for 1 to 3 days.

TO ICE
THE CAKES

First make paper templates for each cake. Using a soft pencil, trace each of the 3 templates from page 66 once on to separate pieces of greaseproof paper, cut to fit the sides of each cake.

Remove all rings and bangles. Brush the marzipan with a little sherry or brandy to moisten, wiping off any

10. Replace dowels and pillars.

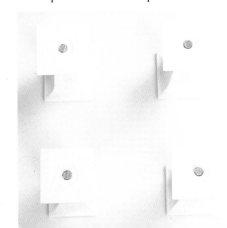

excess. Cover the cake with sugar paste as given for the marzipan (Step 2).

Take particular care not to stretch or tear the icing. If air bubbles form, prick them at one side with a pin, then gently rub bubble to expel the air. With your palm or a smoother, smooth and polish surface and sides of cake – do not press too hard or the icing will become marked (Step 3). Leave the cake to dry for 2 or 3 days.

TO DECORATE
THE CAKES

Pin the template to the cake, with the pencil-marked side facing the cake (Step 4). Carefully draw over the pattern so that a faint outline is marked on to the cake (Step 5). Repeat on each side of the cake, using template 1 for the 15 cm (6 in) cake, template 2 for the 23 cm (9 in) cake and template 3 for the 30.5 cm (12 in) cake.

For the royal icing, whisk the egg white until slightly frothy, and then gradually beat in the icing sugar. Cover the bowl of royal icing with a damp cloth until ready to use.

Using a greaseproof paper icing bag, fitted with a No. 2 piping tube, pipe a 'snail's trail' around the base of each cake (Step 6).

Using a greaseproof icing bag fitted with a No. 1 tube (or a No. 0 tube for the smallest cake), carefully pipe over the traced lines (Step 7), then use a fine paint-brush to correct any errors made when piping. Leave the cake to dry for 1 to 2 days.

The top 2 tiers are supported by wooden dowels, concealed inside hollow pillars to ensure that the cakes do not sink into each other (the paste alone is not strong enough to bear the weight of the top tier). Templates for

positioning the pillars can be made from paper or thin card. Place the 23 cm (9 in) and 30.5 cm (12 in) cake tin on paper or card and draw around the tin. Cut out just inside the line.

A square cake can have 4 pillars arranged either on the cross or on the diagonal: we used pillars placed on the diagonal. Fold the 23 cm (9 in) paper square diagonally in half and in half again (diagonally). Place the template on the cake, making sure the centre of the square is in the centre of the cake. Mark on a fold line 7 cm (2¾ in) from the centre with a pencil, repeat for each pillar, then prick through the paper with a pin to mark the cake. Repeat with the larger cake, but mark 9 cm (3½ in) from the centre (Step 8).

Remove the templates from the cake and push the dowels into the cake where the pin marks are, making sure the dowels are kept straight. Push firmly through the cake until the point touches the cake board. Carefully place the pillars over the dowels and mark each dowel 3 mm (⅛ in) above the top of each pillar (Step 9). Remove the pillars and dowels and, using a small saw, cut each dowel to the same length, using the highest mark as a gauge. Insert them back into the cake the day before the wedding and place the pillars on top. (Step 10).

The wedding cake can be prepared up to this stage, and then delivered to the wedding.

Stick the ribbon to the sides of the cake boards using double-sided sticky tape. When all the cakes have been assembled, place the wired flowers on each of the corners. Place the floral decoration in the centre of the top tier cake, as shown in the main photograph on page 54.

POP IN
TEATIME

SMOKED SALMON ROULADES

MAKES 50 ROLLS

These little sandwich rolls are delicious made with smoked salmon or, for a change, try thinly sliced smoked venison or Parma ham (omit the lemon juice from the butter if using either of these alternative fillings).

25 slices medium-sliced wholemeal bread
140 g (5 oz) butter, softened
85 g (3 oz) watercress, trimmed
and finely chopped
1 teaspoon lemon juice

Freshly ground black pepper or cayenne
455-570 g (1-1¼ lb) thinly sliced
smoked salmon
Watercress and lemon slices,
to garnish

Trim the crusts from the bread and lightly roll each slice with a rolling pin to flatten slightly. Beat together the butter, chopped watercress, lemon juice and pepper, or whizz in a food processor.

Spread the bread with the butter mixture. Arrange slices of smoked salmon on each slice and roll up like a Swiss roll. Cover the finished rolls as you work, then wrap each roll in cling film, to prevent drying out, and chill until required.

When ready to serve, trim the ends of each roll, cutting diagonally, then cut each roll in half, again on the diagonal.

Arrange the roulades on a plate and garnish with watercress and lemon slices.

TO FREEZE: wrap each uncut roll tightly in cling film and pack into a rigid container. Cover tightly with a lid and freeze for up to 2 weeks.

TO USE FROM FROZEN: thaw at room temperature, wrapped, for 3 to 4 hours. Cut and garnish as above.

SAVOURY CHOUX PUFFS

MAKES 40-45

Bite-sized choux puffs are filled with a
choice of three easy fillings, all based on cream cheese
(recipes given on the right).

140 g (5 oz) flour
A pinch each of salt and cayenne
110 g (4 oz) butter

4 eggs, size 3, beaten
A piping bag fitted with a 1 cm (½ in)
plain tube

Set the oven at Gas Mark 7, 425°F, 220°C. Sift the flour, salt and cayenne on to a sheet of greaseproof paper. Put the butter and 280 ml (½ pt) water into a saucepan. Heat gently until the fat has melted, then increase the heat and bring rapidly to the boil. Remove the pan from the heat and immediately tip in all the flour. Beat the mixture thoroughly with a wooden spoon until the flour has absorbed all the liquid.

Continue beating over very low heat until the mixture is smooth and forms a ball in the centre of the pan. Do not overbeat or the mixture will become fatty. Leave to cool for 2 to 3 minutes then gradually beat in the eggs a little at a time (a hand-held mixer is ideal for this). The choux paste should be shiny and of a piping consistency. Spoon the choux into the piping bag and pipe about 40 small bun shapes on greased baking trays, spacing them well apart.

Bake in batches for 15 to 20 minutes until well-risen and golden. (Chill the uncooked puffs in the fridge until the oven is free.) Remove the puffs from the oven, make a small slit in the side of each for the steam to escape and return to the oven for a further 5 minutes to allow the buns to dry out. Cool on a wire rack.

The choux puffs can be filled about an hour before serving.

TO FREEZE: the cooked and cooled puffs can be frozen in a rigid plastic container, layered with greaseproof paper, for 1 week.

TO USE FROM FROZEN: thaw, uncovered, at room temperature for 1 hour before filling. If necessary, crisp up in a low oven on wire racks.

THE FILLINGS

EACH IS SUFFICIENT TO FILL
20 PUFFS

For the cheese and garlic filling:
310 g (11 oz – 4 small packets) garlic and
herb flavoured cream cheese
2 tablespoons soured cream or yogurt
1 tablespoon mayonnaise
Freshly ground black pepper
A piping bag fitted with a small
star-shaped tube

For the cheese and bacon filling:
9 rashers lean bacon, grilled until crisp
225 g (9 oz) full-fat cream cheese
1-2 tablespoons whipping cream
Freshly ground black pepper

For the fish filling:
1 smoked Finnan haddock, about
395 g (14 oz)
255 g (9 oz) full-fat cream cheese
1 tablespoon lemon juice
1 tablespoon mayonnaise
1 tablespoon chopped parsley
Freshly ground black pepper

To make the cheese and garlic filling, beat the cheese until softened, mix in the remaining ingredients and beat until smooth. Taste and adjust the seasoning. Chill until ready to serve – up to 24 hours. Spoon into the piping bag and pipe into the puffs.

To make the cheese and bacon filling, crumble the bacon into small pieces, beat the cream cheese until softened, add the remaining ingredients and mix well. Cover and chill until ready to use – up to 24 hours. Slit the puffs in half and spoon in the filling using a teaspoon.

To make the fish filling, poach the haddock in milk or water for 10 to 15 minutes. Leave to cool. Flake the fish, discarding the skin and any bones. Beat the cream cheese until softened. Add the remaining ingredients and mix well. Taste and adjust the seasoning. Cover and chill until ready to use – up to 24 hours. Slit the puffs in half and spoon in the filling using a teaspoon.

CHEESE AND CRAB NIBBLES

MAKES 25

Crabmeat is mixed with cream cheese, then covered with finely chopped walnuts.

230 g (8 oz) cream cheese
1 tablespoon chopped parsley
1 tablespoon chopped chives
110 g (4 oz) crabmeat, thawed if frozen
2 teaspoons lemon juice
Salt and freshly ground black pepper
110 g (4 oz) walnut pieces

Beat the cheese until soft and fluffy, then beat in the herbs, crabmeat, lemon juice and seasoning. Cover and chill the mixture until firm – about a hour. (The mixture can also be left in a sealed container and chilled overnight.)

Finely chop the walnuts (this can also be done in a processor or blender), then spread out on a sheet of grease-proof paper. Divide the cheese and crab mixture into 25 equal portions, each about the size of a walnut, and form into balls. Roll the cheese balls in the chopped nuts until thoroughly and evenly coated. Chill until ready to serve – up to 4 hours. A cocktail stick can be inserted into each ball for easy serving.

ARBROATH SMOKIE STUFFED CELERY

MAKES ABOUT 50

Arbroath smokies, delicious hot-smoked haddock, can be replaced by cooked haddock or kippers if you prefer.

One head of celery, about 455 g (1 lb)
170 g (6 oz) full-fat cream cheese
170 g (6 oz) flaked Arbroath smokie, free from skin and bones (about 2 large ones)
The juice of 1 lemon
Cayenne pepper

Remove and reserve the celery leaves for the garnish. Scrub the celery stalks, dry thoroughly and then cut into 4 cm (1½ in) lengths.

Beat the cream cheese until soft and fluffy, then beat in the flaked fish (this can be done quickly in a processor). Season to taste with lemon juice and cayenne. Spoon the mixture into the groove in the celery pieces and sprinkle with cayenne pepper. Garnish with the celery leaves. Cover tightly and chill until ready to serve -up to 6 hours.

The filling mixture can be made the day before serving, then stored, tightly covered, in the fridge until required.

SEAFOOD QUICHE

CUTS INTO 24 SQUARES

For the pastry:
170 g (6 oz) flour
85 g (3 oz) butter
The grated rind of 1 lemon
For the filling:
140 ml (¼ pt) whipping cream
140 ml (¼ pt) soured cream
140 ml (¼ pt) milk
4 eggs, size 3
2 tablespoons chopped parsley
Salt and freshly ground black pepper
230 g (8 oz) smoked salmon
100 g (4 oz) prawns, thawed if frozen
A 30.5 by 20.5 by 4 cm (12 by 8 by 1½ in) baking or roasting tin, greased and base-lined with foil

Set the oven at Gas Mark 6, 400°F, 200°C. Heat a baking tray in the oven.

Sift the flour into a bowl. Rub in the butter until the mixture resembles fine breadcrumbs. Stir in the lemon rind and enough cold water to make a soft but not sticky dough. Cover and chill the pastry for 10 minutes. Roll out the pastry and line the prepared tin.

Prick the base with a fork, stand the tin on the hot baking tray and bake the pastry 'blind' for 10 minutes. Remove the baking beans and bake for a further 10 minutes to dry out the base. Reduce to Gas Mark 5, 375°F, 190°C.

Beat together the whipping cream, soured cream, milk and eggs. Season with parsley, salt and pepper.

Chop the smoked salmon into small pieces and arrange with the prawns on the pastry base. Pour over the cream mixture and bake for 40 to 45 minutes. Leave to cool in the tin overnight.

Run a knife round the edge of the tin to loosen the quiche. Quickly tip out the quiche and turn it back on to its base. Cut into 24 squares. Serve hot or cold.
TO FREEZE: turn out and open-freeze whole until firm. Pack and freeze for up to 3 weeks. Use drained, canned prawns or fresh rather than frozen ones if freezing this quiche.
TO USE FROM FROZEN: unwrap and thaw, at room temperature for about 3½ to 4 hours. Reheat at Gas Mark 5, 375°F. 190°C.

PREVIOUS PAGE *Platters from left: Cheese Crab Nibbles, Arbroath Smokie Stuffed Celery and Seafood Quiche; Home-made Pumpernickel Loaf; Herby Goujons and Pork Balls; Smoked Salmon Roulades and Savoury Choux Puffs.*

HERBY CHICKEN GOUJONS WITH SOURED CREAM DIP

MAKES ABOUT 25

Strips of chicken breast are coated in a herby mixture, then fried until crisp to serve hot or cold.

6 boneless chicken breasts,
about 680 g (1½ lb) in weight
30 g (1 oz) seasoned flour
3 eggs, size 3, beaten
One 280 g (10 oz) packet parsley, lemon
and thyme stuffing mix, or stuffing of
your choice
Oil for shallow frying
For the dip:
140 ml (¼ pt) mayonnaise
140 ml (¼ pt) soured cream or yogurt
1-2 cloves garlic, crushed (optional) or
1-2 tablespoons snipped chives
Salt and freshly ground black pepper

Remove any skin from the chicken breasts. Cut the flesh into strips about 2 by 7.5 cm (¾ by 3 in). Toss the strips in seasoned flour, then dip into the beaten egg. Finally, coat evenly with the stuffing mix, pressing it on well. Chill until ready to fry.

To make the dip, mix all ingredients together, then taste and adjust the seasoning as necessary. Cover and chill until required – up to 24 hours.

Heat 2.5 cm (1 in) oil in a frying pan until almost smoking (or use a deep-fat fryer heated to 350°F, 180°C). Fry the chicken for about 2 minutes on each side or until crisp and golden. Drain on absorbent kitchen paper. Serve hot or cold with the dip.

TO FREEZE: the goujons can be made in advance; open-freeze uncooked on a baking tray lined with non-stick baking parchment. When frozen, pack into a rigid container. They can be stored in the rigid container and kept in the freezer for up to 2 weeks.

TO USE FROM FROZEN: fry for 5 to 6 minutes in oil as above.

PORK BALLS WITH SPICY DIP

MAKES 25

Herby sausagemeat balls are quickly fried then served with a mayonnaise-based dip, mildly flavoured with curry paste.

340 g (12 oz) lean pork, minced
2 tablespoons chopped fresh sage
2 tablespoons chopped parsley
1-2 cloves garlic, or to taste, crushed
1 medium onion, finely grated
85 g (3 oz) fresh white breadcrumbs
2 eggs, size 3, lightly beaten
2 tablespoons flour

Salt and freshly ground black pepper
Oil for frying
25 cocktail sticks
For the dip:
280 ml (½ pt) mayonnaise
2 teaspoons curry paste, or to taste
140 ml (¼ pt) soured cream
Freshly ground black pepper

Mix the minced pork with the herbs, garlic, onion, breadcrumbs, eggs, flour and a little seasoning. Beat well. When thoroughly blended, fry a teaspoon of the mixture, taste for seasoning and adjust as necessary. Divide the mixture into 25 portions and roll into small balls. Chill until firm, at least 25 minutes.

Deep- or shallow-fry the pork balls in hot oil, a few at a time, turning frequently, until evenly browned and cooked through – about 4 to 5 minutes. Drain on absorbent kitchen paper and keep warm.

To make the dip, mix together all the ingredients, taste and adjust seasoning as necessary. Put a cocktail stick into each pork ball and serve hot or cold with the dip.
TO FREEZE: open-freeze the uncooked pork balls on baking trays lined with greaseproof paper. When frozen, transfer to a rigid container, and keep for up to 1 month.
TO USE FROM FROZEN: shallow-fry in hot oil for 6 to 7 minutes.

HOME-MADE PUMPERNICKEL LOAF

MAKES THREE 455 G (1 LB) LOAVES

*Pumpernickel squares make a delicious
base for tiny open sandwiches. Choose different
toppings for a nutritious, colourful and attractive alternative
to the usual sandwiches.*

455 g (1 lb) rye flour
455 g (1 lb) strong plain bread flour
2 teaspoons salt
1 tablespoon instant coffee powder
1 tablespoon cocoa powder
2 sachets easy-blend dried yeast
170 g (6 oz) molasses
1 tablespoon vegetable oil
170 g (6 oz) large seedless raisins
Three 455 g (1 lb) loaf tins, greased

Sieve the flours, salt, instant coffee and cocoa powder into a bowl. Stir in the dried yeast and mix well. Stir in 570 ml (1 pt) lukewarm water, the molasses and oil and mix to a soft, pliable dough. Turn out on to a floured work surface and knead thoroughly for 10 minutes. Shape the dough into a ball and place in an oiled bowl. Cover with a piece of oiled cling film and leave to prove in a warm, draught-free place until the dough has doubled in size – about an hour.

Knock down the dough and flatten into a large rectangle, sprinkle over the raisins, roll up the dough and knead gently to evenly distribute the raisins.

Divide the dough into 3 equal portions and shape each portion into a roll to fit the tin. Cover loosely with oiled cling film and leave to prove until doubled in size – this will take about 30 to 45 minutes.

Meanwhile, set the oven at Gas Mark 6, 400°F, 200°C. Bake the loaves for 35 to 40 minutes or until they are dark brown and sound hollow when tapped underneath. Cool completely on wire racks, then wrap. Pumpernickel is best kept for 3 days before cutting.

TO FREEZE: when cold, transfer the loaves to plastic bags. Seal and freeze for up to 3 months.

TO USE FROM FROZEN: thaw the pumpernickel, uncovered, at room temperature overnight.

TOPPINGS

QUANTITIES GIVEN ARE SUFFICIENT FOR ONE LOAF,
WHICH MAKES 48-56 SQUARES

250 g (8 oz) fromage frais or 230 g (8 oz) cream
cheese beaten together
with 4-5 tablespoons milk
About 110 g (4 oz) thinly sliced Parma ham
or salami or beef or smoked salmon or
anchovy fillets or lumpfish roe or
halved green and black grapes

Slice the pumpernickel into 12 to 14 thin slices. Cut each slice into 4 squares and trim off the crusts. Spread with fromage frais or the cream cheese mixture (also try adding chopped herbs, such as chives).

Garnish the squares with thin strips of Parma ham, salami, beef, smoked salmon, anchovy fillets about 2.5 cm (1 in) long, or lumpfish roe. For vegetarians, garnish with halved grapes.

INDIVIDUAL CROUSTADES WITH A CHOICE OF THREE FILLINGS

MAKES 25

Individual croustades are quick to make from sliced bread rather than pastry. Once filled, they will stay crisp for up to three hours.

250 g (8 oz) fromage frais or 230 g (8 oz) cream
cheese beaten together
with 4-5 tablespoons milk

About 110 g (4 oz) thinly sliced Parma ham
or salami or beef or smoked salmon or
anchovy fillets or lumpfish roe or
halved green and black grapes

Set the oven at Gas Mark 6, 400°F, 200°C. Brush the patty or bun tins with a little of the melted butter. Using the cutter, cut a circle from each slice of bread. Use a rolling pin to flatten each circle of bread, then carefully press into the tins to line them completely, as if making jam tarts. Brush with remaining melted butter, then bake 15 to 20 minutes or until golden and crisp – do not overbake. Transfer to a wire rack and leave to cool. Unfilled croustades will keep in an airtight tin for up to 3 days.

CROUSTADE FILLINGS

EACH IS SUFFICIENT TO FILL
25 CROUSTADES

For the mildly curried chicken filling:
230 g (8 oz) cooked chicken meat, free of
skin and bone, finely diced
1 stick of celery, finely chopped
2 spring onions, chopped

140 ml (¼ pt) mayonnaise
2 tablespoons soured cream or yogurt
1-2 teaspoons curry paste, or to taste
Freshly ground black pepper
Green seedless grapes, halved, to garnish

To make the mildly curried chicken filling, mix together the chicken, celery, spring onions, mayonnaise, soured cream or yogurt, curry paste and seasoning. Cover tightly and chill for up to 24 hours. When ready to serve, spoon into the croustades and garnish each with half a grape.

For the creamy pâté filling:
80 g (10 oz) smooth chicken liver pâté
(ready-made)
Two 100 g (3½ oz)pots fromage frais

1 tablespoon sherry or brandy (optional)
Freshly ground black pepper
Stuffed green olives, sliced, to garnish
A piping bag fitted with a large star tube

To make the pâté filling, beat the pâté until slightly softened and smooth. Beat in the fromage frais and sherry or brandy, if using. Taste and adjust the seasoning as necessary. Cover and chill for up to 24 hours. When ready to serve, spoon into the piping bag fitted with the star tube and pipe small swirls or stars in the croustades. This filling is rich so don't overfill. Garnish each with a slice of stuffed green olive.

For the taramasalata filling:
170 g (6 oz) smoked cod roe
40 g (1½ oz) fresh white breadcrumbs
1 clove garlic, or to taste, crushed

1 teaspoon grated onion
The juice of 1 lemon
140 ml (¼ pt) olive oil
Salt and freshly ground black pepper

To make the taramasalata filling, skin the cod roe and put into a processor with the breadcrumbs, garlic, onion and lemon juice. Blend to a smooth paste. With the motor running, gradually pour in oil as if making mayonnaise, to make a thick, emulsified purée. Season to taste. Cover and chill for up to 24 hours. When ready to serve, spoon or pipe into the croustades and garnish each with a little black lumpfish roe.

COCKTAIL MELON AND HAM BALLS

MAKES ABOUT 35

Tiny spheres of melon can be scooped out up to 4 hours in advance, then wrapped in slivers of smoked ham.

8-10 thin slices Parma ham
1 honeydew or ogen melon about
1 kg (2¼ lb) in weight, to yield
340 g (12 oz) flesh
Cocktail sticks
Dill or fennel, to garnish

Trim the fat from the Parma ham and cut each slice into 2.5 cm (1 in) strips. Halve the melon and remove the seeds. Scoop balls from the melon with a melon baller, or cut the melon into small cubes. Place a melon ball at one end of each strip of ham, roll it up and secure with a cocktail stick through the centre. Arrange on a plate and garnish with dill or fennel.

The melon and ham balls can be covered and chilled for up to an hour before serving.

SMOKED MACKEREL DIP

SERVES ABOUT 25

Use as a dip, or as a filling for pieces of celery.

Smoked mackerel fillets, about
340 g (12 oz) total weight
140 ml (¼ pt) soured cream or
Greek-style yogurt
110 ml (4 fl oz) mayonnaise
The grated rind and juice of 1 lemon
1 teaspoon creamed horseradish sauce
1 small onion, very finely chopped
Freshly ground black pepper
A good selection of raw vegetables or
savoury crackers, to serve

Remove the skin from the mackerel and flake the fish into a bowl. Add remaining ingredients and beat thoroughly until smooth (this can also be done in a food processor). Taste and adjust the seasoning as necessary. Spoon into a serving dish, cover tightly and chill until required – up to 24 hours. Arrange the vegetables on a large platter around the dip.

MINI PIZZAS

MAKES ABOUT 25

For the topping:
1 large onion, finely chopped
1-2 cloves garlic, or to taste, crushed
2 tablespoons soya oil
A 425 g (15 oz) can chopped tomatoes
2 teaspoons tomato purée
¼ teaspoon dried oregano
¼ teaspoon dried basil
Salt and freshly ground black pepper
4 pepperami sausages, sliced
(total weight 150 g/6 oz)
110 g (4 oz) Cheddar cheese, grated
110 g (4 oz) mozzarella cheese, diced
For the base:
515 g (1 lb 2 oz) self-raising flour
½ teaspoon salt
85 g (3 oz) butter
3 eggs, size 3, beaten
About 60 ml (2 fl oz) milk
A 6.5 cm (2½ in) plain round cutter

To make the topping, gently cook the onion and garlic in the oil for 5 minutes until the onion is soft and golden. Add the tomatoes with their juice, tomato purée, herbs and the seasoning. Bring to the boil, reduce the heat and simmer for about 20 minutes, uncovered, stirring occasionally. Leave to cool.

To make the base, sift flour and salt into a mixing bowl. Rub in the butter until the mixture resembles bread-crumbs. Make a well in the centre and pour in the eggs and enough milk to mix to a soft but not sticky dough. Set the oven at Gas Mark 6, 400°F, 200°C.

Roll out the dough 6 mm (¼ in) thick on a lightly floured surface. Cut out 25 circles with the cutter, rerolling the trimmings as necessary.

Place on greased baking trays. Spoon a little tomato sauce on each base and arrange the pepperami, Cheddar and mozzarella on top. Bake for 25 to 30 minutes. Serve warm.

TO FREEZE: cool on wire racks. Open-freeze on baking trays lined with greaseproof, then pack into rigid plastic containers and freeze for up to 1 month.

TO USE FROM FROZEN: thaw at room temperature for 1 to 1½ hours or reheat from frozen, at Gas Mark 5, 375°F, 190°C, for 15 minutes.

SAUSAGE CRESCENTS

MAKES 36

These are a tasty and attractive alternative to sausage rolls, but just as easy to make. Use cocktail sausages about 5 cm (2 in) long.

455 g (1 lb) plain flour
2 teaspoons mustard powder
½ teaspoon cayenne
230 g (8 oz) butter
36 cocktail sausages, about
455 g (1 lb)
Beaten egg to glaze

Sift the flour, mustard powder and cayenne pepper into a bowl. Rub in the butter until the mixture resembles fine breadcrumbs. Add enough cold water to bind the pastry, then knead lightly on a floured surface. Wrap and chill the pastry for 10 minutes.

Divide the chilled pastry into 2 equal portions, then roll out each portion on a lightly floured surface to a 30.5 cm (12 in) square. Cut each large square into nine 10 cm (4 in) squares, then cut each square in half diagonally to make 18 triangles – a total of 36.

Brush edges of the pastry triangles with water and put a sausage across the middle of each. Working from the base of the triangle roll up the pastry around the sausage, like a croissant. Pinch the ends of the pastry together and bend them round to form a crescent shape. Transfer to greased baking trays and chill for 10 minutes.

Set the oven at Gas Mark 5, 375°F, 190°C. Brush the sausage crescents with beaten egg and bake for about 25 to 30 minutes until golden. Serve immediately or cool on wire racks and use within a day. Serve cold or warm.

TO FREEZE: the sausage crescents can be made well in advance. Open-freeze the uncooked crescents. When frozen, transfer to a rigid plastic container, seal and keep in freezer for up to 2 weeks.

TO USE FROM FROZEN: transfer the crescents to greased baking trays, glaze, and cook at Gas Mark 6, 400°F, 200°C, for 25 minutes.

LITTLE FILO PARCELS

MAKES 24

Use ready-made sheets of filo or strudel dough.

1 medium onion, finely chopped
15 g (½ oz) butter
1 tablespoon oil
½ teaspoon mixed spice
110 g (4 oz) button mushrooms, finely chopped
280 g (10 oz) lean minced beef
1 tablespoon lemon juice
2 tablespoons chopped parsley
2 tablespoons tomato purée
Salt and freshly ground black pepper
2 hard-boiled eggs, chopped
6 sheets filo pastry
Oil for brushing
Beaten egg to glaze

Gently cook the onion in the butter and oil for 5 minutes or until softened. Stir in the mixed spice and mushrooms and continue cooking for 2 to 3 minutes, stirring frequently. Add the minced beef, lemon juice, parsley and tomato purée, and continue cooking gently for 10 minutes, stirring occasionally. Season well, stir in the chopped eggs and leave to cool. Set the oven at Gas Mark 5, 375°F, 190°C.

Carefully cut each filo sheet into 4 rectangles (cover the filo with a damp cloth while working on each parcel). Brush half the rectangle with oil and fold in half to make a square. Place a teaspoon of filling in the centre. Fold in the sides and corners to meet in the centre and enclose all the filling, over-lapping where necessary.

Place the parcels on greased baking trays, with the tucks underneath. Brush with beaten egg and bake for 10 to 12 minutes or until the pastry is crisp and golden. Serve warm, or cool on wire racks.

TO FREEZE: the filo parcels can be assembled in advance and frozen unbaked for up to a month.

TO USE FROM FROZEN: cook at Gas Mark 6, 400°F, 200°C, for 15 minutes.

CELEBRATION SHORTBREAD HEARTS

Delicate heart-shaped shortbread biscuits are simple and charming.

170 g (6 oz) unsalted butter
85 g (3 oz) caster sugar
230 g (8 oz) flour
30 g (1 oz) rice flour
or ground rice

A little caster sugar for sprinkling
A 5 cm (2 in) heart-shaped cutter,
measured across the widest part
A 2.5 cm (1 in) heart-shaped aspic cutter
(optional)

Cream the butter until soft. Add the sugar and beat until pale and fluffy. Mix in the flour and rice flour or ground rice until the mixture binds together. Knead lightly to form a smooth dough. Roll out 6 mm (¼ in) thick on a lightly floured surface. Cut out heart-shaped biscuits with the large cutter, rerolling the trimmings as necessary. Then, if you wish, use the little aspic cutter to cut out the centre of each biscuit. Place the hearts on baking trays and chill for 15 minutes.

Set the oven at Gas Mark 4, 350°F, 180°C. Bake the biscuits for 15 to 20 minutes until pale golden and just firm to the touch. Cool on a wire rack. Once cool, sprinkle with caster sugar.

TO FREEZE: layer up the biscuits in a rigid plastic container between sheets of greaseproof. Freeze for up to 2 months.

TO USE FROM FROZEN: arrange the biscuits on serving plates and thaw at room temperature for 1 to 2 hours.

VARIATION

To make Lemon Shortbread Rounds, add the grated rind of a lemon to the basic shortbread mixture. Roll out and cut out round biscuits with a plain 4 cm (1½ in) cutter. Bake as above. When cold, spread a teaspoon of home-made lemon curd (recipe on the right) on each biscuit and top with a fresh raspberry.

LEMON CURD

A home-made lemon curd – far superior to curd produced commercially.

230 g (8 oz) caster sugar
110 g (4 oz) unsalted butter
The grated rind and juice of 3 lemons
3 eggs, size 3
Small clean jars, covers and labels

Place the sugar, butter, lemon rind and juice in a double pan or a bowl set over a pan of simmering water. Stir gently until the sugar has dissolved and the butter melted.

Beat the eggs together and strain into the lemon mixture. Cook, stirring constantly, over a very low heat until the mixture has thickened. Do not overheat or allow to boil as the mixture will curdle. Pot the lemon curd, cover and then label.

The lemon curd will keep for up to 3 weeks in the refrigerator.

NON-ALCOHOLIC FRUITY PUNCH

For non-drinkers and those worried about drinking and driving.

The juice of 4 grapefruits
The juice of 2 lemons
The juice of 10 oranges
280 ml (½ pt) apple juice
Two 1 litre bottles tonic water
To serve:
Ice cubes
2 lemons, thinly sliced
Sprigs of fresh mint

Strain all the fruit juices into a large mixing bowl or several jugs. Cover and chill, preferably overnight. Just before serving, add the tonic water. Pour into several large jugs, add plenty of ice cubes plus the lemon slices and mint sprigs. Stir well, then serve.

An average wine glass will hold about 115 ml (4 fl oz) so this quantity will fill 32 glasses. Allow about 3 glasses per person.

Garland of Flowers:
Two-tier Wedding Cake

A cake for that special celebration – for a small wedding, or any other special celebration, such as a birthday or wedding anniversary. This is a classic Madeira-style cake, iced with a garland of exquisite flowers. By following our simple steps and prepare-ahead instructions, you will be amazed how easy this spectacular garland of flowers cake is to make. Make and freeze the orange-flavoured, Madeira-style cakes in advance — the cakes are much easier to ice when frozen. The flowers can be made up to a month before wiring, and stored in cake boxes. The bouquet can be wired two to four weeks before it is required, and arranged on the cake up to six hours before eating.

For the cakes	Round cake 15cm	Round cake 23cm
Ingredients for the cake	(6 in) tin	(9 in) tin
Unsalted butter	110 g (4 oz)	280 g (10 oz)
Golden caster sugar	110 g (4 oz)	280 g (10 oz)
Eggs, size 3	2	5
Plain flour	60 g (2 oz)	140 g (5 oz)
Self-raising flour	110 g (4 oz)	280 g (10 oz)
Grated orange rind	1 orange	2 oranges
Cointreau or Grand Marnier	2 teaspoons	2 tablespoons
White marzipan (if necessary)	40 g (1½ oz)	70 g (2½ oz)
Round cake tin, greased, floured and base-lined	15 cm (6 in)	23cm (9in)
Cake boards (double thick)	15cm (6 in)	0.5cm (12 in) covered with gold paper

For the Buttercream
110 g (4 oz) unsalted butter, softened
340 g (12 oz) icing sugar, sifted
1 to 2 tablespoons freshly squeezed orange juice

For the Sugar Paste
1.1 kg (2½ lb) ready-made, cream-coloured sugar paste
Icing sugar for dusting
A cake decorating smoother

For the royal icing
½ teaspoon egg white substitute; for example,
Mere-white or Renwhite
230 g (8 oz) icing sugar, sifted
Paste edible food colouring – cream

A small greaseproof piping bag fitted with a No 2 writing tube

For the Flowers
Makes 120 flowers
For the flower paste
450 g (15¾ oz) icing sugar, sifted
2 teaspoons cornflour
1 teaspoon gum tragacanth
2 teaspoons powdered gelatine
2 teaspoons white vegetable fat
2 teaspoons liquid glucose
1 egg white, size 2
Paste colouring – cream, gooseberry, mulberry pink

Equipment You Will Need for the Flowers and Leaves

White vegetable fat • Non-stick board or plastic sheets for rolling out flower paste • Small rolling pin with non-stick or metal surface • Cutters – 1 forget-me-not; 1 lily or leaf shape; 1 small, 1 medium rose petal; calyx for roses; 1 small, 1 medium ivy leaf • Ball tool • Assorted stamens – cut one end off (about ⅛ in) to use for pulled flowers; the longer length is used for cutter flowers • 1 egg white, size 3 • Petal dust – cream, pink, apricot, green, yellow, brown • No 4 paint brush • Wooden dowel • Cornflour •

Sharp modelling knife • Green covered wires – Nos 24 and 28, each length cut in 3 • Tweezers • Drinking straws cut in half and fixed into a polystyrene block (make holes for straws with the end of a paint brush) • 1 tablespoon semolina • Artist's palette knife • Cocktail sticks • Leaf veiner to mark ivy (optional) • Confectioner's glaze (optional) • 3 metres (1 yd 10½ in) green 3 mm wide ribbon • 2 metres (6 ft 7 in) pink 3 mm wide ribbon • Stem Tex • Piece of foam • Posy pick • Wire cutters • Scissors.

To Make the Cakes

Set the oven at Gas Mark 2, 300°F, 150°F. Cream the butter with the sugar until pale and light. Beat in the eggs, one at a time, adding a tablespoon of plain flour after each addition. Sieve the remaining flours together and fold into the egg mixture with the grated orange rind, using a large, metal spoon. Fold in the Cointreau or Grand Marnier, then spoon into the prepared cake tin, and smooth the surface.

Bake for 1 hour 30 minutes for the 23 cm (9 in) cake and 1 hour for the 15 cm (6 in) cake, or until golden, firm to the touch, and the cake is shrinking away from the sides of the tin.

Leave to cool in the tin for 5 minutes, then turn out on to a wire rack and leave to cool completely. When cold, wrap tightly in greaseproof paper and store in an airtight container overnight. Alternatively, the wrapped cakes can be frozen in rigid containers, to prevent damage, for up to a month.

The tops of the cakes are to become the bottoms, therefore they must be prepared so that they can sit evenly on the board. Knead the marzipan until smooth and roll out 2 thin 'sausages' to fit on top of each cake. Place a marzipan sausage on the top edge of each cake and smooth gently to the centre with a palette knife. The surfaces of the cakes should now be level. Turn the cakes upside down and place on the cake boards.

To Make the Buttercream

Beat the butter until soft. Gradually beat in the icing sugar and orange juice. Continue beating until pale and creamy. Spread over the cakes evenly, using a large palette knife.

To Ice the Cakes

To cover the cakes, divide the sugar paste so that you have 795 g (1¾ lb) for the large cake and 340 g (12 oz) for the small cake. Ice the cakes one at a time. Keep the sugar paste that you are not working with tightly wrapped in cling film.

Remove all rings and bangles to prevent dents. Gently knead the sugar paste on a clean work surface lightly dusted with icing sugar. Roll out the sugar paste to two circles, each large enough to cover one entire cake. (Calculate the diameter of the cake required by measuring the distance up one side of the cake, across the top and down the other side.) As you roll the sugar paste, move it around to prevent it from sticking to the work surface, but do not turn it over.

Carefully slide your left palm (facing upwards) under the left-hand side of the sugar paste. Take care not to allow too much icing sugar to get on top of the sugar paste. Lift the sugar paste sufficiently to slide your right hand behind the left, keeping both palms upwards and fingers straight. Lift the sugar paste centrally over each cake, allowing the edge furthest away to touch the board first. Withdraw your right hand, using it to smooth the surface as you withdraw your left hand. Flute out the sugar paste flush with the board. Using the cake decorating smoother, polish the top and sides of the cake with an even pressure to eliminate any bumps. If small air bubbles appear, prick them on one side with a pin, then gently rub the bubble to expel the air. Set the cakes aside in a cool, dry place for 1 to 2 days to allow the icing to firm up.

1. Making the cutter flowers.

For the 'Snail's Trail'

To make the royal icing, stir the egg white substitute into 1½ tablespoons of water. Gradually add the icing sugar, beating with an electric whisk on a slow speed for about 5 minutes. Using cream-coloured paste, colour the icing to match the colour of the cake. Place the small cake centrally on top of the main cake. Using a greaseproof paper icing bag fitted with the No 2 writing tube, place a 'snail's trail' around the base of the main cake.

To Make the Flower Paste

Sieve the icing sugar, cornflour and the gum tragacanth into a heatproof bowl and place over a pan of hot water until the sugar is warm.

Sprinkle the gelatine over 5 teaspoons of cold water in a small heatproof basin; leave to sponge then dissolve the gelatine over a pan of hot water, remove from the heat and stir in the vegetable fat and liquid glucose.

Pour the liquid into the centre of the warm sugar. Add the egg white to the mixture and beat with an electric mixer on maximum speed until the paste is white. This will take about 10 minutes. Put the paste into a polythene bag and store in an airtight container in the refrigerator. Keep the flower paste for 24 hours before using.

Flower paste dries quickly, so use only a small amount at a time, and keep the remaining paste tightly covered with cling film. To colour the flower paste, add paste colours, using a cocktail stick, making sure to keep the colouring pale for the flower paste. You can add an extra depth of colour to the finished petals and leaves when they are dry, by dusting them with edible dusting powders.

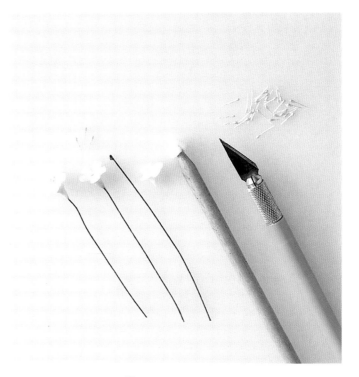

2. Making the pulled flowers.

STEP 1: TO MAKE THE CUTTER FLOWERS
Smear a little white vegetable fat over a small part of a non-stick board and rolling pin. Cut a small quantity of flower paste from the main amount.

Using a tiny amount of the flower paste, and keeping the rest wrapped tightly in cling film, roll out very thinly – the thinner the paste, the more delicate the flower. Cut out several forget-me-not shapes and cover them with a sheet of cling film, while working on individual flowers, to prevent the paste from drying out. Soften the petals of the flower shape with a ball tool, then dip the end of a stamen in egg white and gently push the stalk through the flower. Bend the stalk and hang the flower upside down until the flowers are dry.

When dry, colour the centre with petal dust using a paint brush. Store in a box lined with tissue or kitchen paper. (We used about 120 of these flowers, taped together in threes.)

STEP 2: TO MAKE THE PULLED FLOWERS
Take a piece of flower paste the size of a pea and shape into a cone. Using a sharp modelling knife, make five equal cuts around the cone, cutting about one-third of the way up. Remove the dowel and flatten each of the five sections between the thumb and finger to make the petals. Twist each petal slightly to form a good shape.

Dip the hooked end of No 28 wire into egg white; – insert the straight end of the wire through the centre of the flower head and pull through. Secure the underside of the flower to the wire stem by twisting gently between two fingers. Dip the cut ends of three short stamens into egg white and, using tweezers push into the centre of the flower. Leave to dry standing in straws fixed into a polystyrene block. When dry,

3. Making the arum lily.

dust with petal dust colours in the centre and a green powder on the outside around the flower base. (We used 28 flowers in assorted sizes.)

STEP 3: TO MAKE THE ARUM LILIES
Form a tiny bullrush ('sausage') shape of petal paste about ⅜ inch long. Push the end of a No 28 wire into the paste. Dip a stamen in egg white and coat with semolina. Leave to dry.

Roll out the flower paste thinly and, using a lily or leaf cutter, cut out a petal. Cut off the lower quarter of the leaf. Ball-tool the sides of the petal and brush both sides with a little egg white. Wrap the petal around the dried stamen, tip back the petal and slightly twist the tip. Leave to dry, standing in straws fixed in the polystyrene block. (We used 15 lilies.)

STEP 4: TO MAKE ROSES AND BUDS
Have ready No 24 wires with hooked ends. Colour flower paste cream or pink. Take a piece of flower paste the size of a pea and shape it into an elongated cone no larger than the size of a small petal cutter. Dip the hooked end into egg white and push into the cone. Leave to dry standing in straws fixed into a polystyrene block. Add a little white flower paste to the remaining coloured paste as the centre of the rose is darker than the petals.

Roll paste very thinly using a smear of white fat to prevent it from sticking to the rolling pin or board. Cut out three small rose petal shapes Lift the petal off the board using an artist's palette knife. The first petal is placed sideways across the cone. Brush lower half of the first petal with a little egg white and wrap one end of the petal around the cone, bringing the other end round to the front to enclose the bud.

4. Making roses and buds.

5. Making the ivy leaves.

Using a ball tool, soften the top edge of the second petal. Dampen the base tip of the petal with egg white and place opposite the first petal. Wrap around the bud. Using a cocktail stick, open the petal slightly away from the centre and leave the left-hand edge open. The third petal is formed in the same way, but tucked just inside the second petal, using a cocktail stick. This will form a bud. Cut out three medium rose petals. Ball-tool the top of the petal on the underside to form a lip shape. Tuck the fourth and fifth petal into the previous petals. Allow the petals to open out, and curve back the last petals when they meet, using a cocktail stick. Leave to dry.

Roll out green flower paste thinly and cut out a calyx. Brush the centre with a little egg white before gently pushing the stalk of the rose through the centre of the calyx. Leave to dry. Dust with matching petal dust. (We used 16 rose buds and 12 roses.)

TO MAKE SPRAYS OF BUDS

Using No 28 wire dipped in egg white, and a minute piece of flower paste, shape into a tiny pointed tip and twist the base of the bud between two fingers to fix to the wire stem. (We used 27 buds.)

STEP 5: TO MAKE IVY LEAVES

Roll out green flower paste and cut out small and medium ivy leaves, covering the remaining paste with cling film while working. Place each leaf upside-down, brush the centre with a little egg white and place a No 28 wire on top, securing with a tiny length of green paste. Press the front of the leaf on to a leaf veiner, and leave to dry.

Colour the leaves with a combination of green, brown and yellow petal dust, and brush with confectioner's glaze to give the leaves a shiny appearance. (We used 15 small ivy leaves and 30 medium leaves.)

TO MAKE RIBBON SPRAYS

Form loops of ribbon in a figure of eight about 16.5 cm (6½ in) around each loop. Take a No 28 wire and, holding the centre of the loops, fold the wire across the centre. Twist the wire together tightly to hold the ribbon in place. Fold the loops in half upwards to create 12 loops and twist the wire tightly across the base to secure the loops. (We used 2 green and 1 pink spray.)

TO ASSEMBLE THE FLOWERS

The spray and trail of flowers is formed in the shape of a cross. The north, west and east 'arms' are of equal length, and the southern point is elongated to form a length of wired flowers spiralling from the base of the cake, around the sides and joining the top flowers. The centre of the cross has a tiny posy of ribbons and flowers with tiny sprays of flowers between each main arm of the cross. Make the three arms for the top arrangement of the cake.

STEP 6: TO WIRE THE FLOWERS TOGETHER

Take three tiny buds and wind thin strips of Stem Tex around the stems, adding a group of three cutter flowers and continue winding Stem Tex in the same direction. Add two small ivy leaves on either side to add width to the spray and a little height. Keep wires apart and add flowers, leaves and buds down each short spray until each arm measures about 9 cm (3½ in). Rest the three arms on a piece of foam while working on the centre posy.

STEP 7: TO ASSEMBLE THE GARLAND

Add extra flower sprays around the sides of the posy to make the required shape. Join the three arms and centre posy together by bending the stalk of each arm at just over 90 degrees from the flowers. Push the centre posy in the

6. Wiring flowers together.

7. Assembling the garland.

middle of the three arms and tape securely. Rest on a piece of foam while wiring the long trail.

Working on a large piece of foam, start with an ivy leaf and tiny buds, gradually adding lilies, rose buds, assorted flowers and leaves. The garland of flowers is flat on the underside and the leaves should be kept under the flower heads.

When the garland is the required length, bend the wire stem 90 degrees and add to the top arrangement. Cut wires to a neat shape and cover them with Stem Tex.

STEP 8: TO PLACE THE POSY PICK
Place a plastic posy pick off-centre on the top of the cake, to receive the ends.

STEP 9: TO ARRANGE THE GARLAND
Insert the ends of the flower arrangement into the posy pick. Fix the middle of the garland to the cake by inserting half a cocktail stick against the trail of flowers which rests on the ledge of the main cake.

8. Placing posy pick on the cake.

9. Arranging the garland.

A Perfect Picnic

Tapenade Dip with Crudités

Egg, Mushroom and Herb Tartlets

Royal Game Pie

Picnic Pasta and Pesto Salad

Little Gem Salad

Ratatouille

– * –

Mini Walnut Loaves

to serve with

Cheese and Fruit

– * –

Peaches in Whisky

Dusted Carrot Cake

Strawberry Tart

– * –

Coffee

This is outdoor eating in style – the ultimate picnic for a special celebration or family day out. The art of a good picnic is to choose food that is easy to eat and simple to move. Pack the food in rigid plastic containers and it will be much easier to carry. While cool bags or cool boxes and ice packs are essential for keeping white wine and perishable foods cold, a traditional wicker picnic hamper is not, but it does help to create an image of elegance!

Be stylish – don't serve the food in the containers in which it has been transported. Spend a little extra time choosing and packing plates, dishes, cutlery and glassware (china and glass can be cushioned with rugs and napkins).

And don't forget to pack a rubbish bag to clear away your debris when you leave – do your bit for the environment!

TAPENADE DIP WITH CRUDITÉS

SERVES 8 TO 10

This delicious tapenade dip can be made up to 12 hours in advance and the crudités prepared up to 3 hours ahead.

For the dip:
110 g (4 oz) black olives, pitted
A 50 g (1¾ oz) can anchovy fillets, drained and chopped
4 tablespoons capers, drained
The juice of 1 lemon
A 185 g (6½ oz) can tuna in soya oil, drained
100 ml (3½ fl oz) olive oil
For the crudités:
1 bunch baby carrots, with the tops left on
1 bunch red radishes, with the tops left on
1 bunch baby turnips
1 fennel bulb
½ head celery
280 g (10 oz) cauliflower florets
60 g (2 oz) mange tout
110 g (4 oz) baby corn
Edible flowers, to garnish

To prepare the dip, chop the olives in a food processor until quite fine. Add the anchovy fillets, capers and half the lemon juice and whizz until finely chopped. Add the tuna and process until you have a fine paste. With the processor still running, slowly drizzle in the olive oil a little at a time, so the oil makes an emulsion and the tapenade doesn't separate. Taste the tapenade and add more lemon juice if the flavour needs sharpening. Store in an airtight plastic container for up to 12 hours.

Prepare the crudités; scrub carrots, radishes and turnips, and cut the fennel bulb into 8 equal pieces. Wash and cut the celery in half lengthways and in half across, leaving on as many leaves as possible. Trim the cauliflower into small florets. Blanch the mange tout in boiling water for 30 seconds, plunge into cold water and drain.

Pack all the crudités separately in plastic bags and chill for up to 3 hours before required.

To serve, spoon the tapenade into a small bowl in the centre of a large platter and arrange the crudités around. Garnish with edible flowers.

EGG, MUSHROOM AND HERB TARTLETS

MAKES 18

Use boat tartlet tins, available from kitchen shops, to make these elegant little tarts.

For the pastry:
230 g (8 oz) self-raising wholemeal flour
110 g (4 oz) plain flour
½ teaspoon salt
170 g (6 oz) unsalted butter
2 tablespoons fresh herbs, very finely
chopped – such as chervil, tarragon, chives
and parsley
1 egg yolk, size 3
For the duxelles:
30 g (1 oz) unsalted butter
2 shallots, finely chopped
110 g (4 oz) chestnut mushrooms, wiped
and finely chopped
½ teaspoon salt
½ teaspoon freshly ground black pepper
The juice of ½ lemon
For the filling:
9 quails' eggs
2 eggs, size 3
140 ml (¼ pt) double cream
4 tablespoons fresh herbs, finely chopped
such as chervil, tarragon, chives
and parsley
To garnish:
Paprika
Fresh chives
18 boat tartlet tins

Set the oven at Gas Mark 4, 350°F, 180°C. To make the pastry, sieve the flours and salt together into a bowl, returning any bran collected in the sieve to the bowl. Rub in the butter until the mixture resembles fine breadcrumbs. Mix in the chopped herbs. Add the egg yolk and enough cold water to make a soft but not sticky dough. Wrap in cling film and transfer to the fridge for 1 hour.

Roll out the pastry and use to line the tins. Chill for 30 minutes. Line the pastry cases with greaseproof paper, fill with baking beans and bake 'blind' for 10 to 15 minutes until firm. Remove from the tins and allow to cool. Place on a baking sheet, and return to the oven for 3 minutes. Transfer to a wire rack and leave to cool.

To make the duxelles, melt the butter in a large frying pan and cook the shallots over a low heat until softened but not coloured. Add the mushrooms and cook gently until soft and the liquid has evaporated, then season with salt, freshly ground black pepper and lemon juice. Cook for a further minute.

Cook the quails' eggs for 5 minutes in a large pan of boiling water. Drain and leave in cold water until needed. Shell and halve.

To make the filling, whisk the eggs, cream and herbs together in a jug. Lower the oven temperature to Gas Mark 2, 300°F, 150°C. Place a little of the duxelles in each tartlet case, place half a quail's egg on top and top with the filling mixture. Cook for about 10 to 15 minutes until set, cover with foil if browning. Remove from the oven and transfer to a wire rack to cool completely. Carefully pack them in a rigid plastic container and chill until required. Transfer to a cool bag with ice packs to keep the tartlets cool during transportation.

Just before serving, dust each tartlet with a little paprika using a tea strainer. Garnish with long chives.

LEFT *Picnic spread, including Royal Game Pie, Mini Walnut Loaves with Cheese and Fruit, Little Gem Salad, Egg, Mushroom and Herb Tartlets, Strawberry Tart, Tapenade Dip with Crudités, Dusted Carrot Cake, Ratatouille and Picnic Pasta and Pesto Salad.*
PREVIOUS PAGE RIGHT *Fruit basket.*
PREVIOUS PAGE LEFT *A splendid picnic hamper will turn your picnic into a special occasion.*

ROYAL GAME PIE

MAKES A 23 CM (9 IN) PIE: SERVES 10

A very rich pie with layers of smooth pâté and chopped meat. To make a 15 cm (6 in) pie, use only one-third of the quantities

40 g (1½ oz) shelled pistachio nuts
570 g (1¼ lb) pheasant, grouse, hare, pigeon, venison and rabbit, free from bones, skin and gristle (reserve bones)
170 g (6 oz) chicken breasts, free from skin and bone
Salt and freshly ground black pepper
1 onion
1 stick celery
1 carrot
1 bay leaf
1 sprig thyme
1 tablespoon sunflower oil
1 onion, finely chopped
110 g (4 oz) oyster mushrooms, cut in half if large
30 g (1 oz) unsalted butter
2 tablespoons fresh herbs, finely chopped
For the pâté filling:
1 clove garlic, crushed
60 g (2 oz) unsalted butter
280 g (10 oz) chicken livers, trimmed and roughly chopped
170 g (6 oz) turkey livers, trimmed and roughly chopped
4 tablespoons brandy
1 teaspoon mace
½ teaspoon freshly ground nutmeg
For the hot-water crust pastry:
1.35 kg (3 lb) strong plain white flour, sifted
1 tablespoon salt
210 g (7½ oz) lard, diced
210 g (7½ oz) unsalted butter, diced
455 ml (16 fl oz) water and milk mixed (equal quantity of each)
Beaten egg, to glaze
For the jelly:
½ teaspoons or ½ sachet gelatine
Fresh chervil, to garnish
A 23 cm (9 in) raised pie mould, well-greased with lard

Skin the pistachio nuts by blanching for 1 minute in boiling water, then gently rubbing between 2 dry, clean tea towels; carefully remove any stubborn skins by hand.

Cut the mixed game and chicken into 2.5 cm (1 in) pieces, place in a bowl and season with salt and pepper. Cover and store in the fridge while preparing the rest of the filling.

To make the stock, place the reserved bones, onion, celery, carrot, bayleaf and thyme in a pan, add enough water to cover, bring to the boil, reduce the heat and simmer for 2 hours. Drain, transfer the stock to a clean pan and simmer until reduced to 230 ml (8 fl oz). Reserve.

Heat the oil in a pan, add the onion and cook until softened but not coloured. Fry the mushrooms in butter in a large pan over a high heat, then toss in the herbs. Remove from the heat and cool. Mix with the onions and stir into the game mixture.

To make the pâté filling, fry the garlic with the butter over a low heat. When the butter has melted, turn up the heat until sizzling and add the chopped livers. Stir-fry for 1 to 2 minutes – don't worry if the livers are still pink, as they will cook further during the baking of the pie – then add the remaining ingredients for the pâté. Season well, and place in a food processor and whizz until smooth. Mix in the pistachio nuts.

Set the oven at Gas Mark 6, 400°F, 200°C. To make the hot-water crust pastry, place the flour and salt in a large bowl and rub in 110 g (4 oz) of the lard. Place the remaining lard and the butter in a small pan, add the boiling water and milk and bring to the boil. When it begins to bubble, make a well in the centre of the flour mixture and pour in the liquid. Stir with a wooden spoon, then knead well with your hands.

Take two-thirds of the pastry mixture, roll out to about 1.5 cm (⅝ in) thick and use to line the pie mould. To ensure the pastry lines the mould thoroughly, use a small ball of pastry to press the lining pastry gently into the ridges of the side of the mould. Trim the pastry, leaving 1.5 to 2 cm (⅝ to ¾ in) overlap around the edge.

Place half the pâté filling in the bottom of the pastry case. Add the game and chicken mixture to the pie mould, then top with the remaining pâté mixture. Fold the pastry flap over the pâté mixture and glaze with beaten egg. Roll out the rest of the pastry to form a lid and place on top of the mould. Using a sharp knife, mark the sides of the pie. Trim away the excess pastry and reserve.

Make 2 holes in the top of the pie with a 1.5 cm (⅝ in) plain piping nozzle. Using the reserved pastry trimmings, garnish around the holes. Finally, stamp out pastry leaves using a 4 cm (1½ in) cutter and arrange around the edge of the pastry.

Glaze the pastry case with beaten egg and place the pie on a baking tray. Cook for 20 minutes, cover with foil and cook for a further 10 minutes, then lower the oven to Gas Mark 2, 300°F, 150°C.

Glaze the pie and cover again. Cook for a further 1½ hours (or 1 hour if making the smaller version). Remove from the oven and leave to cool for 15 minutes, then remove the side of the mould. Increase the oven temperature to Gas Mark 6, 400°F, 200°C. Place the pie on a baking tray and glaze the sides. Cover the top and put back into the oven for 15 minutes more to brown the sides. Leave to cool and chill overnight.

To make the jelly, warm the reserved stock slightly. Sprinkle the gelatine on to 4 tablespoons of stock in a small heatproof bowl and leave to sponge for 5 minutes. Dissolve the gelatine by setting the heatproof bowl over a pan of gently simmering water. Add to the remaining stock. When the jelly has cooled and is just on the point of setting, pour into the pie through the holes in the top with the aid of a funnel. Transfer to the fridge to cool completely. Garnish with fresh chervil just before serving.

NOTE: pack the pie in a rigid plastic container and store in a cool bag until required.

RATATOUILLE

SERVES 8 TO 10

A delicious vegetable dish, and the perfect accompaniment for the raised game pies.

2 aubergines
Salt
1 red pepper
1 green pepper
1 yellow pepper
0.9 kg (2 lb) tomatoes, skinned and
deseeded
6 tablespoons extra virgin olive oil
1 clove garlic, crushed
10 small onions, skinned and cut into
8 pieces
1 tablespoon tomato purée
1 tablespoon finely chopped marjoram
2 tablespoons finely chopped parsley
½ teaspoon freshly ground black pepper
Few marjoram leaves, to garnish

Dice the aubergines into small pieces and place in a colander in the sink. Sprinkle with salt to extract the bitter juices. Leave for 30 minutes then rinse well and dry thoroughly on absorbent kitchen paper.

Halve, deseed and dice the peppers. Chop the tomatoes into small pieces, saving any juices. Heat the oil in a wide enamel cooking pot. When hot, add the crushed garlic. Before it colours, add the onions and peppers, stir over a high heat for 3 minutes, add the aubergines and keep stirring for 2 minutes. When melted down and very hot add the tomatoes, tomato purée, marjoram, parsley, 1 teaspoon salt and the black pepper and keep stirring for another 2 minutes to reduce the tomatoes. Cover and simmer for 10 to 15 minutes, stirring occasion-ally. Leave to cool. Pack into a rigid plastic container and chill for up to 12 hours.

PICNIC PASTA AND PESTO SALAD

SERVES 8 TO 10

An interesting, colourful Italian salad that's very quick and simple to make – it is also easy to transport.

230 g (8 oz) penne pasta
2 tablespoons ready-made pesto
4 tablespoons olive oil
1 tablespoon white wine vinegar
170 g (6 oz) baby red tomatoes
60 g (2 oz) black olives, pitted
200 g (7 oz) feta cheese, cubed
A few whole basil leaves to garnish

Cook the pasta in a large pan of salted boiling water for about 10 minutes or according to the packet instructions. Drain and leave to cool. Place the cooked pasta in a large mixing bowl. Whisk together the pesto, oil and wine vinegar and mix into the pasta.

Cut the baby tomatoes in half and carefully remove the hard part of the core. Place on top of the pasta. Cut the olives in half, if wished, and add to the pasta with the feta cheese. Transfer to a rigid plastic container and chill for up to 2 hours before serving.

Tip into a large serving dish and garnish with whole basil leaves just before eating.

LITTLE GEM SALAD

SERVES 8 TO 10

Prepare the salad leaves in advance and pack into a rigid plastic container with a little water. Place the spring onions and slivers of carrot in a plastic bag, and pour the dressing into a screw-top jar. Assemble the salad just before serving.

2 chicory heads
3 little gem lettuce heads
1 bunch spring onions
5 tablespoons pine nuts
3 large carrots
The juice of 1 lime
4 tablespoons sunflower oil
1 tablespoon walnut oil
3 tablespoons concentrated orange juice
½ teaspoon salt
Freshly ground black pepper

Separate the heads of the chicory and little gem lettuce; when the heart is reached, cut in half and arrange on a large plate. Slice the spring onions diagonally and scatter over the leaves with the pine nuts.

Cut the carrots into slivers with a vegetable peeler, toss in a little of the lime juice and add to the salad. Whisk together the oils, orange juice, the remaining lime juice, and salt and freshly ground black pepper and use to dress the salad. Toss together gently when ready to serve.

ABOVE LEFT *Picnic Pasta and Pesto Salad, and Little Gem Salad.*

MINI WALNUT LOAVES TO SERVE WITH CHEESE AND FRUIT

MAKES 12 LOAVES
Ideal to serve with cheese.

230 g (8 oz) strong white flour
230 g (8 oz) wholemeal flour
1 teaspoon salt
1 teaspoon sugar
15 g (½ oz) unsalted butter
2½ teaspoons easy-blend dried yeast
110 g (4 oz) walnuts, chopped
¼ teaspoon clear honey
12 mini loaf tins, oiled

Set the oven at Gas Mark 7, 425°F, 220°C. Sift the flours, salt and sugar together in a large bowl, returning any bran collected in the sieve to the bowl. Rub in the butter until the mixture resembles fine breadcrumbs. Add the yeast and walnuts. Mix the honey with 280 ml (½ pt) tepid water, add to the mixture and blend to form a soft but not sticky dough. Knead for about 8 to 10 minutes until firm and elastic. Divide into 12 pieces and knead into shapes to fit in the mini loaf tins.

Cover with oiled cling film and leave in a warm place to double in size.

Bake for 10 minutes. Remove from the tins, place on a baking sheet and return to the oven for about 5 minutes to brown the bases. Serve with fruit and a selection of cheeses.

TO FREEZE: open-freeze until firm, then pack in polythene bags and freeze for up to 3 months.

TO USE FROM FROZEN: thaw on a wire rack for 3 to 4 hours.

PEACHES IN WHISKY

SERVES 8
Peaches in Whisky are simple to make, easy to transport and the perfect end to any picnic.

170 g (6 oz) caster sugar
18 cardamom pods
370 ml (13 fl oz) Scotch malt whisky
8 ripe peaches
1.7 litre (3 pt) airtight Kilner jar

Dissolve the sugar in 430 ml (¾ pt) cold water over a low heat. Bring to the boil and simmer for 1 minute. Crack the cardamom pods right open, but do not split them, add to the syrup, pour in the whisky and mix well.

Skin the peaches by putting them in boiling water for 1 minute, then plunge into cold water and the skins should be removed easily. Arrange the peaches in a jar and then pour over the whisky mixture. Seal the jar and place in a cool, dark place for at least a week before serving.

Peaches in Whisky may be stored for up to 1 month.

DUSTED CARROT CAKE

MAKES ONE 18 CM (7 IN) ROUND CAKE
A light cake that's ideal to serve with coffee at the end of a meal.

5 egg yolks, size 3, separated
310 g (11 oz) caster sugar
2 teaspoons grated lemon rind
3 carrots, finely grated
230 g (8 oz) ground almonds
85 g (3 oz) self-raising flour, sifted
½ teaspoon salt
Icing sugar, for dusting
A 18 cm (7 in) deep, round cake tin, greased and lined

Set the oven at Gas Mark 4, 350°F, 180°C. Beat the egg yolks with the sugar until pale, thick and creamy. Gently fold in the lemon rind, grated carrot, ground almonds, flour and salt using a large, metal spoon.

Whisk the egg whites until stiff but not dry. Gently fold into the carrot mixture. Pour into the prepared cake tin and bake for 1¼ to 1½ hours; if the cake is overbrowning, cover carefully with a large piece of greaseproof paper. Transfer to a wire rack and allow to cool completely.

Before serving, dust the top of the cake with icing sugar.

TO FREEZE: open-freeze until firm. Wrap in greaseproof paper and foil and freeze for up to 2 months.

TO USE FROM FROZEN: thaw uncovered on a wire rack for 4 hours.

RIGHT *Strawberry Tart*

STRAWBERRY TART

MAKES ONE 23 CM (9 IN) TART

Complete this irresistible classic tart just before you set off on your summer picnic, and transport in a rigid plastic container. Eat within three hours of assembling.

For the pastry:
200 g (7 oz) plain flour, sieved
100 g (3½ oz) ground almonds, sieved
60 g (2 oz) caster sugar, sieved
A pinch of salt
The grated rind of 1 lemon
140 g (5 oz) unsalted butter, diced
1 egg yolk, size 3
For the crème pâtissière:
140 ml (¼ fl oz) milk
140 ml (¼ fl oz) double cream
1 vanilla pod
1 egg, size 3
60 g (2 oz) vanilla sugar
15 g (½ oz) plain flour, sieved
15 g (½ oz) cornflour, sieved
For the glaze:
3 tablespoons redcurrant jelly
2 tablespoons cassis
1 teaspoon lemon juice
For the topping
455 g (1 lb) fresh strawberries, hulled and halved
A few strawberry or mint leaves, for decoration
A 23 cm (9 in) loose-based, fluted flan tin

Set the oven at Gas Mark 5, 375°F, 190°C. Place the flour, almonds, sugar, salt and lemon rind into a food processor, add the butter and process until just beginning to stick together. Add the egg yolk and process until the mixture forms a ball. Wrap in cling film and place in the fridge for 20 minutes.

Roll out the pastry and line the flan tin. Prick the base with a fork and return to the fridge to chill for at least 1 hour.

Line the pastry case with greaseproof paper, fill with baking beans and bake 'blind' for 15 minutes or until a pale golden colour. Remove the baking beans, cover the edges of the pastry case with foil to stop over-colouring, and return to the oven for a further 10 minutes to crisp up the base. Leave to cool. Remove the pastry case from the tin and store it in an airtight container until ready to use.

To make the crème pâtissière, heat the milk, cream and vanilla pod together until just beginning to boil. Leave to infuse for 10 minutes, then remove the vanilla pod. Whisk the egg, the egg yolk and sugar together until pale, thick and creamy, then whisk in the flour and cornflour.

Pour the hot liquid over the egg mixture, mix well and return to the rinsed-out pan. Stir the mixture over a very low heat, taking care it does not stick to the bottom of the pan. When it thickens, remove from the heat and give it a good whisk. Cool and store in an airtight container in the fridge for up to 6 hours.

To make the glaze, mix the ingredients in a small pan over a low heat until the jelly has dissolved – whisk if necessary. Bring to the boil and simmer to form a syrup that will be easy to brush up on to the strawberries.

To assemble, whisk the crème pâtissière, adding a little milk if too thick, and spread evenly over the pastry case base. Arrange the halved strawberries over the top of the tart, in concentric circles. Soften the glaze slightly by adding a drop of extra cassis or water, if necessary, and stir over a low heat. Glaze the top of the tart and decorate with the rinsed and dried leaves of strawberries or mint.

When assembled, store in an airtight container and transfer to the fridge for up to 3 hours. Bring to room temperature before serving the tart.

PICNIC EXTRAS

Tomato Lentil Soup

– ✳ –

Tasty Cheese Baps

Granary Baps

Frinton Pies

– ✳ –

A Selection of Fillings

for Baps and Rolls,

including:

Cheese and Cress,

Club-Style Chicken,

Tangy Beef

– ✳ –

Venison Herb Plaits

Picnic Porkies

– ✳ –

Sprouting Salad

Marinated Courgette Salad

– ✳ –

Chocolate Crinkles

Date Gingerbread

Almond Squares

TOMATO LENTIL SOUP

MAKES 1.45 L (2½ PT),
SERVES 4 TO 6
*A colourful, tasty and
warming soup that's sure to please! Pour
the soup into a thermos flask and
serve in deep mugs.*

110 g (4 oz) red split lentils
1 medium onion, finely chopped
1 clove garlic, crushed (optional)
2 tablespoons vegetable oil
170 g (6 oz) carrots, diced
170 g (6 oz) potatoes, peeled and cubed
1 teaspoon tomato purée
A 400 g (14¼ oz) can chopped tomatoes
990 ml (1¾ pt) chicken or vegetable stock
Salt, pepper and cayenne to taste

Soak the red lentils according to the instructions on the packet. Cook the onion and garlic in the oil over a very low heat until soft.

Add the carrots, potatoes, tomato purée, tomatoes, stock, the drained lentils and a little seasoning. Bring to the boil, then cover and simmer for about 35 to 40 minutes until tender. Purée in a liquidiser or processor. Reheat, taste and adjust the seasoning as necessary.

TO FREEZE: this soup will freeze well for up to 6 months.
TO USE FROM FROZEN: thaw in the refrigerator, reheat and pour into a thermos flask.

OVERLEAF *Picnic Extras, including mugs of Tomato and Lentil Soup, Sprouting Salad, Mixed Courgette Salad, Tasty Cheese Baps (top left) and Granary Baps (bottom right) with a selection of fillings, Frinton Pies, Picnic Porkies, Almond Squares, Date Gingerbread and Chocolate Crinkles, and Venison Plaits.*

TASTY CHEESE BAPS

MAKES 8 LARGE BAPS
The baps are delicious with one of our tasty fillings given below.

455 g (1 lb) strong plain flour, warmed
1 teaspoon salt
1 teaspoon mustard powder
1 sachet easy-blend yeast
170 g (6 oz) Double Gloucester cheese, finely grated
1 small onion, thinly sliced into rings
15 g (½ oz) butter

Sift the flour with the salt and mustard into a warmed bowl. Stir in the yeast and 110 g (4 oz) of the cheese. Mix to a soft but not sticky dough with about 280 ml (½ pt) hand-hot water. Turn on to a floured work surface and knead for about 10 minutes to make a smooth, elastic dough. Place in an oiled bowl, cover and leave in a warm place until doubled in size. Meanwhile, soften the onion rings in the butter over a low heat. Leave to cool.

Knock back the dough and roll or pat out 2 cm (¾ in) thick. Cut out 8 circles 9 cm (3½ in) in diameter, rerolling the trimmings as necessary. Place on greased baking trays. Top the baps with the onion rings and sprinkle with the remaining grated cheese. Cover loosely and leave in a warm place until doubled in size.

Meanwhile, heat the oven to Gas Mark 6, 400°F, 200°C. Bake for 25 minutes until golden and the baps sound hollow when tapped underneath. Cool on a wire rack. Eat within a couple of days or freeze for up to 2 months.
TO FREEZE: wrap in a polythene bag and freeze for up to 3 months.
TO USE FROM FROZEN: loosen wrapping and thaw at room temperature for about 4 to 5 hours.

GRANARY BAPS

MAKES 6 LARGE BAPS

Grated carrot keeps the nutty dough quite light and moist.

455 g (1 lb) Granary flour, warmed
1 sachet easy-blend yeast
1 teaspoon sea salt
110 g (4 oz) carrots, finely grated

1 tablespoon black treacle
30 g (1 oz) butter or white fat, melted
Beaten egg to glaze
Cracked wheat for sprinkling (optional)

Mix the flour with the yeast and salt in a warmed bowl. Stir in the grated carrots.

Mix the treacle and melted fat with 280 ml (½ pt) blood-heat water. Stir into the flour mixture to make a soft but not sticky dough, adding a little more water as necessary. Turn on to a floured work surface and knead for 10 minutes. Put into an oiled bowl, cover and leave in a warm place until doubled in size.

Knock back the dough, and divide into 6. Shape each piece into a bap about 9 cm (3½ in) in diameter. Place on a greased baking tray. Cover and leave in a warm place until doubled in size.

Meanwhile, heat the oven to Gas Mark 6, 400°F, 200°C. Brush the baps with beaten egg, then sprinkle with cracked wheat, if using. Bake for 25 to 30 minutes. Cool on a wire rack. Eat within 2 days or freeze or up to 2 months.

TO FREEZE: as for Tasty Cheese Baps (opposite), for up to 2 months.

FRINTON PIES

MAKES 8 PIES

Light shortcrust pastry encloses a moist, tasty filling of chicken, leeks and mushrooms — and they taste just as good eaten cold as hot.

For the pastry:
340 g (12 oz) plain flour
A pinch each of salt and pepper
85 g (3 oz) butter
85 g (3 oz) white fat or lard
For the filling:
30 g (1 oz) butter
170 g (6 oz) leeks, washed and shredded

85 g (3 oz) button mushrooms, sliced
2 tablespoons flour
200 ml (7 fl oz) milk or chicken stock
340 g (12 oz) cooked chicken meat, free of
skin and bone, diced
Salt, pepper and nutmeg
Beaten egg to glaze
8 Yorkshire pudding tins

To make the pastry, sift the flour and seasonings into a bowl. Dice the fats and rub into the flour, using your fingertips, until the mixture resembles fine breadcrumbs. Bind to a soft but not sticky dough with four to five tablespoons icy water. Wrap and chill for 15 minutes.

Meanwhile, prepare the filling. Melt the butter in a pan. Add the leeks and sliced mushrooms and cook, stirring frequently, until soft but not coloured. Stir in the flour, followed by the milk or stock. Bring to the boil, stirring constantly. Simmer for 1 minute. Stir in the diced chicken and season well. Cool, then coarsely process or chop the filling. Taste, and adjust the seasoning.

Roll out half the pastry and use to line the tins (use a small saucer or bowl of suitable size as a guide to cut out the pastry circles). Fill with the chicken mixture. Dampen the edges of the pastry. Roll out the remaining pastry and cut out 8 'lids'. Cover the pies, sealing the edges firmly. Flute and decorate as wished. Chill for 10 minutes. Meanwhile, heat the oven to Gas Mark 7, 425°F, 220°C.

Brush the pies with beaten egg to glaze, and then bake for 10 minutes. Reduce the temperature to Gas Mark 4, 350°F, 180°C and bake for a further 30 minutes until the pastry is crisp and golden. Cool. Store in the fridge for up to 2 days or freeze for up to 2 months. Delicious served at room temperature or piping hot.

A SELECTION OF BAP FILLINGS

EACH FILLING IS SUFFICIENT FOR SIX BAPS – ADD SALAD IF WISHED

CHEESE AND CRESS

230 g (8 oz) cream cheese (low-fat or full-fat)
2 tablespoons milk or cream
Salt and pepper to taste
1 large bunch watercress, washed

Beat the cream cheese with the milk or cream and seasoning until smooth and spreadable. Spread over the cut surfaces of the baps. Trim the watercress to remove any very thick stalks and roots. Dry thoroughly on kitchen paper. Use to sandwich the baps.

CLUB-STYLE CHICKEN

340 g (12 oz) cooked, boneless chicken
4 rashers back bacon
6 tablespoons mayonnaise
Pepper
3 tomatoes, sliced

Shred the chicken into bite-sized pieces. Grill the bacon until brown and crispy. Drain on kitchen paper, cut into bite-sized pieces. Stir the chicken and bacon into the mayonnaise, adding pepper to taste. Layer up in the baps with the tomatoes (and little salad, if wished).

The chicken filling can be kept tightly covered, in the fridge overnight.

TANGY BEEF

1 pickled cucumber, diced
2 teaspoons creamed horseradish
6 tablespoons mayonnaise
455 g (1 lb) cooked beef, cut in thin strips

Stir the cucumber and horseradish into the mayonnaise. Layer up the beef and mayonnaise in the baps, with a little salad, if wished).

This filling can be kept, tightly covered, in the fridge overnight.

VENISON HERB PLAITS

MAKES 10

Venison is tasty, lean and economical – and is available in most large supermarkets.

For the cheese pastry:
230 g (8 oz) plain flour
A good pinch each of salt, mustard powder
and cayenne
110 g (4 oz) butter
110 g (4 oz) mature Cheddar cheese,
finely grated
For the filling:

340 g (12 oz) lean venison
1 small onion, quartered
230 g (8 oz) good-quality sausagemeat
2 tablespoons chopped parsley
A large pinch of dried thyme
2 tablespoons redcurrant jelly
Salt and pepper
Beaten egg to glaze

To make the pastry, sift the flour with the seasonings. Dice the fat and rub in, using your fingertips, until the mixture resembles fine crumbs. Stir in the cheese, then bind to a stiff dough with 4 or 5 tablespoons of icy water. Wrap and chill for 15 minutes.

Coarsely mince or process the venison with the onion, sausagemeat and parsley. Mix in the thyme, redcurrant jelly and plenty of seasoning.

Roll out the pastry and cut into 10 rectangles about 15 by 12.5 cm (6 by 5 in). Divide the meat mixture into 10 portions. Roll each into a log shape and place down the centre of a pastry rectangle. Cut the long pastry borders diagonally into 1 cm (½ in) strips. Wrap the strips from each side alternately over the filling to resemble small 'plaits'. Seal the ends firmly. Arrange on greased baking trays and chill for about 15 minutes. Meanwhile, heat the oven to Gas Mark 6, 400°F, 200°C.

Brush the pastry with beaten egg. Bake for 20 minutes then reduce the heat to Gas Mark 4, 350°F, 180°C for a further 15 to 20 minutes until the pastry is crisp and golden. Cool. Store in the fridge for up to 2 days or freeze for up to 2 months. Also delicious served at parties, piping hot.

The venison can be replaced by an equal quantity of lean beef. If you wish, roll out the pastry, fill with the venison mixture, and shape as if making sausage rolls, slashing the top before baking.

PICNIC PORKIES

MAKES 8 TO 10

Bite-sized savoury balls of pork and bacon filled with chutney.

230 g (8 oz) lean, boneless pork
170 g (6 oz) rindless streaky bacon
1 small onion, peeled
¼ teaspoon dried sage
Salt and pepper

1 to 2 tablespoons mango chutney
Seasoned flour, for coating
1 egg, size 3, beaten
110 g (4 oz) fresh breadcrumbs
Oil for deep frying

Coarsely mince or process the pork with the bacon and onion. Mix in the sage and season well. Using lightly floured hands, divide into 8 or 10 portions, then roll each portion into a ball, make a hole in the centre and put in half a teaspoon of chutney. Pinch the meat together to enclose the filling and re-roll into a neat ball. Lightly coat the balls in seasoned flour, then dip in beaten egg. Finally, roll each ball in the fresh breadcrumbs to coat completely.

Deep-fry in oil heated to 325°F, 170°C, for 5 to 6 minutes until crisp, golden and cooked through. Drain on kitchen paper. Store the porkies in the fridge for up to 24 hours, and serve cold.

SPROUTING SALAD

SERVES 4 AS A SALAD OR
FILLS 6 BAPS

230 g (8 oz) alfalfa sprouts
1 box of mustard and cress, cut
For the dressing:
3 spring onions, finely chopped
1 tablespoon muscovado sugar
1 tablespoon soy sauce
Salt and pepper to taste
4 tablespoons wine vinegar
4 tablespoons soured cream

Mix the sprouts with the mustard and cress. Put all the dressing ingredients in a screw-topped jar and shake well. Adjust the seasoning to taste. Pour over the salad and toss gently. The salad will remain crisp for several hours, otherwise pack in an airtight container, take the jar of dressing and toss before serving.

MARINATED COURGETTE SALAD

SERVES 4

This will stay crisp for up to 12 hours.

455 g (1 lb) medium-sized courgettes,
trimmed and cut in matchsticks
1 red pepper
1 tablespoon sesame seeds, toasted
For the dressing:
The grated rind and juice of 1 small lemon
1 clove garlic, crushed
1 teaspoon caster sugar
1 teaspoon white wine vinegar
4 tablespoons olive oil
2 tablespoons chopped parsley
Salt and pepper to taste

Place the courgettes into a heatproof bowl, and cover with boiling water for 3 minutes. Drain, refresh with cold water and drain thoroughly. Core, deseed and finely shred the red pepper. Mix with courgettes and sesame seeds.

Put the ingredients for the dressing into a screw-topped jar and shake until emulsified. Pour over the salad and toss gently until thoroughly combined. Keep cool until ready to serve, then toss again, just before serving.

CHOCOLATE CRINKLES

MAKES 24
Chocolate Crinkles are one of those all-time favourite cookie recipes – and if you have children at your picnic, you will have to hide these until the end!

170 g (6 oz) golden granulated sugar
60 ml (2 fl oz) soya oil
60 g (2 oz) plain chocolate, melted and cooled
½ teaspoon vanilla essence
2 eggs, size 3, beaten
140 g (5 oz) self-raising flour
40 g (1½ oz) cocoa powder
A pinch of salt
Icing sugar for coating

Mix the sugar with the oil, chocolate and vanilla essence. When thoroughly blended, gradually beat in the eggs.

Sift the flour with the cocoa and salt and work into the mixture. Cover and chill for 3 hours.

Set the oven at Gas Mark 4, 350°F, 180°C. Shape the dough into 24 even-sized balls. Roll in icing sugar to coat lightly. Place well apart on lightly greased baking trays and flatten lightly. Bake for 10 to 12 minutes, then cool on a wire rack.

TO FREEZE: place in a polythene bag, and freeze for up to 3 months.

TO USE FROM FROZEN: thaw at room temperature for 4 to 5 hours.

DATE GINGERBREAD

MAKES ONE 18 CM (7 IN) SQUARE CAKE
Delicious served with a wedge of Wensleydale cheese.

230 g (8 oz) plain fine wholemeal flour (not bread flour)
1½ teaspoons bicarbonate of soda
½ teaspoon ground cloves
4 teaspoons ground ginger
1 teaspoon mixed spice
95 g (3 oz) butter
110 g (4 oz) muscovado sugar
110 g (4 oz) golden syrup
110 g (4 oz) black treacle
2 eggs, size 3, beaten
5 tablespoons milk
85 g (3 oz) stoned dates, chopped
An 18 cm (7 in) square cake tin, lined and greased

Set the oven at Gas Mark 4, 350°F, 180°C. Mix the wholemeal flour with the bicarbonate of soda, cloves, ginger and mixed spice. Melt the butter with the sugar, syrup and treacle. Leave to cool, then beat in the eggs and milk. Stir into the flour, and beat to a smooth batter. Stir in the chopped dates, and pour into the tin.

Bake for 45 to 50 minutes until a cocktail stick inserted into the centre emerges clean. Cool in the tin. Turn out and remove the greaseproof paper. Wrap the gingerbread and keep for a week before eating.

TO FREEZE: wrap in polythene, and freeze for up to 3 months.

TO USE FROM FROZEN: thaw at room temperature for 4 to 5 hours.

ALMOND SQUARES

MAKES 40 SMALL SQUARES
A very special German recipe.

For the pastry:
170 g (6 oz) plain flour
110 g (4 oz) butter
30 g (1 oz) caster sugar
1 egg yolk, size 3
A couple of drops of vanilla essence
For the topping:
170 g (6 oz) flaked almonds
85 g (3 oz) butter
40 g (1½ oz) golden granulated sugar
40 g (1½ oz) set honey
2 tablespoons single or double cream
A Swiss roll tin 20.5 by 30.5 cm (8 by 12 in)

To make the pastry base, sift the flour, rub in the butter, then stir in the sugar. Add the egg yolk and vanilla essence and knead to a smooth, shortbread-like dough. Press into the tin in an even layer. Prick well and chill for about 10 minutes.

Set the oven at Gas Mark 5, 375°F, 190°C. Bake the pastry for about 10 minutes until firm and golden.

Put the almonds, butter, sugar and honey into a wide, heavy-based pan, preferably non-stick. Cook, stirring, over a low heat until the ingredients have melted and the mixture is a pale straw gold. Stir in the cream. Cook for a few seconds then spread over the pastry base. Bake for about 10 minutes until a deep golden brown. Cool in the tin. Cut into small squares. Store in an airtight tin.

CHAPTER SEVEN

A Christening Tea

A delectable teatime spread is perfect for a relaxed and happy afternoon celebration with family and friends.

Tiny sprays of pastel flowers decorate the sides of a charming cake that's topped with a crib made from pastillage and netting.

The cake – a light Madeira cake, flavoured with orange and Cointreau – can be made well ahead and frozen. The cake is covered with a thin layer of marzipan and cream sugar paste, which is then rolled out like pastry and smoothed into place. This gives an even, professional finish – so much quicker than coating with royal icing.

The pretty pastillage crib is made separately, ready to pop on the cake at the last minute. It can then be carefully removed and kept for many years. The cake can be finished and assembled 2 to 3 days before the christening.

The buffet tea for 20 guests can also be prepared and frozen well ahead, or the recipes divided up between willing helpers to bring along on the day. Choose your favourite sandwiches, cakes and pastries from the selection here – we have included a wide range of traditional and new ideas. Don't forget to borrow a few extra electric kettles, and have a spare tea pot or two to speed up tea making.

Sandwich Selection

Bridge Rolls

Savoury Pinwheels

Miniature Scones

Cheese Straws

Miniature Drop Scones

Gingerbread

Treacle Bread

Malt Bread

Fruit and Nut Loaf

Battenburg Cake

Fresh Fruit Tartlets

Strawberry Tartlets

Iced Fancies

Tiny Chocolate Eclairs

Lemon Swirl Biscuits

Hazelnut Shortbread

Chequered Biscuits

Shortbread

Miniature Brandy Snaps

Coffee Meringue Kisses

Chocolate and Hazelnut Butterfly Cakes

Coffee and Walnut Butterfly Cakes

Madeleines

Cream-filled Swiss Roll

Sumptuous Brownies

Seed Cake

Petal-shaped Christening Cake

Rich Plum Cake

Chocolate Fudge Slab

SANDWICH SELECTION

MAKES 24 SANDWICHES

Tiny sandwiches filled with home-made savoury potted meat, thinly sliced cucumber or freshly picked watercress.

MAKES ABOUT 310 G (11 OZ)

12 slices of white or brown bread, very thinly sliced and buttered
For the potted meat:
230 g (8 oz) stewing steak
85 g (3 oz) belly of pork
1 garlic clove, crushed
A pinch ground mace
Salt

½ teaspoon freshly ground black pepper
½ teaspoon juniper berries
A sprig of fresh thyme
85 ml (3 fl oz) red wine
2 tablespoons port
85 g (3 fl oz) butter, clarified
A medium-sized heatproof terrine

Finely dice the beef and pork, or chop coarsely in a food processor. Layer the meat in the terrine with the garlic, mace, pepper and salt sprinkled over each layer. Arrange the juniper berries and thyme on the top layer. Pour over the red wine, cover dish with foil or a lid. Chill overnight.

Next day set the oven at Gas Mark 3, 325°F, 170°C. Bake the cooked terrine for 1 hour, remove the foil or lid and discard the juniper berries and thyme. Cool.

Next day, process or mince the entire contents of the terrine as smoothly or as coarsely as you wish. Stir in the port, taste and adjust the seasoning. Spoon the mixture into an earthenware dish, pour over the clarified butter and chill for at least 2 days before using.

Use the potted meat to sandwich together the slices of bread. Neatly remove the crusts and cut each round of bread into 4 triangles. Arrange on a serving plate, cover with cling film. Chill up to 1 hour before serving.

VARIATIONS

Cucumber
Peel and thinly slice half a cucumber. Pat dry on absorbent kitchen paper. Arrange on the brown buttered bread. Continue as above.

Watercress
Wash, trim and pat dry one bunch of watercress. Arrange on the brown buttered bread. Continue as above.

ABOVE *Bridge Rolls.*
PREVIOUS PAGE LEFT *Strawberry and Raspberry Tarts, with (from top) Sandwich Selection, Gingerbread, and Iced Fancy.*
PREVIOUS PAGE RIGHT *Iced Fancies (top) and Madeleines.*

BRIDGE ROLLS

MAKES 24 ROLLS

Small enough to be eaten during a bridge game.

455 g (1 lb) strong plain flour
1 teaspoon salt
30 g (1 oz) butter
1 sachet easy-blend yeast
340 ml (12 fl oz) lukewarm milk
Beaten egg to glaze
For the filling:
10 hard-boiled eggs, size 3
140 ml (¼ pt) good-quality mayonnaise
Salt and freshly ground black pepper
Butter for spreading
1 to 2 punnets of mustard and cress

Sift the flour and salt into a warm mixing bowl. Rub in the butter and stir in the yeast. When thoroughly blended add the milk and mix to a soft but not sticky dough. Turn out on to a lightly floured surface and knead well for 10 minutes. Place dough in an oiled bowl and cover with oiled cling film. Leave to prove in a warm place for 45 minutes to 1 hour, or until doubled in size. Knead lightly to knock back the risen dough, then cut into 24 equal pieces. Shape each piece into a tapered roll and place fairly close together on a greased baking tray. Cover with oiled cling film and leave in a warm place until doubled in size (about 15 minutes).

Meanwhile, heat the oven to Gas Mark 8, 450°F, 230°C. Brush the rolls with beaten egg to glaze and bake for 15 to 20 minutes. Cool on a wire rack before carefully separating them, and filling with the egg mixture. Eat within a day.

To make the filling, mash the eggs with a fork until their whites are finely chopped. Mix well with the mayonnaise and plenty of seasoning to taste. Cover and chill for up to 4 hours.

Halve the bridge rolls. Butter them and spread the egg mayonnaise on the half-rolls. Scatter over the snipped mustard and cress evenly. Cover and chill until required.

TO FREEZE: freeze the uncooked shaped rolls on a baking sheet, covered with oiled cling film.

TO USE FROM FROZEN: cook the rolls from frozen for 5 to 7 minutes extra.

SAVOURY PINWHEELS

SERVES ABOUT 20 PER LOAF

An attractive variation on the usual sandwich triangles.

A large, day-old unsliced wholemeal loaf
Softened butter for spreading
For the chicken filling:
230 g (8 oz) cooked chicken meat free of skin and bones, finely diced
85 g (3 oz) cream cheese
3 tablespoons mayonnaise
1 tablespoon mango chutney, or to taste
Salt and freshly ground black pepper
Mustard and cress to garnish
For the cheese filling:
85 g (3 oz) mature Cheddar cheese, finely grated
85 g (3 oz) cream cheese
2 tablespoons mayonnaise
2 tablespoons chopped chives
Salt and freshly ground black pepper
For the prawn filling:
230 g (8 oz) prawns, thawed if frozen, finely chopped
85 g (3 oz) cream cheese
2 teaspoons lemon juice
2 tablespoons mayonnaise
Salt and freshly ground black pepper
Watercress to garnish
For the ham filling:
170 g (6 oz) lean cooked ham, finely diced

85 g (3 oz) cream cheese
1 teaspoon horseradish sauce, or to taste
2 tablespoons mayonnaise
1 tablespoon chopped parsley
Salt and freshly ground black pepper

Choose any two of the fillings to fill 1 loaf, which will serve about 20 people. Mix all the ingredients for the two chosen fillings in a separate bowl, reserving any garnish to sprinkle over before serving.

Using a bread knife, remove all the crust from the bread and cut it into 8 slices lengthways. This is easier to do if the bread is a day old or semi-frozen. Lightly roll each slice of bread with a rolling pin, spread lightly with butter and then with the filling. Each filling recipe is sufficient for 4 slices.

Gently roll up the bread like a Swiss roll and cut it into 8 slices to make pinwheels. Cover the pinwheels tightly and chill for up to 6 hours before serving, then garnish.

TO FREEZE: wrap each roll individually in cling film (don't cut into pinwheels), place in a plastic container and freeze for up to 2 weeks.

TO USE FROM FROZEN: leave wrapped in cling film and thaw at room temperature for 3 to 4 hours. Then cut into pinwheels, arrange on serving plates and garnish. If the pinwheels are cut while frozen, they will dry out by the time they have thawed.

MINIATURE SCONES

MAKES ABOUT 26

455 g (1 lb) self-raising flour
110 g (4 oz) butter
60 g (2 oz) caster sugar
2 eggs, size 3, beaten

About 140 ml (¼ pt) milk
Beaten egg to glaze
A 5 cm (2 in) plain
round cutter

Set the oven at Gas Mark 8, 450°F, 230°C. Sift the flour into a bowl and rub in the butter until the mixture resembles fine breadcrumbs. Add the sugar. Stir in the beaten eggs and enough milk to make a fairly soft dough.

Turn the dough out on to a lightly floured surface and roll out to 2 cm (¾ in) thick. Cut into rounds, rerolling the trimmings as necessary. Transfer to greased baking trays and brush with beaten egg to glaze. Bake for 12 minutes or until the scones are firm and golden.

Cool on a wire rack. Serve split, buttered and spread with home-made jam. As an extra treat serve the buttered scones with jam and topped with clotted cream.

VARIATIONS

Fruit
Add 60 g (2 oz) mixed dried fruit to the dough and continue to bake as above.
Cheese:
Omit the sugar and add ½ teaspoon of dried mustard and 85 g (3 oz) grated mature Cheddar cheese to the dough. Bake as above.
TO FREEZE: pack in a rigid plastic container and freeze for up to 1 month.
TO USE FROM FROZEN: set the scones on a wire rack to thaw at room temperature for 1 to 1½ hours.

CHEESE STRAWS

MAKES 22-24
Use any strong flavoured cheese to make these crisp and deliciously savoury.

230 g (3 oz) ready-made puff pastry
85 g (3 oz) mature Cheddar cheese,
finely grated
1 tablespoon English mustard
Beaten egg to glaze
Poppy seeds, to garnish

Set the oven at Gas Mark 7, 425°F, 220°C. Roll out the puff pastry on a lightly floured surface to make a 28 cm (11 in) square.

Sprinkle the cheese over one half of the pastry and spread the other half with the mustard.

Brush the edges of the pastry with water and fold the mustard half over the cheese half to make a rectangle. Press the edges together and seal by rolling gently over the top with a rolling pin.

Cut into 1 cm (½ in) strips. Twist each strip several times and place on greased baking trays. Brush with beaten egg, sprinkle with poppy seeds and bake for 8 to 10 minutes.

Cool on a wire rack, then store in an airtight container for up to 3 days. Warm the cheese straws in a low oven to crisp up before serving.

Another interesting variation is to replace the mustard with 1 tablespoon anchovy paste.
TO FREEZE: pack in a rigid container and freeze for up to 2 months.
TO USE FROM FROZEN: place in a hot oven for 5 minutes. Cool, and serve.

LEFT *Miniature Scones and Cheese Straws.*
OPPOSITE *Savoury Pinwheels.*

Miniature Drop Scones

*These tiny drop scones
(or pancakes in Scotland) are delicious
freshly made and buttered.*

110 g (4 oz) self-raising flour
A pinch of salt
20 g (1 oz) caster sugar
1 egg, size 3, beaten
140 ml (¼ pt) milk

Lightly grease a griddle or heavy-based frying pan and heat. Sift the dry ingredients into a large bowl, make a well in the centre and add the beaten egg and milk. Mix gently to a smooth paste (don't beat or the mixture will be tough).

Drop spoonfuls of the mixture, 3 or 4 at a time, on the hot griddle or frying pan. When the scones are puffed and bubbling on the surface and golden underneath (after about 2 to 3 minutes), turn them over to brown the other side (a further 2 to 3 minutes).

Place the hot scones in the folds of a clean tea towel until ready to serve. Serve buttered on the same day.

TO FREEZE: pack in a polythene bag and freeze for up to 2 months.

TO USE FROM FROZEN: thaw on a wire rack for 1 hour.

Gingerbread

MAKES ONE 0.9 KG (2 LB) LOAF

*Gingerbread originated in medieval England,
and this delicious sticky bread, sliced and served with or without
butter, has certainly stood the test of time.*

280 ml (½ pt) milk
140 g (5 oz) soft light brown sugar
110 g (4 oz) black treacle
110 g (4 oz) golden syrup
230 g (8 oz) self-raising flour
½ teaspoon bicarbonate of soda
1 tablespoon ground ginger

1 tablespoon cinnamon
1 tablespoon mixed spice
110 g (4 oz) butter
2 eggs, size 3, beaten
A 0.9 kg (2 lb) loaf tin,
greased and lined
with greaseproof paper

Set the oven at Gas Mark 4, 350°F, 180°C. Gently heat the milk and brown sugar in a heavy based pan until the sugar has completely dissolved, stirring occasionally.

Bring to the boil, then remove the pan from the heat. Leave to cool to blood heat.

Put the black treacle and golden syrup in another pan and bring to the boil, then cool to blood heat.

Sift the flour with the bicarbonate of soda and spices into a large mixing bowl. Rub in the butter until the mixture resembles fine breadcrumbs. Stir in the cooled milk, the cooled syrup mixture, followed by the eggs. Using a wooden spoon, beat well to make a smooth batter. Pour into prepared tin.

Bake for 1¼ hours or until a skewer inserted into the centre of the cake comes out clean. Leave to cool in the tin. Turn out and wrap in greaseproof paper and foil. Keep in a cool, dry place for at least 3 days before cutting (during this time the spicy flavours develop). Serve thinly sliced and buttered if wished.

TO FREEZE: wrap and keep for up to 3 months.

TO USE FROM FROZEN: loosen the wrapping and thaw at room temperature for 4 to 5 hours.

TREACLE BREAD

MAKES ONE 0.9 KG (2 LB) LOAF
*This is delicious, served sliced,
with or without butter.*

455 g (1 lb) wholemeal flour
1 teaspoon salt
1 sachet easy-blend dried yeast
110 g (4 oz) stoned dates, chopped
60 g (2 oz) butter, melted
2 tablespoons black treacle
A 0.9 kg (2 lb) loaf tin, greased

Sift the wholemeal flour and salt into a large mixing bowl. Stir in the yeast and the chopped dates.

Mix the butter with the treacle and stir in 280 ml (½ pt) warm water. Stir the liquid into the dry ingredients and mix well to give a fairly soft dough.

Turn out on to a floured work surface and knead for 10 minutes until smooth and elastic. Turn the dough into an oiled bowl and cover with oiled cling film. Leave in a warm place for about an hour, or until the dough has doubled in size.

Knock down the proved dough shape and put into the tin. Cover with oiled cling film and leave in a warm place for about 30 minutes, or until almost doubled in size.

Meanwhile, set the oven at Gas Mark 7, 425°F, 220°C.

Bake the loaf for 35 to 40 minutes until cooked. Turn out on to a wire rack to cool. Serve sliced and buttered.

An interesting variation is to replace 60 g (2 oz) of the dates with an equal quantity of walnut pieces.

TO FREEZE: wrap and freeze for up to 3 months.

TO USE FROM FROZEN: loosen the wrapping and thaw the bread at room temperature for 4 to 5 hours.

MALT BREAD

MAKES THREE

455 G (1 LB) LOAVES
*This moist dark bread is well worth the
effort of making at home.*

680 g (1½ lb) strong white bread flour
1 teaspoon salt
1 sachet easy-blend dried yeast
6 tablespoons malt extract
2 tablespoons black treacle
30 g (1 oz) butter
110 g (4 oz) seedless raisins
For the sweet glaze:
110 g (4 oz) granulated sugar, dissolved
in 140 ml (¼ pt) water
Three 455 g (1 lb) loaf tins, greased

Sift the flour with the salt and yeast into a large bowl.

Melt the malt extract with the treacle and butter. Cool. Add to the dry ingredients with the raisins and 340 ml (12 fl oz) warm (blood heat) water. Beat for about 2 to 3 minutes until well blended and then divide the mixture between the tins. Cover with oiled cling film and leave to prove in a warm place until doubled in size.

Meanwhile, set the oven at Gas Mark 6, 400°F, 200°C.

Bake the loaves for about 35 to 40 minutes, then remove from the tins and brush with the hot glaze. Leave to cool on a wire rack. Serve thickly sliced, spread with butter.

TO FREEZE: wrap and freeze for up to 3 months.

TO USE FROM FROZEN: loosen the wrapping and thaw the bread at room temperature for 4 to 5 hours.

FRUIT AND NUT LOAF

MAKES ONE 455 G (1 LB) LOAF
*Serve this full-flavoured,
old-fashioned tea-bread thinly sliced
and buttered.*

60 g (2 oz) butter
60 g (2 oz) soft light brown sugar
1 egg, size 3, beaten
170 g (6 oz) self-raising flour
½ teaspoon ground mixed spice
¼ teaspoon ground cinnamon
140 ml (¼ pt) milk
The grated rind of 1 lemon
110 g (4 oz) currants
85 g (3 oz) walnut pieces, chopped
A 455 g (1 lb) loaf tin,
greased and lined

Set the oven at Gas Mark 4, 350°F, 180°C. Cream the butter and sugar until pale and fluffy. Gradually beat in the egg. Fold in the flour, spices and milk, followed by the lemon rind, the currants and walnuts.

Spoon the mixture into the tin and bake for 1 to 1¼ hours or until a skewer inserted into the centre of the loaf comes out clean.

Leave to cool in the tin for a few minutes, then turn out and cool on a wire rack. Store the loaf in an airtight container for up to 5 days. Serve the loaf sliced and buttered.

TO FREEZE: wrap in a polythene bag and freeze for up to 3 months.

TO USE FROM FROZEN: loosen the wrapping and thaw the loaf overnight at room temperature.

BATTENBURG CAKE

MAKES ONE 18 CM (7 IN)
RECTANGULAR SHAPED CAKE

*This popular cake is named after Prince Henry of Battenburg,
but was also known as the Chapel Window or Tennis Cake because of its
chequered appearance.*

110 g (4 oz) butter
110 g (4 oz) caster sugar
2 eggs, size 3, beaten
85 g (3 oz) self-raising flour, sifted
30 g (1 oz) ground almonds
A few drops of almond essence
1 to 2 tablespoons milk

A little red food colouring paste
170 g (6 oz) warmed, sieved
apricot jam
350 g (12 oz) almond paste
Caster sugar for sprinkling
An 18 cm (7 in) square tin, greased
A strip of foil

Set the oven at Gas Mark 4, 350°F, 180°C. Using a double strip of foil, divide the tin in half, folding the edges of the foil over the side of the tin to secure.

Cream the butter with the sugar until pale and light. Gradually beat in the eggs, beating well after each addition. Gently fold in the flour, followed by the almonds with a few drops of the almond essence. Add enough milk to give the batter a soft dropping consistency.

Spoon half the mixture into the prepared tin and smooth the surface. Stir the red food colouring paste into remaining mixture. Spoon this mixture into the other half of the tin and smooth the surface. Bake for 20 to 25 minutes or until firm to the touch in the centre. Carefully turn the cake out on to a wire rack to cool.

Neatly trim the edges of the cake, making sure they are of equal size and cut in half lengthways. Spread the sides of each strip of cake with some of the warmed, sieved apricot jam and stick the cakes together to form a two-layer chequerboard. Coat the outside of the cake (but not the ends) with the remaining apricot jam.

Roll almond paste to a rectangle 30.5 by 18 cm (12 by 7 in) and wrap neatly over and around the cake, leaving the ends of the cake visible. Flute the top edges of the almond paste and lightly score the top in a diamond pattern. Store the cake in an airtight tin for 1 to 2 days. Sprinkle with caster sugar just before serving.

FRESH FRUIT TARTLETS

MAKES 24 TARTLETS

*Dainty little tartlets, made from rich
pastry filled with lightly whipped cream
and topped with seasonal fruits, are
a teatime favourite.*

60 g (2 oz) butter
110 g (4 oz) plain flour, sifted
15 g (½ oz) caster sugar
1 egg yolk, size 3
For the filling:
140 ml (¼ pt) double cream, lightly
whipped
280 g (10 oz) prepared red summer fruit,
such as strawberries and raspberries
A 6.5 cm (2½ in) fluted cutter
24 patty or mince pie tins

Rub the butter together with the flour into a mixing bowl until the mixture resembles fine breadcrumbs. Stir in the sugar. Add the egg yolk with about 2 to 3 teaspoons of cold water and mix to make a soft but not sticky dough. Wrap and chill the pastry for 15 minutes.

Set the oven at Gas Mark 6, 400°F, 200°C. Roll the dough out on a lightly floured work surface. Using the fluted cutter stamp out 24 rounds. Line the patty or mince pie tins with the pastry.

Lightly prick the pastry with a fork and chill for 10 minutes. Line the pastry with greaseproof paper and fill with baking beans. Bake 'blind' for about 7 to 10 minutes. Remove the beans and paper from the tin and bake the pastry for a further 5 to 10 minutes or until cooked. Leave to cool.

To complete, place a little lightly whipped cream in each pastry case and arrange the summer fruits on top.

LEFT *Battenburg Cake*
OPPOSITE *Strawberry Tartlets, and
Chocolate and Hazelnut Butterfly Cakes*

STRAWBERRY TARTLETS

MAKES 20-22

*Elegant and attractive, these tiny discs of rich pastry
are topped with a dab of cream cheese and a
glazed strawberry.*

For the pastry:
110 g (4 oz) plain flour
A pinch of salt
60 g (2 oz) caster sugar
60 g (2 oz) unsalted butter, softened
2 egg yolks, size 3
For the topping:
85 g (3 oz) full-fat cream cheese
1½ teaspoons milk
110 g (4 oz) strawberries, hulled and halved
(cut large ones into 3 or 4 pieces)
3 tablespoons redcurrant jelly
A 5 cm (2 in) plain round biscuit cutter

Sift the flour with the salt on to a cool work surface. Make a well in the centre and add the sugar, butter and egg yolks. With the tips of your fingers work the sugar, butter and yolks together until they resemble scrambled eggs, then gradually work in all the flour from round the sides. Knead the pastry lightly until smooth (it can also be made in a processor), cover with cling film and chill for an hour.

Roll out the pastry 3 mm (⅛ in) thick on a lightly floured surface and cut out 20-22 rounds, rerolling the trimmings as necessary. Transfer to greased baking trays, prick with a fork and chill for 5 to 10 minutes. Meanwhile, set the oven at Gas Mark 5, 375°F, 190°C. Bake the pastry rounds for about 7 to 10 minutes or until golden. Cool on a wire rack.

Beat the cream cheese until softened then gradually beat in the milk. Spread over the pastry rounds and arrange half a strawberry on each. Melt the redcurrant jelly over gentle heat, stirring constantly to make a smooth glaze. Brush over the strawberries using a pastry brush, and leave to set for a few minutes. Arrange on serving plates and serve within an hour.

The cream cheese topping can be made the previous day, then covered and stored in the fridge until required. To melt the redcurrant jelly in the microwave, cook on full power ('high') for 1 minute.

TO FREEZE: the pastry rounds can be made in advance and frozen. Open-freeze then pack into a plastic container and store in freezer for up to 3 months.

TO USE FROM FROZEN: thaw at room temperature on wire racks for about an hour.

ICED FANCIES

These dainty little cakes are the very essence of femininity.
A classic 'must' for a celebration tea. For a professional touch,
top the cakes with sugar decorations.

170 g (6 oz) butter
170 g (6 oz) caster sugar
The grated rind of a large lemon
3 eggs, size 3, beaten
230 g (8 oz) self-raising flour, sifted
2 to 3 tablespoons lemon juice
310 g (11 oz) warmed, sieved apricot jam
735 g (1 lb 10 oz) almond paste
625 g (1 lb 6 oz) icing sugar, sifted
Food colouring paste, optional
To decorate:
Sugar flower violets or crystallised seeds
(mimosa style)
30 little paper cases
A 20.5 cm (8 in) square cake tin, greased and lined

Set the oven at Gas Mark 4, 350°F, 180°C. Cream the butter, sugar and lemon rind until pale and light. Gradually beat in the eggs, beating well after each addition. Gently fold in the sifted flour, stir in enough lemon juice to make the cake batter of a soft dropping consistency. Spoon into the prepared tin and smooth the surface. Bake for 25 to 35 minutes. Leave to cool in the tin for 15 minutes. Turn out on to a wire rack, remove the lining paper and leave to cool completely.

Brush the top of the cake with the warm, sieved apricot jam. Cut the cake into 30 small squares. Brush the sides of the cakes with apricot jam. Roll the almond paste out on a work surface, lightly dusted with icing sugar. Cut the almond paste to fit the top and sides of each cake. Leave the cakes in an airtight container for a day to let the almond paste firm.

Next day, sift the icing sugar into a bowl, then gradually add enough cold water to make a glacé icing of coating consistency, then add a little food colouring paste to the icing, if using.

Arrange the cake squares on a large wire rack set over a sheet of greaseproof paper to catch any icing that runs off the cakes. Carefully and evenly spoon the icing over each cake until completely coated. Leave in a cool, dry place until the icing sets. Decorate the top of each cake with sugar flower violets or crystallised seeds. Store in an airtight container for about 1 to 2 days and serve in paper cases.

TO FREEZE: the cake base can be wrapped in greaseproof paper and foil and frozen for up to 1 month. Do not freeze the cakes once they have been iced.

TO USE THE CAKE BASE FROM FROZEN: thaw, unwrapped at room temperature for 1½ to 2 hours.

TINY CHOCOLATE ECLAIRS

MAKES ABOUT 24 ÉCLAIRS

French finger-sized pastries filled with lightly whipped cream and topped with a chocolate icing.

For the choux pastry:
65 g (2¼ oz) plain flour, sifted
A pinch each of salt and sugar
50 g (1¾ oz) unsalted butter
2 eggs, size 3, beaten
For the filling:
280 ml (½ pt) double cream, lightly whipped
For the glacé icing:
2 teaspoons cocoa powder
170 g (6 oz) icing sugar, sifted
A piping bag and a plain (½ in) tube and star tube

Set the oven at Gas Mark 5, 375°F, 190°C. Sift the flour with the salt and sugar, twice. Heat the butter gently in a medium-sized pan with 140 ml (¼ pt) water until the butter has melted, then bring to a rapid boil. Tip in the flour, all at once, and beat vigorously with a wooden spoon over a low heat until the dough leaves the sides of the pan and looks smooth. Cook for a minute longer, stirring.

Stand the pan in cold water for 5 minutes to cool. Gradually whisk in the eggs, whisking well after each addition (an electric whisk is ideal). The finished choux paste should be thick enough to hold its own shape and stiff enough to pipe.

Using a piping bag and a small plain tube, pipe éclairs about 5 cm (2 in) long on a dampened baking tray. Bake for about 20 minutes until crisp. Make a small hole in the side of each éclair to let out the steam. Return to the oven for 2 to 3 minutes. Remove from the baking tray and leave to cool on a wire rack.

Spoon the lightly whipped cream into a piping bag fitted with the small star tube. Halve the éclairs and pipe the cream in the bottom half.

Finally, make the glacé icing by dissolving the cocoa powder in 2 tablespoons of boiling water until it forms a paste. Gradually stir in the sifted icing sugar. Dip the top half of each eclair into the icing. Leave to set. Place it on top of the cream filled half. Eat within 4 hours.

TO FREEZE: place the unfilled éclairs in a rigid plastic container and freeze for up to 3 months.

TO USE FROM FROZEN: place in a hot oven for 5 minutes. Allow to cool completely before filling and icing.

LEFT: *Iced Fancies.*

ABOVE: *Tiny Chocolate Eclairs.*

LEMON SWIRL BISCUITS

MAKES ABOUT 30

Rich lemon biscuits decorated with tiny pieces of glacé cherry.

230 g (8 oz) butter
60 g (2 oz) caster sugar
The grated rind of 1 lemon
1 tablespoon lemon juice
230 g (8 oz) plain flour
A few glacé cherries, to decorate
A piping bag fitted with a star tube

Cream the butter and sugar until pale and fluffy. Beat in the lemon rind and juice. Gently fold in the flour. Spoon the mixture into the piping bag and pipe about 30 swirls on greased baking trays. Decorate with tiny pieces of glacé cherry, then chill for about 10 to 15 minutes. Set the oven at Gas Mark 4, 350°F, 180°C.

Bake the biscuits for about 15 to 18 minutes or until barely golden. Leave to cool on the baking trays for about a minute, then transfer to a wire rack to cool completely. Store the biscuits in an airtight container for up to 4 days.
TO FREEZE: open-freeze then pack in a rigid container and store in freezer for up to 3 months.
TO USE FROM FROZEN: place the biscuits on serving plates and thaw at room temperature for about an hour.

HAZELNUT SHORTBREAD

MAKES 24

Rich, buttery shortbread fingers flavoured with roasted hazelnuts.

230 g (8 oz) butter, softened
60 g (2 oz) soft light brown sugar
170 g (6 oz) plain flour
30 g (1 oz) rice flour or ground rice
110 g (4 oz) hazelnuts, roasted and chopped in a liquidiser or processor
A 30.5 by 20.5 cm (12 by 8 in) shallow cake tin, greased and lined

Set the oven at Gas Mark 3, 325°F, 170°C. Cream the butter and sugar together. Fold in the flour, rice flour or ground rice and nuts. Knead the mixture to form a firm shortbread dough, and press evenly into the tin with a palette knife. Bake for about 35 to 45 minutes or until golden and firm to the touch. Mark into 24 fingers.

Leave the shortbread to cool in the tin for 15 minutes, then transfer to a wire rack to finish cooling. Store in an airtight container for up to 4 days.
TO FREEZE: open-freeze, then pack in a plastic container and freeze for up to 2 weeks.
TO USE FROM FROZEN: thaw the shortbread fingers, uncovered, at room temperature for about an hour, then crisp in a warm oven. Cool and serve.

CHEQUERED BISCUITS

MAKES ABOUT 35

These unusual orange and chocolate chequerboard biscuits are made by rolling the mixture into sausages then layering them up.

230 g (8 oz) butter
110 g (4 oz) icing sugar
340 g (12 oz) plain flour
1 egg yolk, size 3
The grated rind of 1 orange
30 g (1 oz) cocoa powder
Beaten egg white

Beat the butter with the sifted icing sugar until pale and fluffy. Fold in the flour and egg yolk. Mix well to form a firm dough. Divide the dough in half. Knead the orange rind into 1 half and the cocoa powder into the other. Wrap each half in cling film and chill for about 2 hours.

Divide the chocolate dough into 4 equal portions and the orange dough into 3 equal portions.

On a lightly floured surface with your hands roll all the orange portions and 3 of the chocolate portions into thin rolls about 25.5 cm (10 in) long. Arrange the rolls alternately in 2 layers of 3 to give a chequerboard effect. Seal each roll with a little beaten egg white.

Using a rolling pin, roll out the remaining chocolate portion very thinly on a surface lightly dusted with icing sugar to a rectangle large enough to wrap round the chequerboard dough to make a brick shape.

Seal with egg white, cover and chill for 15 to 20 minutes. Meanwhile, set the oven at Gas Mark 5, 375°F, 190°C.

Cut the dough into about 35 slices, place on greased baking trays and bake for 15 to 16 minutes or until golden. Transfer to a wire rack to cool. Store in an airtight container for up to 4 days.
TO FREEZE: pack into a plastic container and freeze for up to 2 months.
TO USE FROM FROZEN: thaw on wire racks or on serving plates at room temperature for about an hour.

SHORTBREAD

Traditionally, shortbread was served as a flat round cake and marked into segments.

170 g (6 oz) unsalted butter
85 g (3 oz) caster sugar
230 g (8 oz) plain flour, sifted
30 g (1 oz) rice flour or ground rice
A little caster sugar for sprinkling
A baking tray, greased

Set the oven at Gas Mark 3, 325°F, 170°C. Cream the butter until soft. Add the sugar and beat until pale and light. Work in the flour and rice flour or ground rice until the mixture binds together, and knead lightly to form a smooth dough.

Roll out the dough on to a lightly floured surface to a circle 18 cm (7 in) diameter. Lightly mark the rim of the shortbread with a fork and mark into 8 segments. Lightly prick the surface with a fork and carefully transfer to the prepared baking tray.

Bake the shortbread for about 20 to 25 minutes until pale golden and just firm to the touch.

Leave to cool on the baking tray for about 2 to 3 minutes before cutting right through the petticoat markings. Transfer the shortbread to a wire rack to cool completely. Sprinkle with the caster sugar just before serving.

TO FREEZE: open freeze until firm. Pack into a rigid plastic container and freeze for up to 2 months.

TO USE FROM FROZEN: transfer to a wire rack. Thaw at room temperature for 2 hours.

MINIATURE BRANDY SNAPS

These brandy snaps are the size of a little finger – with the end of each one dipped in chocolate. For an extra treat, fill the little brandy snaps with whipped cream.

60 g (2 oz) butter
60 g (2 oz) caster sugar
2 tablespoons golden syrup
60 g (2 oz) plain flour
½ teaspoon ground ginger
The grated rind of 1 lemon
1 teaspoon brandy
60 g (2 oz) plain chocolate
2 or 3 wooden spoons

Set the oven at Gas Mark 4, 350°F, 180°C. Grease the handles of several wooden spoons (these will be used for rolling up the cooked brandy snaps).

Melt the butter, caster sugar and golden syrup over a gentle heat. Stir until smooth, then sift the flour with the ginger and stir into the melted mixture with the grated lemon rind and the brandy. Mix well.

Put teaspoons of the mixture about 10 cm (4 in) apart on baking trays lined with non-stick baking parchment. Bake for about 7 to 10 minutes or until bubbly and golden.

Leave to cool for a minute, then lift off the tray, one at a time, using a palette knife, and roll them loosely round a spoon handle. Leave until set, then gently twist off and cool on a wire rack. (If the biscuits set before they have been rolled return to the oven for a minute until pliable again.)

Break up the chocolate and melt in a bowl over simmering water. Beat in 1 tablespoon of water until smooth and glossy. Dip the ends of each brandy snap in the chocolate. Leave them to set on a wire rack or on waxed paper in a cool place.

NOTE that the undipped brandy snaps will keep in an airtight container for up to a week. However, the dipped ones should be eaten within 24 hours.

ABOVE *Coffee Meringue Kisses*
OPPOSITE *Chequered Biscuits (top), Hazelnut Shortbread (right) and Lemon Swirl Biscuits.*

COFFEE MERINGUE KISSES

Meringues can be made well ahead and stored in an airtight container in a warm, dry place.

3 egg whites, size 3
170 g (6 oz) caster sugar
1 tablespoon instant coffee powder
140 ml (¼ pt) double or whipping cream, lightly whipped
A piping bag fitted with a large star tube

Set the oven at Gas Mark ¼, 225°F, 110°C, then stiffly whisk the egg whites in a large, spotlessly clean and grease-free bowl. Gradually whisk in the sugar and coffee powder to make a thick glossy meringue.

Spoon into the piping bag and pipe 40 small swirls on baking trays lined with non-stick baking parchment. Bake for 2 to 2½ hours or until the meringues are crisp and dry.

Cool the meringues, then lift them off the trays and store in an airtight container for up to 3 weeks. Sandwich the meringues together in pairs with a little whipped cream up to an hour before serving.

CHOCOLATE AND HAZELNUT BUTTERFLY CAKES

MAKES 20-22

A sophisticated combination of nuts and chocolate gives a new twist to a favourite recipe.

For the cakes:
110 g (4 oz) butter
110 g (4 oz) caster sugar
2 eggs, size 3, beaten
60 g (2 oz) hazelnuts, toasted and chopped
1 tablespoon cocoa powder, dissolved in
1 tablespoon boiling water
170 g (6 oz) self-raising flour
For the buttercream:
85 g (3 oz) butter
230 g (8 oz) icing sugar, sifted
1 tablespoon cocoa powder, dissolved in
1 tablespoon boiling water
Icing sugar to dredge
20-22 bun tins, greased, or paper
bun cases

Set the oven at Gas Mark 6, 400°F, 200°C. Cream the butter and sugar together until the mixture is pale and fluffy. Gradually beat in the eggs, beating well after each addition.

Carefully fold in the hazelnuts, cooled cocoa liquid and sifted flour. Using a teaspoon, half fill the bun tins or cases. Bake for 10 to 15 minutes or until well-risen and firm. Cool on a wire rack.

Beat together all the buttercream ingredients until smooth. Cut a slice from the top of each cake and pipe or spoon a little buttercream on each. Cut each slice in half and insert in the buttercream at an angle to resemble butterfly wings. Dredge with icing sugar just before serving.
TO FREEZE: open-freeze the cakes, then pack in a plastic container layered with greaseproof paper. They can be stored in freezer for up to a fortnight.
TO USE FROM FROZEN: arrange on serving plates and thaw at room temperature for 1 to 1½ hours. When completely thawed, dredge with icing sugar.

COFFEE AND WALNUT BUTTERFLY CAKES

MAKES 20-22

Nutty, coffee fairy cakes.

For the cakes:
110 g (4 oz) butter
110 g (4 oz) caster sugar
2 eggs, size 3, beaten
60 g (2 oz) walnut pieces, finely chopped
2 teaspoons instant coffee, dissolved in
1 tablespoon boiling water
170 g (6 oz) self-raising flour
For the buttercream:
85 g (3 oz) butter
250 g (8 oz) icing sugar, sifted
1 teaspoon instant coffee, dissolved in
1 tablespoon boiling water
Walnut pieces, to decorate
Icing sugar to dredge
20-22 bun tins, greased, or paper
bun cases

Make and bake as for Chocolate and Hazelnut Butterfly Cakes (recipe on the left), substituting chopped walnuts and cooled coffee liquid for the hazelnuts and chocolate liquid.

Make the buttercream and assemble the butterfly cakes as in the recipe on the left, substituting the coffee liquid for the chocolate. Decorate the cakes with walnut pieces.
TO FREEZE: open-freeze the cakes, then pack in a plastic container layered with greaseproof paper. They can be stored in freezer for up to a fortnight.
TO USE FROM FROZEN: arrange on serving plates and thaw at room temperature for 1 to 1½ hours. When completely thawed, dredge with icing sugar.

MADELEINES

MAKES 20-25

The French version of fairy cakes.

110 g (4 oz) self-raising flour
110 g (4 oz) caster sugar
The grated rind of 1 lemon
2 eggs, size 3, beaten
110 g (4 oz) butter, melted
Icing sugar to dust
Madeleine moulds or bun tins,
greased or paper bun cases

Set the oven at Gas Mark 5, 375°F, 190°C. Sift the flour into a bowl, stir in the sugar and lemon rind. Gradually add the beaten eggs, mixing well. Fold in the melted butter a little at a time. Spoon into the moulds (fill two-thirds full) and bake for 12 to 15 minutes until well-risen and golden - don't overcook.

Cool on a wire rack then store in an airtight container for up to a day. Dust with icing sugar and serve.
TO FREEZE: open-freeze, then pack in a rigid plastic container and store in freezer for up to 2 weeks.
TO USE FROM FROZEN: thaw the Madeleines on a wire rack for about 1 to 1½ hours at room temperature.

CREAM-FILLED SWISS ROLL

MAKES ONE 20.5 CM (8 IN)
SWISS ROLL

Deliciously light sponge that can be filled with jam and cream, or a lemon buttercream.

3 eggs, size 3
85 g (3 oz) caster sugar
85 g (3 oz) self-raising flour
For the filling:
4 tablespoons good quality strawberry
or raspberry jam
140 ml (¼ pt) double or whipping cream,
lightly whipped

Caster sugar for sprinkling
A 30.5 by 20.5 cm (12 by 8 in) Swiss roll
tin, greased and lined
For the lemon buttercream:
85 g (3 oz) butter, softened
170 g (6 oz) icing sugar, sifted
The grated rind of 1 lemon
1-2 tablespoons lemon juice

Set the oven at Gas Mark 7, 425°F, 220°C. Whisk the eggs with the sugar until very thick indeed - the whisk should leave a distinct ribbon-like trail when lifted out of the mixture. Carefully fold in the flour using a metal spoon. Pour the mixture into the tin and bake for 12 to 15 minutes until the cake is golden and springy to the touch.

Turn out on to a piece of greaseproof lightly dusted with caster sugar. Quickly peel off the greaseproof lining. Trim the edges of the sponge with a large, sharp knife. Loosely roll up the sponge in the clean greaseproof and leave to cool.

When cold, unroll the sponge and spread evenly with jam and then whipped cream. Reroll and dust with a little caster sugar. Eat within a day.

To make the lemon buttercream, beat together all the ingredients and use to fill the lemon Swiss roll. Roll up and dust lightly with caster or icing sugar.

VARIATIONS

Lemon Zesty Swiss Roll
Add the grated rind of 1 lemon to the Swiss roll mixture with the sugar and bake as above. Fill with lemon buttercream.

Lemon Curd Swiss Roll
You can also fill with Lemon Curd (recipe page 79) and whipped cream.

TO FREEZE: freeze unfilled sponge, rolled up in greaseproof paper and wrapped, for up to 3 months.

TO USE FROM FROZEN: loosen outer wrapping and thaw at room temperature for 2 to 3 hours. Unwrap and fill before serving.

SUMPTUOUS BROWNIES

MAKES 16 SQUARES
Everyone's favourite!

170 ml (6 fl oz) soya oil
170 g (6 oz) soft dark brown sugar
A few drops vanilla essence
3 eggs, size 3, beaten

110 g (4 oz) plain flour
40 g (1½ oz) cocoa powder
½ teaspoon baking powder
60 g (2 oz) walnut pieces

Set the oven at Gas Mark 4, 350°F, 180°C. Mix the oil with the sugar and vanilla essence, then beat in the eggs. Sift the flour with the cocoa and baking powder and gradually blend into the egg mixture. Stir in the walnuts. Spread evenly in the tin. Bake the brownies for 25 to 30 minutes. Do not overcook – mixture should be slightly soft in centre. Cool, turn out and cut into squares.

TO FREEZE: wrap and freeze for up to 1 month.

TO USE FROM FROZEN: thaw, unwrapped at room temperature for about 3 hours.

SEED CAKE

MAKES ONE 20.5 CM (8 IN) CAKE
Flavoured with caraway seeds, whose distinctive taste combines perfectly with tea, this now unusual cake was enormously popular at the turn of the century.

230 g (8 oz) butter, softened
230 g (8 oz) caster sugar
4 eggs, size 3, beaten
280 g (10 oz) self-raising flour, sifted
The grated rind of 1 orange
2 tablespoons caraway seeds
2 tablespoons orange juice
A 20.5 cm (8 in) deep, round cake tin,
greased and lined

Set the oven at Gas Mark 4, 350°F, 180°C. Beat all the ingredients for the cake together in a large bowl until well mixed and smooth; this will take about 1 minute by hand or 30 to 40 seconds in a mixer. Spoon the mixture into the prepared tin and smooth the surface. Bake for 40 minutes to 1 hour, or until golden and the cake springs back when lightly pressed. Leave to cool in the tin for 5 minutes. Turn out on to a wire rack to cool completely. Store in an airtight tin and eat within 3 days.

Petal-shaped Christening Cake

For the cake:
110 g (4 oz) self-raising flour
110 g (4 oz) plain flour
60 g (2 oz) ground almonds
230 g (8 oz) unsalted butter
230 g (8 oz) caster sugar
4 eggs, size 3
The grated rind of 2 oranges
2 tablespoons Cointreau or Grand Marnier
A 20.5 cm (8 in) petal-shaped tin, greased and lined

For the marzipan:
795 g (1¾ lb) ready-made white marzipan
110 g (4 oz) apricot jam, lightly beaten, boiled and sieved
Icing sugar for rolling
A 28 cm (11 in) petal-shaped cake board

For the sugar paste:
A little vodka
1.25 kg (2¾ lb) cream Regalice (sugar paste),
plus 30 g (1 oz) for the crib

For the royal icing:
3 teaspoons egg-white substitute:
for example,
Meri-white or Renwhite
455 g (1 lb) icing sugar
Cream and peach paste colouring

For the pastillage:
¾ level teaspoon gelatine
230 g (8 oz) icing sugar
¼ teaspoon gum tragacanth
(bought from cake decorating suppliers)
A little cornflour

For the flowers:
85 g (3 oz) flower paste
(from Cake Decorating Suppliers)
Cream, peach and yellow
paste colouring
A little egg white
A little white vegetable fat

EQUIPMENT

A cake decorating smoother
A small greaseproof paper piping bag
No. 1 piping nozzle
Lengths of number 28 florists' wire
30 gauge wire
Dry oasis or polystyrene covered in cling film
Small daisy cutter
6 mm (¼ in) blossom cutter
Small palette knife
Tweezers and cocktail sticks for shaping flowers
Ball tool
Small piece of foam
Artist's paint brush, size 4

Florists' tape
Piece of Perspex
Tiny baby doll for the crib
3 cm (1¼ in) rolling pin
Non-stick board
10 cm (4 in) oval cutter
Tracing paper and thin card
1 m (39 in) length of cream ribbon, 5 cm (⅝ in) wide, to go
around edge of the cake board
Double-sided sticky tape
50 by 15 cm (19½ by 6 in) white net or tulle
Non-toxic pencil
Pink petal dust

TO MAKE THE CAKE
Set oven at Gas Mark 4, 350°F, 180°C. Sift the flours and ground almonds together. Cream the butter and sugar until pale and light. Gradually beat in the eggs. Fold in orange rind, Cointreau and flour mixture. Spoon into the tin and level the surface. Bake for 40 minutes. Reduce the oven to Gas Mark 3, 325°F, 170°C. Bake for a further 45 minutes until golden, firm to touch, and a skewer inserted into the cake comes out clean.

Cool in the tin for 10 minutes, then turn out on to a wire cake rack to cool completely. Wrap in greaseproof paper and store in an airtight container for 1 to 2 days, or wrap and freeze for up to 1 month. (Defrost the cake overnight before decorating).

TO COVER CAKE BOARD
Using 340 g (12 oz) of the cream sugar paste, roll out to fit the width of the cake board. Prepare a little royal icing (see basic method on page 118) and spread on the surface of the board. Place the sugar paste on top. Smooth the surface and trim the edges with a knife. Leave to dry for 2 or 3 days.

TO MARZIPAN THE CAKE
Knead the marzipan until smooth and roll out a thin 'sausage'. Place around the top edge of the cake and smooth gently to the centre with a palette knife to form a level surface. Turn the cake

upside down and place on a non-stick board or work surface. Spread with apricot jam glaze. Take off any rings or bangles to avoid marking the marzipan.

On a work surface lightly dusted with icing sugar, roll out the remaining marzipan to a circle large enough to cover the entire cake. Lift the marzipan over the cake to cover (see page 68). Flute out the marzipan at the sides and carefully unfold any pleats. Gently press the marzipan into the indentations of the petal-shaped sides. Using the palm of your hand only, ease marzipan around the sides of the cake with an upward movement. Using the cake decorating smoother, smooth the top and sides of the cake with even pressure to remove bumps. Trim off excess with a knife. Leave to dry for 24 hours.

TO SUGAR PASTE THE CAKE
Brush a little vodka over the marzipan. Cover the cake with 0.9 kg (2 lb) of cream sugar paste, using the same method as for the marzipan, smoothing top and sides of the cake. Trim off excess with a knife. Place the cake on the covered petal-shaped board.

TO MAKE THE ROYAL ICING
Dissolve the Meri-white or Renwhite in 70 ml (2½ fl oz) cold water. Gradually add the icing sugar to the liquid, beating thoroughly until it is the consistency of whipped meringue. Leave one quarter of the icing white, and colour another quarter of the icing a fairly deep shade of peach for writing the baby's name. Colour the remaining icing cream to match the colour of the sugar paste. Keep the royal icing covered. Spoon a little cream icing into a greaseproof paper piping bag fitted with a No. 1 piping nozzle and pipe a 'snail's trail' around the base of the cake.

TO MAKE THE PASTILLAGE
Put 5 teaspoons of cold water into a small, heatproof bowl, and sprinkle over the gelatine. Leave to sponge. Dissolve over hot water, but do not stir. Put the icing sugar into a small mixing bowl and mix in ¼ teaspoon of gum tragacanth. Add the dissolved gelatine and mix with a fork. (If the mixture is

very dry, add a drop of hot water.) Turn out on to a non-stick board and knead for 5 to 10 minutes until very smooth.

Place the pastillage into 2 plastic bags, seal them tightly and keep at room temperature for at least 24 hours (but no longer than 10 days) before using.

TO MAKE CRIB AND PLAQUES
Trace the crib templates on to thin card. Lightly dust the non-stick board with cornflour and roll out a portion of pastillage fairly thinly. Cut out the crib sections using the templates. Place the base of the crib lengthwise over a rolling pin. Cut out 2 plaques using a 10 cm (4 in) oval cutter. Leave the pieces to dry on Perspex.

TO ASSEMBLE THE CRIB
Using a No. 1 nozzle and white royal icing, pipe round the shortest edges of the base of the crib and fix the top and bottom in place, following the dotted lines shown on the templates. Pipe round the seams to strengthen them. Leave to dry. Pipe a 'snail's trail' round the headboard. To make a pillow, form a small piece of sugar paste into a sausage-shape and 'frill' edges using a cocktail stick. Place the baby doll on top of the pillow. Make a sugar paste quilt to match the pillow and place over the doll. Cut a piece of net 10 by 15 cm (4 by 6 in) to fold over the top of the headboard; gather at the centre with thread. Fix the net to the crib with a little royal icing. Leave to dry.

TO CAKE NAME PLAQUE
Using a non-toxic pencil, trace the baby's name on to the plaque. Do not press hard as plaque may break. Use peach royal icing and a No. 1 nozzle to pipe the name. Fix the plaque on to the cake with a little royal icing.

TO MAKE FLOWER SPRAYS
Cutter flowers
Divide the flower paste into 3 and colour ⅓ yellow, ⅓ cream and ⅓ peach. Smear a little vegetable fat on the non-stick board and the rolling pin. Thinly roll out a small amount of coloured flower paste (cover the remaining paste

with cling film). Cut out flowers with a blossom cutter, and depress on to a piece of foam to cup the flower. Cut the 30 gauge wire into short lengths (you will need 96 in all). Dip one end of a piece of wire in egg white and gently push through the centre of a flower. Repeat for all flowers and leave to dry on the foam. When dry, tape 2 cutter flowers together to form a spray and store carefully. We used 18 peach sprays, 18 yellow and 12 cream. Make 30 peach cutter flowers for the top of the cake. Fix on to top of the cake with dots of royal icing. Pipe a small dot of icing on to the centre of each flower.

Daisies
Cut each piece of 28 florists' wire into 4 (you will need 6 pieces of wire). Make a hook at right angles in 1 end. Flatten a pea-sized piece of yellow paste, dip the hook of the stem in egg white, then push it into the centre. Mark over a fine wire mesh and leave to dry in the oasis. Using white paste, roll out and cut 2 daisy shapes (keep one well covered while working on the other). Make a slit in the centre of each petal and carefully roll each petal with a cocktail stick. Press on to foam with a ball tool. Paint the centre with egg white, and push the petals along the stem to join the prepared yellow centre. Repeat with the second layer. Leave to dry in the oasis. The tips can then be brushed with pink petal dust. Makes 6 daisies. Cut 12 net strips 5 by 10 cm (2 by 4 in), twist fine wire into centre of each. Secure tightly to make net sprays; trim net to round-off edges. Make 2 for each indentation of the petal cake (12 in total).

TO COMPLETE
Fix a piece of flower paste to each indentation using royal icing. Arrange flowers and net, cutting the stems of the flowers to the required length (make sure that no wires stick into the surface of the cake). Finally, secure the ribbon round the edge of the cake board using double-sided sticky tape.

NOTE: Eat the Christening Cake within 2 days of icing. The wired flowers are not edible and should be kept away from children.

RICH PLUM CAKE

MAKES ONE 20.5 CM (8 IN) ROUND CAKE

A traditional English plum cake, packed with fruit soaked in liquor and given a touch of spice. Deliciously moist, it will keep well in an airtight tin.

170 g (6 oz) pitted prunes, chopped
170 g (6 oz) currants
170 g (6 oz) sultanas
170 g (6 oz) raisins
140 ml (¼ pt) rum or brandy
60 g (2 oz) mixed peel, finely chopped
200 g (7 oz) self-raising flour

½ teaspoon each of grated nutmeg, ground cinnamon and ground cloves
170 g (6 oz) butter, softened
170 g (6 oz) soft light brown sugar
3 eggs, size 3, beaten
A 20.5 cm (8 in) deep round cake tin, greased and lined

Wrap a double layer of newspaper or brown paper around the outside of the cake tin - this prevents the cake from drying out during cooking.

Thoroughly rinse the dried fruit and drain well. Tip into a large bowl, pour over the rum or brandy and stir well. Cover and leave in a cool place for at least 6 hours, stirring occasionally. Stir in the mixed peel.

Set the oven at Gas Mark 2, 300°F, 150°C. Sift the flour with the spices. Cream the butter and sugar together until pale and light. Gradually beat in the eggs, beating well after each addition; and a little of the flour to prevent the mixture from curdling, if necessary. Using a large metal spoon, fold in the sifted flour and spices. Add the soaked fruit with the liquid and mix gently but thoroughly. Spoon into the prepared cake tin and level the surface. Bake for 3 to 3½ hours or until a skewer inserted in the centre comes out clean. Leave to cool in the tin. Turn out, remove the greaseproof paper, wrap in fresh greaseproof paper and foil. Store in a cool, dry place for at least 2 weeks before cutting.

STENCILS FOR THE PETAL-SHAPED CHRISTENING CAKE

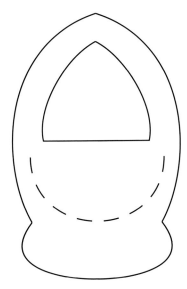

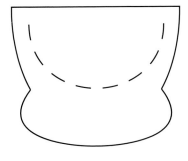

ABOVE: *Crib headboard.*
TOP RIGHT: *Foot of crib.*
BOTTOM RIGHT: *Curved base of crib.*

CHOCOLATE FUDGE SLAB

MAKES 20 SQUARES

The chocolate sponge base can be frozen for up to two months.

2 tablespoons instant coffee
170 g (6 oz) butter
170 g (6 oz) golden granulated sugar
2 tablespoons golden syrup
455 g (1 lb) plain flour
2 tablespoons cocoa powder
4 tablespoons hot milk
2 teaspoons bicarbonate of soda
A few drops vanilla essence
For the topping:
255 g (9 oz) plain chocolate
110 g (4 oz) unsalted butter
340 g (12 oz) icing sugar
A 34 by 28 cm (13½ by 11 in) deep roasting tin, greased and lined

Set the oven at Gas Mark 4, 350°F, 180°C. Put the coffee, butter, sugar and syrup into a heavy pan with 455 ml (16 fl oz) boiling water. Stir over a low heat until smooth and melted. Boil, then simmer for 5 minutes. Cool.

Sieve the flour with the cocoa and beat into the cooled mixture. Mix together the milk, bicarbonate of soda and vanilla essence, then stir into the cake mixture. Spoon into the prepared tin and bake for 20 minutes, then reduce the temperature to Gas Mark 3, 325°F, 170°C, and bake for a further 10 minutes. Cool in the tin.

To make the topping: melt the chocolate with the butter then stir in 115 ml (4 fl oz) water. Then, still over the heat, gradually beat in the icing sugar to make a thick but pourable icing, adding a little extra water if necessary. Spread the topping over and leave to set. Serve cut into squares.

TO FREEZE: wrap the sponge base, and freeze for up to 2 months
TO USE FROM FROZEN: thaw at room temperature for about 1 hour then cover with topping.

A Vegetarian Dinner

The days are long gone, thankfully, when having vegetarians around to dinner meant serving up 'meat and two veg' without the meat! The era of nut roasts and lentil burgers has been consigned to the dustbin of history, too – and now even the most militant carnivore knows that vegetarian food doesn't have to be dull and boring.

Here's a fantastic feast that will be enjoyed by vegetarians and meat eaters alike – gourmet recipes for everyone who loves good food.

SERVES 8

Stuffed Tomatoes

or

Russian Herb Blinis with Crème Fraîche and Asparagus

– ∗ –

Leek and Pine Nut Pilau

Celebration Pie

Mushrooms, Mange Tout and Chestnuts

– ∗ –

Baked Alaska

Cranberry and Port Torte with Whipped Cream

– ∗ –

Coffee

STUFFED TOMATOES

SERVES 8

To make this light and refreshing starter, choose the special tomatoes called 'stuffing tomatoes', or other large varieties, such as 'Beefsteak'.

8 stuffing tomatoes
For the filling:
4 spring onions, sliced
4 sticks celery, washed and sliced
170 g (6 oz) fennel, washed and diced
170 g (6 oz) baby sweetcorn,
blanched and quartered
1 eating apple, cored and diced
6 tablespoons mayonnaise
2 tablespoons freshly chopped parsley
Salt and freshly ground black pepper
A little salad or herbs, to garnish

Slice the top off the tomatoes and reserve. Scoop out the flesh and leave the tomatoes upside down to drain while preparing the filling.

Then, to make the filling, mix all the ingredients together and season to taste.

Stuff the tomatoes with the filling and replace the tops. Leave in the fridge to chill for up to 3 hours before serving. Garnish with a little salad or herbs, if wished.

122

RIGHT *Stuffed Tomatoes, and Russian Herb Blinis with Crème Fraîche and Asparagus.*
PREVIOUS PAGE LEFT *Wonderful fruits and cheeses – a treat for vegetarians and non-vegetarians alike.*
PREVIOUS PAGE RIGHT *Candlelight makes any dinner a special occasion.*

RUSSIAN HERB BLINIS WITH CRÈME FRAÎCHE AND ASPARAGUS

SERVES 8

Delicate pancakes make a colourful and unusual starter. Traditionally they are served with chilled vodka or crisp, dry white wine

85 g (3 oz) strong plain white flour
85 g (3 oz) wholemeal flour
1 egg, size 3, separated
½ teaspoon salt
½ packet easy-blend yeast
4 tablespoons freshly chopped mixed herbs

200 ml (7 fl oz) milk
A little butter, for frying
230 g (8 oz) asparagus spears
140 ml (¼ pt) crème fraîche
To garnish:
Sprigs of chervil
Paprika

To the make the blinis, sift the flours, returning any bran left in the sieve to the bowl. Whisk the egg yolk with 200 ml (7 fl oz) of lukewarm water. Combine the flours in a warmed mixing bowl and stir in the salt and yeast. Gradually beat in the yolk mixture, beating thoroughly to make a smooth batter. Stiffly whisk the egg white and beat into the mixture. Cover and leave in a warm place or until the batter has doubled in size – about 30 minutes.

Add the mixed herbs to the milk, heat to just below boiling point and quickly fold into the batter. Cover the batter and leave to rise again as before. (The batter can be stored in the fridge overnight at this stage.) To cook, heat a small knob of butter in a non-stick frying pan. Fry tablespoonfuls of batter to make pancakes about 9 cm (3½ in) in diameter, cooking each one for about 2 minutes on each side until puffy and golden. Cover and keep warm, in a low oven while cooking the rest. The blinis can be made up to 12 hours in advance, then warmed through in a foil-covered dish in a low oven.

Trim the asparagus spears to the same length. Remove the hard outer skin and v-shaped scales with a sharp knife. Rinse gently, then tie the asparagus in a bundle with fine string, taking care not to damage the spears. Stand the bundle upright, with the heads uppermost, in a small, deep pan of boiling, salted water. Cover with a domed lid of foil and cook gently for 5 to 10 minutes until tender. Remove carefully and drain.

To serve, place 2 blinis and a few asparagus spears on each warmed serving plate, and top with a spoonful of the crème fraîche mixture. Garnish with a sprig of chervil and a pinch of paprika.

TO FREEZE: the blinis can be cooked, cooled, layered between sheets of grease-proof paper, and frozen. Freeze for up to 1 months.

TO USE FROM FROZEN: warm through from frozen as above.

LEEK AND PINE NUT PILAU

Rice with a difference.

2 to 3 tablespoons sunflower oil
1 medium onion, finely chopped
1 clove garlic, or to taste, crushed
A few strands saffron
230 g (8 oz) brown rice
About 710 ml (1¼ pt) good-quality chicken
or vegetable stock
Salt and freshly ground black pepper
110 g (4 oz) leeks, washed and cut into
thin matchsticks
110 g (4 oz) carrots, scrubbed and cut into
thin matchsticks
60 g (2 oz) French beans, topped, tailed
and halved
To complete:
60 g (2 oz) pine nuts, toasted
3 tablespoons freshly chopped coriander
or parsley

Heat the oil in a large, heavy-based saucepan and gently cook the chopped onion and garlic until softened but not coloured. Soak the saffron in a couple of tablespoons of boiling water for a minute, then add to the pan. Stir in the rice and cook for 2 minutes. Add the stock and a little seasoning and bring to the boil. Cover the pan tightly and cook over a very low heat for 30 minutes.

Arrange the prepared vegetables on top of the rice and cook for about 10 to 20 minutes or until the rice is tender and the liquid has all been absorbed (the vegetables will cook in the steam).

To complete, stir in the pine nuts and coriander, and serve immediately.

CELEBRATION PIE

SERVES 8
This rich pie with its four colourful layers will be the highlight of the day – loved by vegetarians and meat-eaters alike.

3 large red peppers
3 large yellow peppers
60 g (2 oz) unsalted butter
340 g (12 oz) finely chopped onion
Salt and freshly ground black pepper
A few strands of saffron soaked in
2 tablespoons water
A pinch each of ground ginger and nutmeg
1 teaspoon ground cinnamon
2 tablespoons freshly chopped parsley
The juice of ½ lemon
280 ml (½ pt) good-quality vegetable stock
455 g (1 lb) Quorn, cubed
12 sheets of filo pastry about
565 g (1 lb 4 oz)

110 g (4 oz) blanched almonds,
toasted and chopped
110 g (4 oz) unsalted butter, melted
Two 395 g (14 oz) cans of artichoke hearts,
drained and sliced
12 quails' eggs, or 6 hens' eggs,
hard boiled
For the sauce:
A 10 cm (4 in) piece cucumber,
coarsely grated
140 ml (¼ pt) Greek-style yogurt
A pinch of ground cumin
A few drops Tabasco
A 21.5 cm (8½ in) round, loose-based
cake tin

Rinse and dry the peppers, then grill on both sides, turning frequently until the skin is blistered and blackened. Wrap in a clean tea towel and leave to cool for about 10 minutes. Carefully peel. Halve and deseed the peppers, and cut into thin slices. Leave the pepper slices to drain in a sieve set over a bowl.

Melt the butter in a large frying pan. Add the chopped onion and cook gently until softened but not coloured. Add the seasoning, the saffron and its liquid, all the spices, parsley, lemon juice and stock. Simmer for 15 minutes, stirring frequently until almost all the liquid has evaporated. Add the Quorn.

Set the oven at Gas Mark 5, 375°F, 190°C. To assemble, line the tin using 4 sheets of filo pastry to cover the sides and base of the tin. Place the chopped almonds in the bottom. Cover with 2 sheets of filo and brush with a little melted butter. Place the sliced peppers on top. Cover with 2 sheets of filo pastry and brush with melted butter. For the next layer, place the sliced artichokes and quails' eggs on top. Cover with another 2 sheets of filo and brush with butter. Then place the Quorn and onion mixture on top. Cover with the remaining filo pastry and drizzle over the remaining melted butter.

Bake in the oven for 50 to 60 minutes, or until a skewer inserted into the centre is hot through when removed. Cover the pie with a sheet of foil after 15 minutes to prevent over-browning.

Meanwhile, to make the sauce, mix all the ingredients together and chill until ready to serve.

RIGHT *Celebration Pie, a cornucopia of good things, wrapped in delicious papery filo pastry – a vegetarian dish which is sure to impress the most confirmed meat-eater.*

MUSHROOMS, MANGE TOUT AND CHESTNUTS

SERVES 6 TO 8

Quick, easy and delicious

8 tablespoons ground nut or vegetable oil
30 g (1 oz) slices of fresh root ginger, peeled
4 spring onions, cut into 2.5 cm (1 in) lengths, with white and green parts separated
455 g (1 lb) fresh white mushrooms, trimmed and cut into 6 mm (¼ in) slices
455 g (1 lb) mange tout, topped, and tailed
230 g (8 oz) chestnuts
4 to 6 teaspoons light soy sauce
Salt, to taste

Heat a wok over a high heat until smoke rises. Add the oil and swirl it around to cover a large area.

Add the ginger and let it sizzle for a few seconds, then add the white spring onion and stir together for a few more seconds. Add the mushrooms, stir for about 30 seconds and then add the mange tout and chestnuts. With a scoop or spatula, go to the bottom of the wok, and flip and turn the vegetables, then reduce the heat to medium.

Add the soy sauce and continue to stir for about 2 minutes or until the mange tout are cooked yet still crunchy. Add salt to taste. Add the green spring onions, stir, and place on a serving dish. Serve at once.

BAKED ALASKA

SERVES 8

A luxurious iced dessert, studded with fruit and nuts, flavoured with brandy and covered with fluffy meringue.

85 g (3 oz) currants
85 g (3 oz) sultanas
60 g (2 oz) glacé cherries
1 teaspoon ground cinnamon
2 teaspoons ground mixed spice
1 teaspoon grated nutmeg
70 ml (2½ fl oz) brandy
1 tablespoon cocoa powder
60 g (2 oz) flaked almonds, toasted
4 egg yolks, size 3
85 g (3 oz) soft, light brown muscovado sugar
430 ml (¾ pt) milk
430 ml (¾ pt) double cream
A 1.7 litre (3 pt) pudding basin lined with cling film
For the sponge base:
1 egg, size 3
60 g (2 oz) caster sugar
60 g (2 oz) self-raising flour
60 g (2 oz) butter
An 18 cm (7 in) round, loose-based cake tin
For the meringue:
6 egg whites, size 3
340 g (12 oz) caster sugar

Mix the dried fruits with the cherries, spices and brandy. Cover and chill overnight, stirring occasionally.

The next day, dissolve the cocoa powder in 1 tablespoon of boiling water. Stir the toasted almonds into the marinated fruit mixture. Whisk the egg yolks and sugar together until thick enough to leave a ribbon-like trail for 8 seconds when the whisk is lifted. Heat the milk until scalding hot then gradually pour into the whisked egg mixture, stirring constantly. Pour the milk mixture back into the rinsed-out pan, and heat very gently until the custard is thick enough to coat the back of a wooden spoon. Strain and leave to cool.

Lightly whip the cream and fold into the cooled custard mixture with the fruit and cocoa mixture. Pour into a rigid plastic container and freeze until firm.

When firm, beat the mixture well and pour into the lined pudding basin. Cover and freeze again until required. The day before you are going to serve the pudding, briefly dip the mould in hot water and unmould the ice-cream.

Set the oven at Gas Mark 6, 400°F, 200°C. To make the sponge base, cream together the egg, sugar, flour and butter. When combined, pour into the prepared tin and bake for 12 minutes until well risen and golden. Remove from the tin and leave to cool on a wire rack.

To make the meringue, whisk the egg whites until stiff, about 2 to 3 hours before serving, then beat in the sugar a tablespoon at a time, keeping the meringue stiff and glossy. Place the sponge on a baking tray or ovenproof serving dish. Place the unmoulded ice-cream on top. Swirl or pipe the meringue over the ice-cream to cover completely. Return to the freezer until ready to serve.

Set the oven at Gas Mark 8, 450°F, 230°C. Bake for 3 to 4 minutes until the meringue is browned evenly. Serve at once.

NOTE: it is not advisable to serve mixtures containing raw or partially cooked eggs to the very young, the elderly, the sick or to pregnant women.

OPPOSITE *A spectacular Baked Alaska, and a Cranberry and Port Torte with Whipped Cream.*

CRANBERRY AND PORT TORTE WITH WHIPPED CREAM

SERVES 8

This can be made up to 2 days in advance.
Serve warm or cold, with lashings of whipped cream.

For the filling:
340 g (12 oz) cranberries
400 ml (14 fl oz) port
60 g (2 oz) brown sugar, or to taste
340 g (12 oz) cranberry jelly or jellied cranberry sauce
For the torte:
230 g (8 oz) butter, softened
85 g (3 oz) soft, light brown muscovado sugar
2 tablespoons sunflower oil
2 teaspoons vanilla essence
2 eggs, size 3, beaten
455 g (1 lb) plain flour
2 teaspoons baking powder
2 tablespoons ground mixed spice
Icing sugar, to decorate
Lightly whipped cream
A 20.5 cm (8 in) loose-based cake tin, greased and lined

Simmer the cranberries, port and sugar together in a small, heavy-based pan for about 10 to 15 minutes or until thickened and syrupy. Remove the pan from the heat, stir in the cranberry jelly and leave to cool. Divide the cranberry mixture in half, and reserve one-half for serving with the torte. Set the oven at Gas Mark 2, 300°F, 150°C.

To make the torte, cream the butter and sugar together until pale and light. Gradually beat in the oil, vanilla essence and eggs. Sift in the flour, baking powder and mixed spice, and gently fold in using a large, metal spoon. Work the dough together and knead until smooth. Divide in half, and finely dice. Sprinkle half the dough over the base of the tin. Spoon half of the cranberry mixture over the dough. Add the remaining dough and use to cover the cranberry mixture evenly. Bake for about 1¼ hours or until lightly golden. Remove the torte from the oven and leave to cool in the tin.

Wrap the torte in a layer of greaseproof paper and then in foil for up to 2 days before serving.

Dust the torte with icing sugar, and serve with the reserved cranberries and whipped cream.

CHAPTER NINE

A Cocktail Party

On a chilly evening, hot savoury nibbles and a glass of something warming are the perfect welcome to a party. Hand around tiny individual cheese pastry quiches with delicious fillings of mushrooms, cheese and anchovy; miniature kebabs of bacon, cocktail sausages, and chicken livers with prunes and dates. Your guests will love the crisply fried sandwich triangles filled with a savoury anchovy and egg mixture and the melt-in-the-mouth cubes of fried cheese mixture.

For cold cocktail savouries, sliced dark pumpernickel spread with mayonnaise is an excellent, tasty, non-soggy, well-flavoured base for quick toppings and open sandwiches. Discs of pâté or liver sausage, smoked fish (especially smoked trout), thinly sliced cold meat or hard-boiled egg slices sprinkled with paprika are all simple and effective. Use up puff pastry trimmings to make flaky savoury palmiers, or bouchées filled with crabmeat mayonnaise or cream cheese and walnuts. For a really speedy yet elegant delicacy, try hard-boiled quails' eggs accompanied by a tasty dip of mayonnaise, yogurt and grated cucumber.

Marinated Olives
Sausages with Honey and Mustard
Spinach and Cream Cheese
Roulade
Ricotta and Spinach Filo Bundles
Parma Parcels
Savoury Cheese Bites
Nutty Shapes
Crispy Croustades with Two
Fillings
Sun-dried Tomatoes and
Olives in Oil
Guacamole Tacos
Mini Cheese Fondues
Anchovy and Mushroom Tartlets
Celery Bites
Citrus Cooler
Smoked Mackerel Dip
Walnut Nibbles
Hazelnut and Cheese Sables
Mini Bacon and Fruit Kebabs
Scandinavian Sandwiches
Quails' Eggs with Herby
Cucumber Dip
Stuffed Vineleaves
Savoury Palmiers
Walnut Puffs
Pumpernickel Triangles
Pumpernickel Rounds

*— * —*

Cocktails:
Lychee Fizz
Bellinis
Kir
Pink Camellia
Sangria
Daiquiris
Winter Sunset

MARINATED OLIVES

MAKES ABOUT 230 G (8 OZ)

Marinated olives are delicious served as a canapés and make a great present too!

30 g (8 oz) black olives, drained weight
2 to 3 cloves garlic, crushed
2 fresh sprigs rosemary
1 teaspoon yellow mustard seeds
The pared rind of 1 lemon, cut into thin strips
Good quality olive oil to cover
A screw-top jar

Pack the drained olives into the jar, layering them up with the garlic, the rosemary sprigs, mustard seeds and pared lemon rind. Pour over enough olive oil to cover well. Seal the jar and leave for at least 2 weeks (not more than a month) in a cool dark place before using. Once opened, store in the fridge. Reserve the flavoured oil from the marinated olives and use it for making salad dressings.

SAUSAGES WITH HONEY AND MUSTARD

SERVES 6

Be organised – buy your cocktail sausages ahead and freeze them. The dressing takes little or no time to prepare and makes these little party bites absolutely irresistible.

0.9 kg (2 lb) good quality cocktail sausages
4 tablespoons clear honey
1 tablespoon coarse grain mustard

Set the oven at Gas Mark 6, 400°F, 200°C. Place the sausages in a roasting tin and roast for 10 to 15 minutes until golden. Mix the honey and mustard together and pour over the sausages, toss well to cover and return to the oven for a further 10 minutes until cooked.

SPINACH AND CREAM CHEESE ROULADE

MAKES 32 PIECES

Colourful, simple and easy to prepare – these are a must for any party platter.

230 g (8 oz) frozen chopped spinach, thawed
4 eggs, size 3, separated
½ teaspoon finely grated nutmeg
Salt and freshly ground black pepper
For the filling:
110 g (4 oz) cream cheese
salt and freshly ground black pepper
A 20.5 by 30.5 cm (8 by 12 in) Swiss roll tin, greased and lined
4 rectangles of greaseproof paper about 10 to 15 cm (4 by 6 in)

Set the oven at Gas Mark 7, 425°F, 220°C. To make the roulade, drain the spinach, squeezing well to remove as much water as possible. Tip the spinach into a large bowl. Add the egg yolks, nutmeg and seasoning and mix well. Whisk the egg whites until stiff but not dry. Carefully fold into the spinach mixture. Pour into the prepared Swiss roll tin and level the surface. Bake for about 15 to 20 minutes until well risen and golden, then leave to cool in the tin.

Turn the roulade out on to a clean work surface or chopping board and remove the backing paper. Divide into 4 rectangles and lay each piece on top of a rectangle of greaseproof paper. To make the filling beat the cream cheese with the seasonings until softened, and spread over the 4 roulade rectangles. Roll each rectangle up tightly like a Swiss roll. Wrap each roll in cling film, twisting the ends tightly and refrigerate for at least 30 minutes before serving. Unwrap the roulades, trim the ends and cut each roll into 8 pieces. Arrange on a large platter with the other canapés.

TO FREEZE: the unfilled roulade can be frozen for up to 1 month.

TO USE FROM FROZEN: defrost the roulade in the fridge overnight before filling and completing.

RICOTTA AND SPINACH FILO BUNDLES

MAKES ABOUT 16

*These are the ideal party canapé.
They look pretty and taste delicious – and
can be prepared in advance
and frozen.*

For the filling:
230 g (8 oz) ricotta cheese
110 g (4 oz) frozen chopped
spinach, thawed
Salt and freshly ground black pepper
12 sheets of filo pastry, thawed

Set the oven at Gas Mark 4, 350°F, 180°C. To make the filling, beat the ricotta cheese until softened. Squeeze the spinach thoroughly to extract the moisture, beat into the ricotta cheese with the seasoning.

Cut each sheet of filo into 4 squares. Allow 2 squares for each bundle and place 1 on top of another. Place a teaspoonful of the mixture in the centre of each square and bring up the corners to form a bundle.

Place the bundles on baking trays and bake for 5 to 10 minutes until pale golden. Serve warm.

TO FREEZE: place in a rigid plastic container and freeze for up to 2 weeks.
TO USE FROM FROZEN: defrost for about 1 hour then reheat in an oven for 10 minutes, Gas Mark 4, 350°F, 180°C.

131

LEFT *A selection of canapés,
including Marinated Olives, Sausages with
Honey and Mustard, Spinach and Cream
Cheese Roulade, and Ricotta
and Spinach Filo Parcels.*
PREVIOUS PAGE RIGHT *Pumpernickel
Rounds with a selection of toppings.*
PREVIOUS PAGE LEFT *Bellini, Lychee
Fizz and Sangria.*

PARMA PARCELS

SERVES 8

Tastes of the Mediterranean sunshine.

8 slices of Parma ham
For the filling:
200 g (7 oz) Boursin cheese with peppers
2 tablespoons Greek yogurt
8 long chives

Place the slices of Parma ham on a clean work surface. Beat the cheese with the yogurt until smooth and creamy and place a spoonful of the mixture in the centre of each slice of ham. Draw up the ends of the Parma ham to enclose the filling. Tie each bundle with a chive. Chill the parcels for up to 4 hours, until ready to serve.

SAVOURY CHEESE BITES

MAKES ABOUT 24

A selection of colourful canapés which are quick and easy to make – and taste absolutely delicious spread on toast.

230 g (8 oz) goats' cheese
Salt and freshly ground black pepper
2 tablespoons sesame seeds, toasted
2 tablespoons freshly chopped mixed herbs

Beat the goat's cheese until soft, season with salt and freshly ground black pepper. Cover and chill the mixture until firm – about an hour. (The mixture can also be left in a sealed container and chilled overnight.)

Divide the cheese mixture into 24 equal portions, and roll into walnut sized balls. Roll half the balls in the sesame seeds, and the other half in the chopped herbs. Chill until ready to serve, up to 4 hours. Arrange the canapés on a large platter.

ABOVE RIGHT *Parma Parcels, Nutty Shapes, Crispy Croustades with Two Fillings and Nutty Shapes.*

132

NUTTY SHAPES

MAKES ABOUT 100

No one will be able to resist these delicious savoury biscuits, so make plenty and serve warm or cold.

230 g (8 oz) unsalted butter, softened
110 g (4 oz) semolina
200 g (7 oz) self raising flour
170 g (6 oz) mature Cheddar, finely grated

60 g (2 oz) cashew nuts, roughly chopped
Salt and freshly ground black pepper
Pinch of paprika

Place the butter in a food processor and process until softened, add the semolina, flour and cheese and process until the mixture starts to come together. Remove from the processor and add the nuts and seasoning. Wrap and chill for 30 minutes.

Set the oven at Gas Mark 5, 375°F, 190°C. Roll out on a lightly floured work surface and using a variety of cutters cut out various shapes. Transfer to a baking tray and bake for 15 to 20 minutes. Serve the biscuits warm or cold.

TO FREEZE: allow to cool, then place the biscuits in a rigid plastic container and freeze for up to 1 month.

TO USE FROM FROZEN: thaw at room temperature for about 1 hour. and reheat in the oven, set at Gas Mark 4, 350°F, 180°C, for 5 minutes.

CRISPY CROUSTADES WITH TWO FILLINGS

*These individual croustades are perfect for a
cocktail party. They are quick to make from sliced bread,
rather than pastry, and both the croustades and their fillings can be
prepared in advance and frozen ready to be reheated on the
day of the party. Once filled they will stay crisp for
up to three hours.*

For the croustades:
85 g (3 oz) unsalted butter, melted
24 slices of wholemeal bread
24 patty or bun tins
An 8.5 cm (3¼ in) plain cutter

For the chicken liver filling for 24 cases:
1 shallot, finely chopped
30 g (1 oz) unsalted butter
110 g (4 oz) chicken livers,
trimmed and sliced
2 tablespoons dry sherry
2 tablespoons double cream

For the ratatouille filling for 24 cases:
1 small aubergine, finely diced
Salt
2 tablespoons olive oil
1 green pepper, deseeded and diced
1 clove garlic, crushed
1 small onion, finely chopped
230 g (8 oz) tomatoes, skinned, deseeded
and chopped
1 tablespoon tomato purée
1 tablespoon finely chopped marjoram
1 tablespoon finely chopped parsley
Freshly ground black pepper

Set the oven at Gas Mark 6, 400°F, 200°C. Brush the patty or bun tins with a little of the melted butter.

Using the plain cutter, cut out 2 circles from each slice of bread. Use a rolling pin to flatten each circle of bread, then carefully press into the tins to line them completely as if you are making jam tarts.

Brush with the remaining melted butter, then bake for about 15 to 20 minutes or until golden and crisp. Do not over bake. Transfer to a wire rack and leave to cool.

The unfilled croustades will keep in an airtight tin for up to 3 days. Alternatively they can be frozen for up to a month. Warm through in a low oven to make them crisp.

TO FREEZE: allow to cool completely, then layer them in a rigid plastic container, packing the layers between sheets of greaseproof paper, and freeze for up to 1 month.

TO USE FROM FROZEN: place on a wire rack for 2 hours at room temperature. To crisp, warm through in a low oven .

FOR THE CHICKEN LIVER FILLING

Gently cook the shallot in the butter, until softened but not coloured. Add the chicken livers and stir fry for 3 to 5 minutes. Remove from the heat, place in a liquidiser or food processor and process until smooth. Add the sherry and cream. Spoon into the croustades.

TO FREEZE: allow to cool completely, then spoon into a rigid plastic container and freeze for up to 1 month.

TO USE FROM FROZEN: place in the fridge overnight.

FOR THE RATATOUILLE FILLING

Place the aubergine in a colander and sprinkle with salt to extract the bitter juices. Leave for 30 minutes, then rinse well and roughly dry on absorbent kitchen paper.

Heat the oil in a heavy-based pan. Add the pepper, garlic, onion and stir over a high heat for 3 minutes. Add the aubergine and continue stirring for 2 minutes. When softened, add the tomatoes, tomato purée, herbs and seasoning and cook for a further 2 minutes, stirring constantly.

Cover and simmer for about 10 to 15 minutes, stirring occasionally until slightly thicker. Spoon into the croustades.

TO FREEZE: allow to cool completely, then place in a rigid plastic container and freeze for up to 1 month.

TO USE FROM FROZEN: place overnight in the fridge, then reheat in a saucepan until piping hot.

SUN-DRIED TOMATOES AND OLIVES IN OIL

MAKES ABOUT 455 G (1 LB)

Sun-dried tomatoes are widely available from supermarkets and delicatessens.

200 g (7 oz) Italian sun-dried tomatoes
85 g (3 oz) black olives
1 clove garlic, or to taste, crushed
2 sprigs of marjoram
About 570 ml (1 pt) good-quality olive oil
A 455 g (1 lb) airtight jar, sterilised

Place the tomatoes in a large, heatproof bowl and pour over boiling water to cover. Leave to stand for 20 minutes. Drain thoroughly and mix in with the olives and garlic. Spoon into the jar and add the marjoram. Pour over enough olive oil to cover. Seal, label and store in a cool, dark place for up to 1 month.

GUACAMOLE TACOS

MAKES ABOUT 20

Packets of cocktail-sized tacos and tortilla chips are available in supermarkets.

4 tomatoes, peeled, deseeded and diced
½ small onion, finely chopped
1 green chilli, deseeded and very finely chopped
The juice of 1 lime or lemon
2 large ripe avocados
Salt and pepper to taste
One 100 g (3½ oz) packet taco or tortilla chips
Coriander leaves to garnish

Mix the diced tomato with the onion, chilli and half the citrus juice. Peel the avocados and remove the stones. Chop roughly, add the remaining citrus juice and mash coarsely using a fork. Stir the avocados into the tomato mixture and taste for seasoning (at this point, the mixture can be tightly covered and chilled for up to 3 hours). Spoon a little guacamole on to each taco or tortilla chip and garnish with coriander. Serve as soon as possible, as the bases lose their crispness after an hour.

MINI CHEESE FONDUES

MAKES 36

These tiny cubes of deep-fried cheese mixture are ideal to serve to vegetarians – and your other guests will love them too.

45 g (1½ oz) butter
60 g (2 oz) flour
280 ml (½ pt) milk
2 egg yolks, size 3
Salt and pepper
A generous pinch each of nutmeg and cayenne pepper
85 g (3 oz) strong Cheddar cheese, grated
85 g (3 oz) Gruyère cheese, grated
Seasoned flour for coating
2 eggs, size 3, beaten
170 g (6 oz) fine fresh breadcrumbs
Oil for deep frying
Parmesan cheese, grated
A non-stick 18 cm (7 in) square container, greased and base-lined

Melt the butter in a small pan, stir in the flour and cook for 1 minute. Remove from the heat and gradually whisk in the milk. Bring to the boil and simmer for 4 minutes, stirring all the time, until very thick.

Take off the heat, and beat in the egg yolks, seasonings and cheeses. Spoon into the prepared tin and smooth the surface. Cover the tin with buttered greaseproof paper and leave to cool. Chill the mixture for at least 2 hours, preferably overnight.

Turn the cheese mixture out on to a floured board and cut into 36 cubes. Carefully coat in seasoned flour, then egg and breadcrumbs. Chill again for up to 24 hours until firm.

Deep-fry in batches in hot oil until golden - about 2 or 3 minutes. Drain on kitchen paper and keep warm in a low oven until ready to serve.

Just before serving, sprinkle with Parmesan cheese.

The mini fondues can be cooked then reheated in a microwave for about 2 minutes.

ANCHOVY AND MUSHROOM TARTLETS

MAKES 18 TO 20

Individual quiches made with a crisp, cheese pastry and filled with a delicious moist cheese and mushroom mixture.

For the pastry:
170 g (6 oz) plain flour
¼ teaspoon mustard powder
Salt
Cayenne pepper
85 g (3 oz) butter
40 g (1½ oz) strong Cheddar cheese, grated
For the filling:
110 g (4 oz) button mushrooms, sliced
15 g (½ oz) butter
3 egg yolks, size 3
280 ml (½ pt) single cream or milk
Black pepper
Cayenne pepper
50 g (1¾ oz) can anchovy fillets, drained
4 tablespoons Parmesan cheese, grated
20 patty or mince pie tins

To make the pastry, sift the flour with the mustard and seasonings. Rub in the butter and stir in the cheese. Bind to a soft but not sticky dough with 2 to 3 tablespoons iced water. Wrap and chill for 15 minutes.

Set the oven at Gas Mark 5, 375°F, 190°C. Roll out the pastry. Cut out 20 rounds 7.5 cm (3 in) across and use to line the patty tins. Cook the sliced mushrooms in the butter for 3 minutes until soft. Pour off any excess liquid and divide the mushrooms between the patty tins. Beat the egg yolks with the cream and seasonings. Cut the anchovy fillets in half down the backbones. Pour the cream mixture over the mushrooms, sprinkle over the cheese, and arrange the anchovies to form crosses on top of each tartlet. Bake for 25 to 30 minutes until the pastry is cooked, and the filling puffy and golden. Cool on wire racks. Serve warm or cold.

TO FREEZE: as for Ricotta and Spinach Filo Bundles on page 131

LEFT *Anchovy and Mushroom Tartlets and Mini Cheese Fondues.*

CELERY BITES

MAKES ABOUT 32

The hollow in celery stalks is just made for creamy cheese. For extra flavour, use cream cheese made with herbs, pepper or garlic. Another interesting variation uses tiny cherry tomatoes.

One head celery, about 455 g (1 lb)
Two 85 g (3 oz) packets cream cheese
Salt, pepper and cayenne to taste
To garnish:
Paprika
Celery leaves

Reserve the celery leaves for garnish. Scrub the celery stalks, dry thoroughly then cut into 2.5 cm (1 in) lengths.

Thoroughly blend the cream cheese with the onions and seasonings – this can be done in a food processor. Spoon or pipe the mixture into the groove in the celery. Sprinkle with paprika, then arrange on serving plates and garnish with celery leaves. Cover and chill until ready to serve.

Tiny cherry tomatoes can be filled with the same mixture of cheese and spring onions. Just slice off the tops, scoop the seeds, pipe or spoon in the filing, and replace the tops.

CITRUS COOLER

SERVES 8 TO 12

Serve this thirst quencher in tall glasses with plenty of ice and sprigs of mint.

570 ml (1 pt) fresh orange juice
570 ml (1 pt) dry vermouth
570 ml (1 pt) lemonade
1 lemon, thinly sliced
Sprigs of fresh mint

Mix together the orange juice, the dry vermouth and lemonade. Pour into chilled glasses filed with ice and add lemon slices and sprigs of fresh mint.

As a variation, add a splash of gin to the mixture, to taste.

SMOKED MACKEREL DIP

SERVES 15 TO 20

This very tasty dip can also be served as a first course with brown bread.

2 smoked mackerel fillets, total weight about 340 g (12 oz)
140 ml (¼ pt) soured cream
2 tablespoons mayonnaise
The grated rind and juice of 1 lemon
1 tablespoon milk
½ teaspoon horseradish sauce
½ small onion, finely chopped or grated
Salt and pepper to taste
To serve:
A selection of crudités: sliced carrots, celery, peppers, spring onions, cauliflower, mushrooms, radishes

Remove the skin from the mackerel and flake the flesh into a bowl. Add the remaining ingredients and beat the mixture thoroughly until smooth.

Taste and adjust the seasoning as necessary. Spoon into a serving bowl and chill. Arrange the vegetables on a large plate, around the dip.

WALNUT NIBBLES

MAKES 12 TO 16

These walnut-covered cream cheese balls, can also be served with fresh fruit at the end of a meal instead of dessert.

Two 85 g (3 oz) packets garlic and herb flavoured cream cheese
60 g (2 oz) walnut pieces
To garnish:
A few small lettuce leaves
Quartered tomatoes

Unwrap the cheese, place on a plate and freeze for 5 minutes. Meanwhile, finely chop the walnuts, then spread them out on a sheet of greaseproof paper. Cut the cream cheese into 12 to 16 equal pieces, and roll to form small balls. Roll the cheese balls in the chopped walnuts until thoroughly and evenly coated. Chill until ready to serve, then garnish with lettuce leaves or tomato quarters.

HAZELNUT AND CHEESE SABLES

MAKES ABOUT 64

Lovely, rich, crumbly cheese biscuits.

85 g (3 oz) flour
A pinch of salt
¼ teaspoon each cayenne pepper and mustard powder
85 g (3 oz) butter
85 g (3 oz) mature Cheddar cheese, grated
Beaten egg to glaze
40 g (1½ oz) toasted hazelnuts, chopped

Sift the flour with the salt, pepper and mustard powder. Rub in the butter, and stir in the grated Cheddar cheese. Knead the mixture together to form a paste as for shortbread (this can also be done in a processor). Wrap and chill the sables for 10 minutes. Set the oven at Gas Mark 5, 375°F, 190°C.

On a floured surface, roll out the paste to a 20.5 cm (8 in) square. Cut into 16 squares. Cut each square into 4 triangles. Transfer to baking sheets and chill for 5 minutes.

Brush the biscuits with beaten egg and sprinkle with nuts. Bake for about 10 minutes until golden. Cool on the baking sheets for a few minutes then transfer the biscuits to a wire rack to cool completely. The biscuits can be stored in an airtight tin for 2 days, or frozen for up to 3 months. Crisp the sables in the oven before serving.

SCANDINAVIAN SANDWICHES

MAKES 24

Tiny, crispy, hot sandwiches with a savoury filling.

12 slices day-old bread, thinly sliced
50 g (1¾ oz) can anchovy fillets, drained
2 tablespoons milk
60 g (2 oz) butter, softened
1 tablespoon Dijon mustard
2 eggs, size 3, hard-boiled and shelled
2 tablespoons parsley, chopped
Pepper
Oil and a little butter or frying

Remove the crusts from the bread. Soak the anchovies in the milk for about 10 minutes. Pound or process the anchovies until the mixture is fairly smooth. Beat into the butter with the mustard, mashed eggs, parsley and pepper. Spread this mixture thickly over half of the bread slices. Top with the other slices and press firmly together. Wrap in cling film and chill for up to 24 hours.

To cook, heat 3 mm (⅛ in) oil in a frying pan with a knob of butter until it is foaming. Quickly fry the sandwiches on both sides until crisp and golden. Drain on kitchen paper. Cut each slice into 4 triangles and serve hot. (Keep fried sandwiches warm in a low oven while cooking the remainder).

MINI BACON AND FRUIT KEBABS

MAKES 24

A hot, savoury snack that's a variation of sausages on sticks and devils on horseback.

12 large prunes
12 dessert dates
4 tablespoons mango chutney
110 g (4 oz) chicken livers

12 rashers rindless streaky bacon
12 cocktail sausages
24 wooden cocktail sticks

Stone the prunes and dates and stuff the cavity of each with a little mango chutney. Wash the chicken livers, pat dry, and cut to make 12 chunks.

Stretch the bacon rashers with the blade of a knife and cut each in half. Wrap a piece of bacon round a prune and a piece of chicken liver so that the ends of the bacon meet in the middle. Thread on to a cocktail stick. Repeat the process with combinations of prune and cocktail sausage, date and chicken liver, and date and cocktail sausage. Chill until ready to serve – for up to 3 hours.

Preheat the grill and cook the mini-kebabs on all sides for 10 to 12 minutes until the bacon is crispy and well browned. Drain on kitchen paper and serve hot.

ABOVE LEFT *Mini Bacon and Fruit Kebabs and Scandinavian Sandwiches.*

QUAILS' EGGS WITH HERBY CUCUMBER DIP

An attractive display that's deceptively simple to prepare.

2 dozen quails' eggs
Celery salt
Cayenne pepper
Lettuce, shredded
For the cucumber dip:
3 tablespoons mayonnaise
3 tablespoons Greek yogurt
60 g (2 oz) cucumber, grated
2 tablespoons chopped fresh herbs
A few drops of Tabasco
1 clove garlic, crushed (optional)
Salt and pepper

Put the quails' eggs into a pan of cold water, bring to the boil and simmer for 3 minutes. Drain and run under cold water until cool. Shell carefully. Insert a cocktail stick into the pointed end of each egg and dip the other end into a little celery salt and cayenne. Arrange the eggs on a bed of shredded lettuce. Cover and chill until ready to serve.

To make the dip, mix together all the ingredients, reserving some of the herbs for garnish, and season to taste. Cover and chill until ready to serve. Sprinkle the herbs over the dip and serve with the quails' eggs.

LEFT *Quails' Eggs with Herby Cucumber Dip.*
OPPOSITE *Savoury Palmiers and delicious Walnut Puffs.*

STUFFED VINELEAVES

Vacuum-packed vine leaves are available from delicatessens and large supermarkets. Serve with small squares of cheese that have been marinated in pimento-flavoured olive oil.

A 110 g (4 oz) packet vine leaves in brine
680 g (1½ lb) feta cheese
Salt and freshly ground black pepper
A 400 g (14½ oz) can of pimentos, drained
570 ml (1 pt) good-quality olive oil
6 sprigs of rosemary
A 1.7 litre (3 pt) airtight jar, sterilised

Place the vine leaves in a large bowl and pour boiling water over them, ensuring that the water penetrates between the layers. Leave to soak for 20 minutes, then drain thoroughly. Rinse well under cold water, drain, and repeat the process. This will remove excess salt. Carefully pat the leaves dry using absorbent kitchen paper.

Cut the feta cheese into twenty-eight 2.5 cm (1 in) cubes.

Lay the vine leaves vein side up on a work surface. Place a cube of feta cheese in the centre of each vine leaf and season to taste. Fold the stem of the leaf over the cheese and bring the edges up around the side. Continue wrapping the vine leaf round the cheese to cover it completely.

Pack the cheese parcels into the jar. Add the pimentos, pour over the olive oil to cover and add the sprigs of rosemary. Seal and store the jar in a cool, dark place for at least 1 week (up to a month) before use. The longer the storage, the better the flavour.

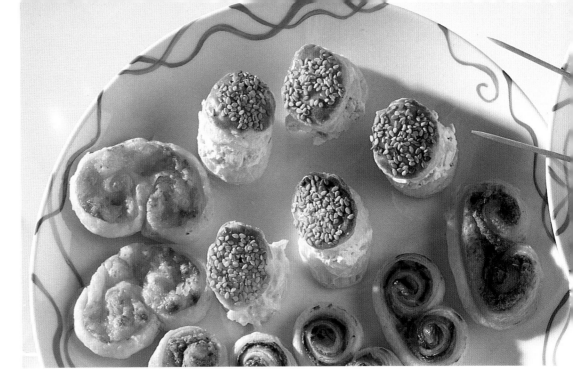

SAVOURY PALMIERS

MAKES 34

170 g (6 oz) ready-made puff pastry, thawed if frozen
For the Marmite filling:
110 g (4 oz) Philadelphia cream cheese
1 to 2 teaspoons Marmite, to taste
For the cheese filling:
1 tablespoon English mustard
170 g (6 oz) Gouda cheese, grated
Cayenne pepper
For the sardine filling:
60 g (2 oz) butter
A 130 g (4½ oz) can sardines in oil, drained

Set the oven at Gas Mark 7, 425°F, 220°C. Roll the pastry out to a rectangle about 30.5 by 23 cm (12 by 9 in).

For the Marmite filling, beat the cream cheese with the Marmite. Spread over the pastry with a palette knife. For the sardine filling, beat the sardines and butter together, then spread over the pastry as before. Bake 12 to 15 minutes until crisp and golden. Cool on a wire rack. Serve while still warm.

For the cheese filling, spread the pastry with mustard, scatter with cheese and cayenne. Roll up, chill, cut and cook as for the Marmite-filled palmiers.

The palmiers can be frozen for up to a month, and then reheated straight from the freezer.

WALNUT PUFFS

110 g (4 oz) puff pastry trimmings, thawed
Beaten egg to glaze
Sesame seeds
For the cream cheese filling:
110 g (4 oz) cream cheese
3 tablespoons single cream
40 g (1½ oz) walnut pieces, finely chopped
For the crab filling:
85 g (3 oz) crabmeat, flaked
3 tablespoons mayonnaise
3 tablespoons soured cream
Salt, pepper and cayenne

Set the oven at Gas Mark 7, 425°F, 220°C. Roll out the pastry 3 mm (⅛ in) thick and cut out 2.5 cm (1 in) rounds. Place on damp baking sheets. Brush the rounds with beaten egg and sprinkle each one thickly with sesame seeds. Bake for 10 minutes until puffy and golden. Cool on wire racks.

To make the cream cheese filling, beat the cheese with the cream until smooth, then stir in the walnuts.

To make the crab filling mix the crab with the mayonnaise, soured cream and seasoning.

Split the pastry rounds in two and spoon a little filling on to each bottom half. Replace top half and serve.
TO FREEZE: freeze uncooked rounds on baking trays covered with cling film.
TO USE FROM FROZEN: cook from frozen.

PUMPERNICKEL TRIANGLES

MAKES 50 TO 60

Thinly sliced pumpernickel, dark rye bread originally from Germany, makes an ideal base for a cocktail snack as it stays moist without becoming soggy. Cream cheese and smoked salmon is a classic combination – cocktail pieces or trimmings of smoked salmon are good value.

**One 250 g (8¾ oz) packet pumpernickel
230 g (8 oz) cream cheese
4 tablespoons double cream
3 tablespoons milk
Salt and pepper
Toppings:
30 to 60 g (1 to 2 oz) smoked salmon trimmings
Lumpfish roe (black or red), or caviar
A few anchovy fillets, thinly sliced
Green or black grapes, halved and deseeded**

Separate the slices of pumpernickel, then cut each slice into small bite-sized triangles. Beat the cream cheese with the cream and milk until smooth. Season with a little salt, and plenty of pepper. Spoon the mixture into a piping bag fitted with a plain tube, and pipe a small blob of the cheese mixture on to each triangle.

The triangles can be garnished with thin strips of smoked salmon, a little lumpfish roe or caviar, small pieces of anchovy fillet or grapes.

PUMPERNICKEL ROUNDS

MAKES 40

Dices of dark rye pumpernickel with colourful toppings

8 slices pumpernickel	**15 g (½ oz) butter**
3 tablespoons mayonnaise	**110 g (4 oz) cream cheese**
10 slices of rare beef, ham or tongue or smoked salmon or German-style sausage, very thinly cut	**2 to 3 teaspoons horseradish sauce, to taste**
	To garnish:
1 small onion, very thinly sliced	**4 gherkins, sliced**
1 tablespoon vegetable oil	**1 quail's egg, hard-boiled and sliced**

Spread the pumpernickel with mayonnaise and cut out 40 rounds 3 cm (1¼ in) across using a biscuit cutter.

For the meat topping, cut the beef, ham or tongue into 2.5 by 7.5 cm (1 by 3 in) strips. Fry the onion in oil and butter over a medium heat until golden brown and crisp. Drain on kitchen paper, leave to cool. Crumble the fried onion, beat into the cream cheese with the horseradish. Put a tea-spoonful of the cheese mixture on each strip of meat and roll up. Place 1 roll on each pumpernickel round and garnish with a piece of gherkin.

For the salmon topping, place a slice of smoked salmon on top of each of the pumpernickel rounds, and garnish with a slice of quail's egg.

For the spicy sausage topping, place a slice of German-style sausage on top of each pumpernickel round. Cover all the prepared pumpernickel rounds, and keep cool until served.

ABOVE RIGHT Pumpernickel Rounds with a selection of toppings.
OPPOSITE Pink Camellia.

LYCHEE FIZZ

FILLS 8 TO 10 GLASSES

A 425 g (14 oz) can of lychees
2 bottles of chilled champagne

Drain the lychees, reserving the juice. Place a lychee in the bottom of each glass, pour a tablespoon of the reserved lychee juice over the top and fill with chilled champagne.

BELLINIS

FILLS ABOUT 8 GLASSES

A 425 g (14 oz) can of peaches in natural
juice, drained
Lemon juice to taste
1 bottle of chilled champagne

Purée the drained peaches in a food processor or liquidiser together with a little lemon juice. Sieve the mixture, and then chill the peach purée until required. Divide the peach mixture between the glasses and top up with chilled champagne.

KIR

FILLS ABOUT 6 GLASSES

2 tablespoons Crème de Cassis
1 bottle chilled champagne

Place 1 to 2 teaspoons of Crème de Cassis in the bottom of each glass. Top up with the chilled champagne.

PINK CAMELLIA

SERVES 4

60 ml (2 fl oz) gin
60 ml (2 fl oz) apricot brandy
60 ml (2 fl oz) Campari
280 ml (10 fl oz) freshly squeezed
orange juice
2 tablespoons lemon juice

Pour all the ingredients into a cocktail shaker and shake well. Pour into 4 icy glasses and serve.

SANGRIA

SERVES 6

60 ml (2 fl oz) brandy
60 ml (2 fl oz) Martini
30 ml (1 fl oz) Cointreau
115 ml (4 fl oz) red wine
The juice of ½ lemon
The juice of 1 orange
570 ml (1 pt) lemonade
Orange and lemon slices, and ice to serve.

Mix the brandy and Martini with the Cointreau and red wine in a jug. Stir in the fruit juices and the lemonade. Add slices of orange and lemon, and ice to serve.

DAIQUIRIS

SERVES 2 TO 4

230 g (8 oz) strawberries, washed
and hulled
85 g (3 oz) ice
The juice of a lemon
2 teaspoons caster sugar
115 ml (4 fl oz) white rum

Place the strawberries in the bowl of a food processor and process until smooth, then pass through a sieve to remove the pips. Return to the rinsed out processor bowl with the ice, lemon juice and sugar and 'pulse' until the ice is coarsely crushed. Add the rum and 'pulse' to combine. Pour into 2 to 4 chilled glasses and serve at once.

WINTER SUNSET

(non-alcoholic)

SERVES 6

20 ice cubes, roughly crushed
430 ml (¾ pt) chilled, freshly squeezed
pink grapefruit juice
280 ml (½ pt) chilled, freshly squeezed
orange juice
A few drops of Angostura bitters
280 ml (½ pt) chilled sparkling
white grape juices

Place all the ingredients in a punch bowl, mix well and serve in tall glasses and decorate with fresh mint.

CHAPTER TEN

Classic Christmas Lunch

For our truly spectacular Christmas meal we have kept the food simple and traditional. Spend time decorating your table, choose a simple colour scheme, polish the china, the silver, cutlery and glass until they gleam, and search out unusual crackers, Christmas foliage, nuts and a selection of sweets. Whether you choose to serve it as lunch, or as dinner by candlelight, follow our Christmas Countdown to create this simple but stylish meal for all the family to enjoy.

Curried Parsnip and Apple Soup

Crispy Smoked Trout Mousse

— * —

Roast Turkey with

All the Trimmings:

Sausagemeat and Chestnut Stuffing

Bacon and Cocktail Sausage Rolls

Lemon and Thyme Stuffing

Cranberry Sauce

Roast Potatoes and Shallots

Classic Bread Sauce

Mustard Glazed Ham

Creamy Gratin of Brussels Sprouts

Mixed Baby Vegetables with

Parsley Butter

— * —

Double Chocolate Iced Soufflé

— * —

Luxury Christmas Pudding

Brandy Butter

Orange Flower Water Cream

— * —

Christmas Cake

COUNTDOWN

BEGINNING OF DECEMBER
- Make Christmas Pudding and Christmas Cake.

ONE WEEK BEFORE
- Make and freeze the Curried Parsnip and Apple Soup.
- Buy and freeze bread rolls.
- Make, shape and freeze the stuffing balls.
- Make and freeze Double Chocolate Iced Soufflé.

DECEMBER 23
- If using a frozen turkey, thaw in the refrigerator (check chart for thawing times).
- Make the bread bases for the Crispy Trout Mousse, Cranberry Sauce and Brandy Butter, and store in separate airtight plastic containers in the refrigerator.

CHRISTMAS EVE
- Thaw the soup overnight in the refrigerator.
- Make and chill Smoked Trout Mousse.
- Thaw stuffing balls overnight in the refrigerator.
- Make cocktail sausages and chill.
- Peel the potatoes and store immersed in cold water in an airtight plastic container.
- Prepare and blanch the carrots and courgettes. Place the vegetables in an ovenproof serving dish, dot with herb butter, cover with foil and chill overnight.
- Prepare Creamy Brussels Sprouts Gratin, cover and chill.
- Soak the ham overnight in cold water to cover.
- Make Classic Bread Sauce, cool and store in an air tight plastic container in the refrigerator overnight.
- Set the table for lunch.

CHRISTMAS DAY
- Based on a 3.6 kg (8 lb) turkey to be served at 1 pm.

4½ HOURS BEFORE SERVING
- Set oven at Gas Mark 4, 350°F, 180°C.

4 HOURS BEFORE SERVING
- Place turkey in the oven.
- Drain the ham and cook.
- Steam the Luxury Christmas Pudding (check water level regularly).
- Make Orange Flower Water Cream, place in serving dish and chill.
- Remove gratin and prepared vegetables from the refrigerator.

2 HOURS BEFORE SERVING
- Part boil roast potatoes and place on the top shelf in the oven.

1 HOUR BEFORE SERVING
- Increase oven temperature to Gas Mark 7, 425°F, 220°C.
- Pipe the Smoked Trout Mousse on to the croustades.

45 MINUTES BEFORE SERVING
- Place the ham in the oven, with the prepared vegetables, gratin, stuffing balls and Bacon and Cocktail Sausage Rolls.

30 MINUTES BEFORE SERVING
- Make the gravy.
- Reheat the soup and add the cream.
- Reheat the bread sauce and cranberry sauce.

1 PM
- Serve the meal.

TURKEY THAWING TIMES

Place turkey on a tray and thaw in the refrigerator.

Weight of Turkey	Thawing Time	No of Servings
1.35 to 2.3 kg (3 to 5 lb)	20 hours	4 to 6
2.7 to 3.2 kg (6 to 7 lb)	30 hours	7 to 9
3.6 to 4.1 kg (8 to 9 lb)	36 hours	10 to 14
4.5 to 5 kg (10 to 11 lb)	45 hours	15 to 16
5.4 to 5.8 kg (12 to 13 lb)	48 hours	17 to 18
6.3 to 7.7 kg (14 to 17 lb)	48 hours	19 to 25
8.1 to 9.9 kg (18 to 22 lb)	48 hours	26 to 37

CURRIED PARSNIP AND APPLE SOUP

SERVES 6 TO 8

2 tablespoons sunflower oil
1 large onion, chopped
1 teaspoon hot curry powder, or to taste
110 g (4 oz) carrots, scrubbed
and chopped
680 g (1½ lb) parsnips, scrubbed
and chopped
340 g (12 oz) Bramley cooking apples,
peeled, cored and chopped
1.45 litres (2½ pt) good-quality vegetable
or chicken stock
2 tablespoons Calvados (optional)
140 ml (¼ pt) double cream
Salt and freshly ground black pepper
Fresh coriander, to garnish

Heat the oil in a large, heavy-based saucepan. Add the chopped onion and cook for 5 minutes or until softened but not coloured. Add the curry powder and cook for another 1 minute, stirring occasionally. Add the carrots and the parsnips, and continue cooking until all the vegetables are golden. Add the apples and stir in the stock. Bring to the boil, reduce the heat and simmer gently for about 30 to 40 minutes or until the vegetables are tender.

 Pour the soup into a liquidiser and blend until smooth. Return to the rinsed-out pan. Add the Calvados, if using,*and the double cream. Season to taste. Reheat the soup gently and serve, garnished with coriander.

TO FREEZE: *do not add the cream. Cool, pour into a rigid plastic container and freeze for up to 1 month.

TO USE FROM FROZEN: thaw the soup overnight in the fridge. Reheat, add the cream, and season to taste.

RIGHT *Curried Parsnip and Apple Soup.*
PREVIOUS PAGE LEFT *The Christmas Table, including Stilton, Creamy Gratin of Brussels Sprouts, Mixed Baby Vegetables with Parsley Butter, Cranberry Sauce, Bread Sauce, and Roast Turkey with all the Trimmings.*
PREVIOUS PAGE RIGHT *Christmas Cheer, with nuts and glacé fruits.*

SAUSAGEMEAT AND CHESTNUT STUFFING

SERVES 8

Classic, simple and a favourite with all the family.

1 large onion, chopped
30 g (1 oz) unsalted butter
1 large cooking apple, cored and grated
230 g (8 oz) pork sausagemeat
110 g (4 oz) fresh wholemeal breadcrumbs
Half a 350 g (12½ oz) can of whole
chestnuts, drained and chopped
Salt and freshly ground black pepper
1 tablespoon sunflower oil, for roasting

Cook the chopped onion in the butter until softened but not coloured. Leave to cool, then, mix with the remaining ingredients.

When thoroughly combined, shape the mixture into walnut-sized balls and chill overnight. Set the oven at Gas Mark 7, 425°F, 220°C.

Place the stuffing balls in a greased roasting tin, pour over the oil and cook in the oven for 20 minutes. Serve with the turkey.

TO FREEZE: place the cold stuffing balls in an airtight plastic container and freeze for up to 1 month.
TO USE FROM FROZEN: thaw in the fridge overnight.

CRISPY SMOKED TROUT MOUSSE

SERVES 6 TO 8

It can be made the day before, and is excellent served with well-chilled vodka.

For the croustades:
16 thin slices wholemeal bread
110 g (4 oz) unsalted butter, melted
For the mousse:
170 g (6 oz) smoked trout, chopped
60 g (2 oz) cream cheese
1 teaspoon horseradish sauce, or to taste
140 ml (¼ pt) double cream, lightly

whipped
Cayenne pepper, to taste
A 6.5 cm (1½ in) plain cutter
A piping bag fitted with a large star nozzle
To garnish:
Lumpfish roe
A little mixed salad
Dill

Set the oven at Gas Mark 6, 400°F, 200°C. To make the croustades, using the cutter, cut out 16 circles from the wholemeal bread. Brush both sides of the bread circles with melted butter and place on a baking tray. Bake in the oven for 10 minutes or until golden and crisp. Remove from the oven and transfer on to wire racks to cool completely. When cool, store in an airtight container for up to 3 days before using.

To make the mousse, whizz the smoked trout in a blender or food processor briefly. Add the cream cheese and horseradish sauce and whizz until smooth – do not over-process. Fold the whipped cream into the trout mixture and season to taste. Chill for 1 hour or overnight.

You may need to add 1 to 2 tablespoons of double cream to the mousse mixture if it has been chilled overnight. Fill the prepared piping bag with the trout mousse mixture and pipe on to the croustades before serving. Garnish with a little lumpfish roe, mixed salad and dill.

BACON AND COCKTAIL SAUSAGE ROLLS

SERVES 8

Traditional accompaniments for roast turkey and always a firm favourite.

12 rashers back bacon, rind removed
24 cocktail sausages
A little sunflower oil

Gently stretch the rashers of bacon with the back of a knife. Cut each rasher in half and tightly wrap each piece of bacon around a sausage to form a roll. Transfer to a roasting tin, drizzle over a little oil and cook for about 20 minutes with the stuffing.

ROAST TURKEY WITH ALL THE TRIMMINGS

SERVES 8

Choose a plump fresh turkey, or if using a frozen bird make sure it is thoroughly defrosted (see the chart on page 144 as a guide).

For the turkey:	8 rashers back bacon
A 4.5 kg (10 lb) turkey	A piece of muslin large enough to
Salt	cover the bird completely
Freshly ground white pepper	*For the gravy:*
2 onions, quartered	30 g (1 oz) flour
2 cloves garlic	About 430 ml (¾ pt) good-quality turkey
2 lemons, pricked and quartered	or chicken stock
A bunch of thyme	3 to 4 tablespoons port or sherry
A bunch of parsley	Salt and freshly ground black pepper
30 g (1 oz) unsalted butter, melted	Bayleaves, to garnish

Set the oven at Gas Mark 4, 350°F, 180°C. Wipe the inside of the bird, season and stuff the neck and body cavity with the onion, garlic, lemons and herbs. (It is not wise to stuff the body cavity with the edible stuffing because there may be some risk of salmonella). Pull the skin flap over and secure with cocktail sticks.

Carefully truss the turkey with the wings folded under the body and the legs tied together. Weigh the turkey to calculate the cooking time, allowing 20 minutes per 455 g (1 lb), plus 20 minutes. Transfer to a large roasting tin and brush with half the melted butter. Arrange the bacon rashers on top of the bird. Cover the legs and breast of the turkey with the muslin and brush liberally with the remaining butter. (The muslin soaked in butter helps keep the turkey breast moist).

Roast for the calculated time, basting frequently. The bird is cooked when a sharp knife or skewer is inserted into the thickest part of the thigh and the juices run clear. If the juices run pink, return to the oven.

Remove the turkey from the oven, cover completely with foil and leave to stand for at least 15 to 20 minutes. This makes carving easier.

To make the gravy, spoon off all the fat from the turkey roasting tin, leaving the sediment and meat juices. Stir in the flour and heat gently on the hob for about 1 minute. Gradually stir in the stock, bring to the boil, reduce the heat and simmer gently for 1 minute, stirring constantly. Add the port or sherry and seasoning, and continue simmering gently for about 1 to 2 minutes. Taste and adjust the seasoning if necessary. Serve piping hot in a warmed gravy boat.

Remove the foil, muslin and bacon rashers from the turkey and garnish with bay leaves. Serve with all the trimmings (recipes on pages 146, 147 and 148).

LEFT *Crispy Smoked Trout Mousse, garnished with lumpfish roe, mixed salad and dill.*

LEMON AND THYME STUFFING

SERVES 8

30 g (1 oz) unsalted butter
1 large onion, chopped
230 g (8 oz) fresh white breadcrumbs
3 tablespoons freshly chopped parsley
1 tablespoon freshly chopped lemon thyme
The grated rind of 1 lemon
2 tablespoons lemon juice
1 egg, size 3, beaten
Salt and freshly ground black pepper
1 tablespoon sunflower oil, for roasting

Melt the butter in a small, heavy-based pan. Add the onion and cook until it is softened but not coloured. Leave to cool. Mix in the remaining ingredients. Shape the mixture into walnut-sized balls, cover and chill until required. Place in a roasting tin, sprinkle over the sunflower oil and roast for 20 minutes. TO FREEZE: freeze in a rigid plastic container for up to 1 month, then thaw in the fridge overnight.

CRANBERRY SAUCE

SERVES 8

340 g (12 oz) fresh or frozen cranberries
170 g (6 oz) golden caster sugar
The grated rind of 2 oranges
60 ml (2 fl oz) orange juice
1 tablespoon Cointreau (optional)
¼ teaspoon mixed spice
Freshly ground black pepper

Place all the ingredients in a heavy-based pan. Heat gently to dissolve the sugar, stirring frequently. Bring to the boil, reduce the heat and simmer, while stirring occasionally, for about 20 to 25 minutes until the cranberries are tender. Serve hot with ham or turkey.

The sauce can be made up to 2 days in advance, left to cool and stored in an airtight container in the fridge. Reheat gently when ready to use, addng a little more orange juice, if necessary.
TO FREEZE: for up to 1 month and reheat from frozen.

ROAST POTATOES AND SHALLOTS

SERVES 8

Use waxy potatoes rather than floury ones for this recipe, as they will hold their shape much better. The shallots cook in their skins and become very sweet.

1.8 kg (4 lb) potatoes, peeled
85 g (3 oz) dripping or lard
455 g (1 lb) shallots

Chop the potatoes into even-sized pieces. Place in a large pan of salted water and bring to the boil. Reduce the heat and simmer gently for 5 minutes.

Set the oven at Gas Mark 6, 400°F, 200°C. Melt the fat in a roasting tin. Place the potatoes in the roasting tin, baste thoroughly and roast for about 1½ hours, basting frequently. Add the shallots after 30 minutes.

The potatoes can be peeled in advance and kept immersed in a bowl of cold water overnight, but do not part-boil them at this stage, because they will go brown.

BREAD SAUCE

SERVES 8

1 large onion, peeled, quartered and studded with 8 cloves
1 bayleaf
280 ml (½ pt) milk
280 ml (½ pt) single cream
Salt and freshly ground black pepper
Grated nutmeg, to taste
110 g (4 oz) fresh white breadcrumbs
30 g (1 oz) unsalted butter

Place the onion studded with cloves in a heavy-based pan with the bayleaf, milk and cream and bring slowly to the boil. Remove from the heat, cover and leave to infuse for 30 minutes.

Remove and discard the onion, cloves and bayleaf. Season to taste. Bring the mixture slowly to the boil. Then add the breadcrumbs, stirring constantly. Reduce the heat and simmer gently for 10 to 15 minutes, stirring to prevent the mixture from sticking, and stir in the butter. Spoon into a warmed bowl and serve with the turkey.

MUSTARD GLAZED HAM

SERVES 8

A combination of mustard and sugar make a delicious glaze for the ham, which can be served hot or cold.

A middle gammon joint, weighing about 2.05 kg (4½ lb)
2 onions, each studded with 4 cloves
2 carrots, quartered
3 bayleaves
10 peppercorns
570 ml (1 pt) dry cider
For the glaze:
2 to 3 tablespoons ready-made English mustard
3 tablespoons demerara sugar
Whole cloves
A few sprigs of flat-leaf parsley, to garnish

Weigh the ham so that you are able to calculate the cooking time accurately. Soak the ham overnight in enough cold water to cover.

The next day, place the ham, the onions, the carrot, the bayleaves and peppercorns in a preserving pan. Pour over the cider and add enough water to cover. Bring to the boil and simmer for 20 minutes per 455 g (1 lb). Cover the pan with a baking tray.

Set the oven at Gas Mark 7, 425°F, 220°C. Line a large roasting tin with foil. Drain the ham and discard the vegetables and stock.

To make the glaze, remove the skin from the ham and score the fat into a diamond pattern. Place in the prepared roasting pan and drizzle liberally with mustard. Sprinkle over the demerara sugar and stud with cloves. Roast the ham for 25 to 30 minutes until golden. Transfer to a warmed ham stand or serving platter and garnish with sprigs of flat-leaf parsley.

LEFT *Mustard Glazed Ham, with Roast Potatoes and Shallots.*
OPPOSITE *Spend time decorating your Christmas table, and serve Christmas Dinner by candlelight.*

CREAMY GRATIN OF BRUSSELS SPROUTS

SERVES 8

An alternative way of serving Brussels sprouts. Make and chill the day before serving.

1.35 kg (3 lb) Brussels sprouts
570 ml (1 pt) milk
1 onion studded with 6 cloves
A bayleaf
6 peppercorns
30 g (1 oz) unsalted butter
30 g (1 oz) flour
Salt and freshly ground black pepper
Freshly grated nutmeg, to taste
For the topping:
60 g (2 oz) fresh white breadcrumbs

Trim the sprouts and cook in a pan of boiling, lightly salted water until tender – about 5 to 7 minutes. Drain and refresh under cold water, then drain again thoroughly. Place them in a liquidiser or food processor and blend until smooth.

Place the milk, onion, bayleaf and peppercorns in a pan, and heat slowly until scalding hot but not boiling. Remove from the heat, cover and leave to infuse for 20 minutes. Strain.

Melt the butter in a heavy-based pan and stir in the flour, followed by the flavoured milk. Bring to the boil, stirring constantly, until thickened. Season to taste.

Add the sprouts and spoon into a greased, ovenproof serving dish. Sprinkle over the breadcrumbs. Cool, cover and chill for up to 4 hours. Cook in the oven with the turkey for about 30 to 45 minutes until bubbling and lightly browned.

OPPOSITE Luxury Christmas Pudding, served with Brandy Butter and Orange Flower Water Cream, and Double Chocolate Iced Soufflé.

MIXED BABY VEGETABLES WITH PARSLEY BUTTER

SERVES 8

The parsley butter enhances the colourful combination of the baby vegetables. Prepare and blanch the vegetables the day before serving. The butter can be made up to 2 days before using.

1.35 kg (3 lb) baby carrots
0.9 kg (2 lb) baby turnips
1.35 kg (3 lb) baby courgettes
For the butter:
110 g (4 oz) unsalted butter, softened
3 tablespoons freshly chopped parsley
1 tablespoon freshly chopped chervil
Salt and freshly ground black pepper

Scrub and top-and-tail the carrots and turnips. Turn the courgettes and cut any large ones in half.

Either steam or cook the carrots and turnips in boiling, lightly salted water for 2 to 3 minutes until *al dente*. Drain and immediately plunge into ice-cold water. Leave to cool completely, then drain. Steam or cook the courgettes for 1 minutes. Drain and immediately plunge into ice-cold water. Place in warmed ovenproof serving dishes or a roasting tin.

To make the butter, place all the ingredients and seasoning in a food processor and blend together until well combined. Dot the herb butter over the vegetables, cover the dishes with lids or foil and place in an oven heated to Gas Mark 5, 375°F, 190°C for 20 minutes.

Spoon into warmed serving dishes and serve at once.

DOUBLE CHOCOLATE ICED SOUFFLÉ

SERVES 10

340 g (12 oz) good-quality white chocolate
30 g (1 oz) unsalted butter
110 g (4 oz) amaretti biscuits, broken into pieces
3 tablespoons Amaretto liqueur
The grated rind and juice of 1 orange
1 tablespoon powdered gelatine
8 eggs, size 3, separated
230 g (8 oz) golden caster sugar
430 ml (¾ pt) double cream, lightly whipped
To decorate:
Cocoa powder, sifted
White chocolate curls
A 23 cm (9 in) deep-sided cake tin, oiled and lined

Melt chocolate and butter in a bowl set over a pan of barely simmering water. Remove from the heat, and beat until smooth and glossy. Using a large pastry brush, brush chocolate over the inner sides and base of the tin. Leave to set.

Soak the biscuits in Amaretto while preparing the filling. Place juice in a heatproof bowl, sprinkle with gelatine and leave to soak for 5 minutes. Dissolve, standing the bowl in a pan of hot water.

Whisk the egg yolks, orange rind and sugar together until pale and thick enough to leave a ribbon-like trail for 8 seconds when the whisk is lifted. Fold into the biscuit mixture, followed by the gelatine and cream. Whisk the egg whites until stiff but not dry, and carefully fold into the amaretti mixture. Spoon the soufflé mixture into the chocolate lined tin and freeze for at least 12 hours or up to 2 weeks.

To serve, quickly dip the tin in a pan of hot water to loosen, then remove the soufflé. Carefully remove the grease-proof paper. Just before serving dust with cocoa powder and decorate with white chocolate curls. Serve slightly frozen cut into slices.

NOTE: it is not advisable to serve mixtures containing raw or partially cooked eggs to the very young, the elderly, the sick or to pregnant women.

LUXURY CHRISTMAS PUDDING

MAKES ONE 1.7 LITRE (3 PT) PUDDING
No Christmas Dinner is complete without it!

170 g (6 oz) pitted prunes, quartered
170 g (6 oz) sultanas
170 g (6 oz) raisins
170 g (6 oz) currants
140 ml (¼ pt) brandy
140 ml (¼ pt) orange juice
110 g (4 oz) plain flour
1½ teaspoons mixed spice
½ teaspoon grated nutmeg
½ teaspoon ground cinnamon
110 g (4 oz) fresh white breadcrumbs

170 g (6 oz) shredded beef or vegetarian suet
230 g (8 oz) soft, dark brown sugar
60 g (2 oz) almonds, toasted and chopped
The grated rind of 2 oranges
1 eating apple, cored and grated
2 tablespoons black treacle
2 eggs, size 3, beaten
60 ml (2 fl oz) brandy to ignite the pudding (optional)
Icing sugar, sifted
A 1.7 litre (3 pt) pudding basin, greased

Wash the dried fruit thoroughly and drain well. Soak the washed fruit overnight in the brandy and orange juice, stirring occasionally.

Next day, sift the flour and spices together and stir in the breadcrumbs, suet, sugar, nuts, orange rind and apple. Beat in the treacle and eggs, followed by the soaked fruit and their liquid. Mix thoroughly and spoon into the prepared basin. Cover with greaseproof paper and foil, and pleat it across the middle to allow for expansion. Tie securely with string around the rim and over the top to form a handle.

Place the pudding in a steamer or on a trivet in a pan of boiling water (the water level should come two-thirds of the way up the basin). Cover and steam for 8 hours, topping up the pan with boiling water as necessary. Leave to cool.

Remove foil and greaseproof paper. Wrap well with a new sheet of greaseproof paper and foil. Store in a cool, dry place for 2 weeks to allow the pudding to mature.

When ready to reheat, steam as above for 4 hours. Turn out on to a warmed serving plate. Warm the brandy gently (it is important not to boil it), pour over the pudding and carefully ignite. Dust with icing sugar and decorate with a sprig of holly. Serve with Brandy Butter or Orange Flower Water Cream.

BRANDY BUTTER

SERVES 8
A favourite with Christmas Pudding – and excellent with mince pies too.

170 g (6 oz) unsalted butter, softened
170 g (6 oz) icing sugar
3 tablespoons brandy

Beat the butter until pale and light. Gradually beat in the icing sugar and brandy, beating well between each addition. Spoon into a serving dish, cover and chill until ready to serve.

ORANGE FLOWER WATER CREAM

SERVES 8
A delicately flavoured cream to serve with the Christmas Pudding.

430 ml (¾ pt) double cream
1 teaspoon orange flower water
30 g (1 oz) icing sugar, sifted

Place the cream with the orange flower water and icing sugar in a cold bowl. Whisk until thick, then spoon into a serving bowl. Chill until required, or for up to 4 hours.

CHRISTMAS CAKE

No Christmas would be complete without Christmas cake – a delicious British tradition. This recipe is one of our favourites – and the resulting fruit cake is rich and moist. It is sumptuously iced in white and attractively decorated in royal blue and white. First, it is covered in marzipan and then in sugar paste. We have chosen a decoration which is attractive, easy to do, unusual and very stylish. A posy of white roses and sparkly silver leaves is tied with curling ribbons in royal blue and white. Just follow our step-by-step guide to success. Topping it all is a white Christmas candle – light it and bring the cake to the table as a spectacular grand finale to this most special of family occasions.

For the cake:
625 g (1 lb 6 oz) sultanas
170 g (6 oz) pitted prunes, chopped
170 g (6 oz) raisins
255 g (9 oz) glacé cherries, quartered
140 g (5 oz) mixed peel, finely chopped
310 g (11 oz) plain flour
1 teaspoon ground cinnamon
2 teaspoons ground mixed spice
½ teaspoon grated nutmeg
230 g (8 oz) unsalted butter
230 g (8 oz) soft, light brown sugar
5 eggs, size 3, beaten
1½ tablespoons black treacle
5 tablespoons brandy
140 g (5 oz) walnuts, chopped
A 23 cm (9 in) round cake tin, greased and lined

To marzipan the cake:
110 g (4 oz) apricot jam,
lightly beaten, boiled and sieved, for glazing
795 g (1¾ lb) white marzipan
Icing sugar, for dusting
A 28 cm (11 in) and a 35.5 cm (14 in) round
silver cake board

For the royal icing:
3 teaspoons egg white substitute: for example,
Meri-white or Renwhite
455 g (1 lb) icing sugar

To sugar paste the cake:
1 teaspoon vodka or gin
1.1 kg (2½ lb) sugar paste
Icing sugar, for dusting

For the decoration:
A circle of thin silver card,
10 cm (4 in) in diameter
60 g (2 oz) flower paste bought
from cake decorators'
shops or made up
Yellow paste colouring
Yellow stamens
Non-toxic silver food colouring
1.8 cm (2 yd) royal blue ribbon,
3 mm (1.8 in) wide
A white candle 1 cm (½ in) in diameter,
cut to 8.5 cm (3¼ in) high
2.3 m (2½ yd) white ribbon,
as wide as the cake
board is deep

*Flower paste for the silver leaves
and Christmas roses:*
450 g (15¾ oz) icing sugar
2 teaspoons cornflour
1 teaspoon gum tragacanth
2 teaspoons powdered gelatine
2 teaspoons white vegetable fat
2 teaspoons liquid glucose
1 egg white, size 2

EQUIPMENT

A cake decorating smoother
Non-stick board or plastic sheet
A small rolling pin
White vegetable fat
Cornflour
Five-petal flower cutter
3 cm (1¼ in) rose leaf cutter/veiner
Size 7 ball tool
A small palette knife

Tweezers
Artist's paint brush, size 4
Empty quails' egg boxes or
similar containers
Silicone paper
Double-sided tape
Small greaseproof paper piping bags
No. 1 piping tube
Cocktail sticks.

1. Cover the cake with sugar paste.

2. Smooth the top and sides of the cake.

3. Cover the silver card for decoration.

Decorating the Christmas Cake

Make the cake and the royal icing, then roll out the marzipan and cover the cake, as described in the box below. To decorate the Christmas cake, follow these step-by-step directions:

STEP 1: TO COVER THE CAKE WITH SUGAR PASTE

Brush a little vodka or gin over the marzipan to make it slightly sticky. Roll out the sugar paste, in the same way as for the marzipan (see below). Lift the sugar paste over the cake to cover, and ease it around the sides of the cake.

STEP 2: TO SMOOTH THE CAKE

With a cake smoother, smooth the top and sides with an even pressure to remove any bumps. Trim off any excess with a knife. Reserve the trimmings. Leave the cake in a cool place for about 24 hours before decorating it.

STEP 3: COVERING THE SILVER CARD FOR DECORATION

Spread a little royal icing over the non-silver side of the circle of card. Roll out reserved sugar paste to cover the card. Using a smoother, smooth the surface and trim the sugar paste around the edges. Leave to dry for at least 24 hours.

MAKING FLOWER PASTE

Sift the icing sugar, cornflour and the gum tragacanth into a heatproof bowl and place over a pan of hot water until the icing sugar is warmed through.

Sprinkle gelatine over 5 teaspoons of cold water in a heatproof basin; leave to sponge. Dissolve over a pan of hot water, remove from the heat and stir in the fat and glucose. Pour the liquid into the centre of the warm sugar. Add egg white; beat with an electric mixer until the paste is white (about 10 minutes). Store in a polythene bag in an airtight container; chill 24 hours before using.

Keep the flower paste wrapped in cling film to prevent drying; use only a small amount at a time.

TO MAKE THE CAKE

Make the cake at least 1 month, or up to 2 months before Christmas.

Set the oven at Gas Mark 2, 300°F, 150°C. Line the outside of the cake tin with a sheet of brown paper. Wash and drain the fruits well. Sift the flour into a bowl with the spices.

Cream the butter and sugar until pale and light. Gradually beat in the eggs, then the treacle. Fold in the flour, then mix in the brandy, walnuts and fruit. Spoon into the cake tin and smooth the surface, then make a slight hollow in the centre.

Cook for 3½ to 4 hours. Cover with greaseproof paper after 1½ hours to avoid overbrowning. The cake is cooked when a skewer inserted into the centre comes out clean. Leave the cake to cool in the tin.

Remove the lining paper and wrap the cake first in fresh greaseproof paper and then in foil. Store the cake in a cool, dry place for up to 2 months.

TO MAKE THE ROYAL ICING

Dissolve the egg white substitute in 70 ml (2½ fl oz) of cold water. Then gradually beat the icing sugar into the liquid, beating thoroughly until the royal icing mixture is the consistency of whipped meringue.

TO MARZIPAN THE CAKE

Stick the smaller cake board on top of the larger one with a little royal icing. Place the cake centrally on the smaller board and spread with the apricot glaze.

Remove rings and bangles to avoid marking the cake. Roll out the marzipan on to a surface dusted with icing sugar to a circle large enough to cover the entire cake. Lift marzipan over the cake to cover. Using the palm of your hand only, ease marzipan around the sides of the cake. With a cake smoother, smooth the top and sides with even pressure to remove bumps. Press marzipan into the cake board and trim off excess with a knife. Leave to dry for 24 hours.

4. Make the Christmas roses.

STEP 4:
MAKING THE CHRISTMAS ROSES

Cut 24 pieces of silicone paper into squares 4 cm (1½ in) in size.

Cut almost into the centre of the square from each corner so that the paper will fold into the cup shape of the tiny quails' egg boxes or similar small containers. Smear a little vegetable fat over a small area of a non-stick board and a small rolling pin.

Roll out a small piece of flower paste very thinly. Then, using the flower cutter, cut out a few roses at a time. Dust the palm of your hand with a little cornflour, place a flower in the palm and, using the ball tool, elongate and frill the petals.

Place a rose on to the centre of the prepared paper square and carefully push into the egg-shaped container, using the ball tool to depress the centre. You will need to make 24. Leave to dry for 24 hours before adding the centres.

To make the flower centres, colour a small piece of flower paste yellow by adding the colour with the tip of a cocktail stick. Knead it well until the paste is evenly coloured. Then take a tiny piece of yellow paste; roll it into a ball and press against a fine sieve to give the centre texture. Using a spot of royal icing, fix the centre into the dried rose. With tweezers, push the cut ends of the stamens into the centre. Leave a slight gap in the middle of each centre and bend the stamens with tweezers to give a natural look. Leave to dry for a further 24 hours.

5. Cover the board with Royal Icing.

MAKING THE SILVER LEAVES

Thinly roll out the flower paste. Using the leaf cutter/veiner, cut out 12 leaves. Dry the leaves for 24 hours over a curved shape such as a pencil, then colour the leaves with silver non-toxic food colouring.

MAKING THE RIBBON CURLS

Cut the royal blue ribbon into six lengths, 12.5 cm (5 in) each. Run the ribbon over the edge of a scissor-blade to curl it, and then wind the curl around a cocktail stick.

STEP 5:
COVERING THE BOARD WITH ROYAL ICING

With a palette knife, spread a layer of icing over the top of the boards. Leave to dry for 24 hours.

STEP 6:
COMPLETING THE TOP DECORATION

Roll 10 g (¼ oz) flower paste into a ball. Fix it to the centre of the covered card with royal icing. Push the candle into the flower paste. Using a dot of royal icing, fix 12 silver leaves around the circle of paste, then push the ends of the ribbon curls into the flower paste using a cocktail stick.

Finally, using royal icing, fix 6 of the Christmas roses around the base of the candle. Leave the decoration to dry for 2 hours before positioning it on top of the cake with a little royal icing.

6. Complete the top decoration.

7. Position the ribbons and roses.

STEP 7:
POSITIONING THE RIBBONS AND THE CHRISTMAS ROSES

Using double-sided tape, carefully secure the royal blue ribbon around the base of the Christmas cake, and then fix the white ribbon around the edges of the cake boards.

Measure the circumference of the cake and cut a strip of paper to that length and the same depth as the cake. Fold the paper into 6 even sections.

Unfold the paper, place it around the cake and use the fold lines as a guide for marking the base of the cake into 6. At each of the 6 points, fix 3 Christmas roses – positioning 2 at the base and 1 on top.

Use a spot of royal icing to secure the flowers in place. Finally, position 3 of the silver leaves between each group of 3 Christmas roses.

INDEX

INDEX

NOTES

Both metric and imperial measurements have been given in all recipes. Use one set of measurements only, and not a mixture of both.

Standard level spoon measurements are used in all recipes.
1 tablespoon = one 15ml spoon
1 teaspoon = one 5ml spoon

Milk should be full fat unless otherwise stated.

Pepper should be freshly ground black pepper unless otherwise stated.

Fresh herbs should be used unless otherwise stated. If unavailable use dried herbs as an alternative, but halve the quantities stated.

Ovens should be preheated to the specified temperature – if using a fan-assisted oven, follow the manufacturer's instructions for adjusting the time and temperature.

Freezing instructions are included for those recipes which are suitable for freezing. Any recipes which do not have these instructions are not suitable for freezing.